Too dirty for the Windmill

Caryl Brahms and Ned Sherrin

Too dirty for the Windmill

a memoir of Caryl Brahms

Constable · London

First published in Great Britain 1986
by Constable and Company Limited
10 Orange Street, London WC2H 7EG
Copyright © 1986 by Caryl Brahms and Ned Sherrin
Set in Linotron Ehrhardt 10pt by
Rowland Phototypesetting Limited
Bury St Edmunds, Suffolk
Printed in Great Britain by
St Edmundsbury Press
Bury St Edmunds, Suffolk

British Library CIP data
Brahms, Caryl
Too dirty for the Windmill: a memoir of Caryl Brahms.
1. Brahms, Caryl – Biography   2. Authors, English
– 20th century – Biography
I. Title   II. Sherrin, Ned
823'.912   PR6052.R264/

ISBN 0 09 466380 7

Dear Caryl,

I hope 'the heavy hand of Ned'
does not lie too leaden across
your memories . . .

Ned.

Contents

Illustrations

between pages 238 and 239

Caryl and Joyce Weiner at the Akropolis
Caryl on the balcony of her Regent's Park flat
The Levi brothers (*photograph by Sandra Lousada*)
Caryl and Ned: in a garden near Chichester; and eating oysters in
    Whitstable (*photograph by Michael York*)
Caryl and Ned during a rehearsal of *Beecham* (*photograph by Roger
    Elliott*)
Caryl and Anton Dolin (*photograph by Peter Ramsey*)
Caryl at work on her memoirs (*copyright The Radio Times*)
Caryl, Ned, and a line-up from *I Gotta Shoe* (*photograph by Zoë
    Dominic*)
Caryl and the *Song by Song* team (*photograph by Doug Mckenzie of PPS*)
Caryl in her flat, with cherubs (*copyright The Guardian*)

Acknowledgements

I started to sort through the pages of Caryl Brahms's autobiographical notes at Champneys, a health resort near Tring, in the early summer of 1983, some few months after her death in December 1982. I had long wanted to pay such a visit in the interests of fitness: but I could never persuade Caryl that it was other than selfish to interrupt our working schedule for that reason, or that she might benefit from joining me. In the two and a half years since then many of her family, friends and colleagues have helped me to fill in some of the gaps in her manuscript. Completing the task now, back at the same place (still 28 pounds lighter), I am reminded of my debt to them.

Caryl's contemporary cousins, Tana Lowe and Pearl Welch, have died since 1982 but I was able to have a long – indeed, ribald – lunch with Mrs Lowe in 1983, and I have many memories of Mrs Welch's kindness and some of her reminiscences during Caryl's lifetime. Professor Anthony Levi has generously allowed me to read the early manuscript pages of his book *Changes of Faith* and to adjust his side of the Levi family's history against that handed down through Caryl's and Mrs Lowe's parents. Peter Levi has kindly permitted me to reprint his fine poem 'Lament', which appeared in his collection of poems, *Shakespeare's Birthday*, at the end of the book; and Zoë Dominic, another favourite cousin, has been a source both of family lore and of encouragement. Mrs Drapkin, a cousin on the Abrahams side of Caryl's family, came up to London and identified some photographs and confirmed and corrected facts over the not particularly good lunch which I gave her. Max and Helen Landau, friends of Caryl's for more than fifty years, have done much the same: but I had the pleasure of being entertained by them.

I must also thank Hugh Bergel, the younger brother of Caryl's fiancé, for the photograph of his brother, for permission to quote from his book *Fly and Deliver*, and for other information; and I am indebted

[xi]

to Caryl's friends, Doris Barry, John Byron, Thelma Chadwick, James Cairncross, Christopher Fry, Valerie Hovenden, Dame Alicia Markova, Herbert Sidon, Maudie Pike, Mervyn Stockwood, and Doris Toye for replying to my various letters and telephone calls and allowing me to quote them. Sir Robert Lusty has taken the time and trouble to comment on an incident of which he has no recollection, and the late Joyce Weiner read through and commented on the whole of the manuscript (as it then stood) just before she died.

In the last years of her life, Caryl was lucky in the people who interviewed her (though she wasn't a bad subject). I have been happy to use more objective and wittier perceptions of her than mine would have been from the pens of Janet Watts (the *Guardian*), Sheridan Morley (the *Radio Times*), Ruth Gorb (the *Ham and High*), Pauline Peters (the *Sunday Express*), Philip Oakes (the *Sunday Times*), Maureen Cleave (the *Observer*) and Michael Billington (the *Guardian*).

Caryl worked with a great number of secretaries over her life, doyenne of these being Mrs Margaret Daniel, whose help in keeping the threads of her life and therefore of this book together was incalculable. Shirley Mowbray has contributed a vivid vignette of her period at Cambridge Gate; and Charlotte Darwin, her last secretary, has done this too, and is also the person who typed, re-typed and re-re-typed hundreds of yellow quarto pages as Caryl revised, re-wrote, re-selected and re-arranged. Julia Bankover has typed two drafts of the book for me and still come up smiling.

I am grateful to David Higham for permission to publish the lines from Edith Sitwell's *Look the Sun*; and to Robert Heber-Percy for permission to quote the poetry of Lord Berners.

I should like also to cram into a few lines some of the people whose names may not appear in this book but who did much to ease Caryl's path in her last years: Jessie Pearce, William Gray, Bill and Margaret Lacy, Barry Ayres, Jack Tinker, Nicholas Dromgoole, David Kernan, Tom and Daphne Clinch, Robert Maas, Douglas and Laura Bunn, Terry Sheppard, Deke and Jill Arlon, and their son, Jamie, whose permission I have also received to publish his correspondence with Caryl.

Caryl started her memoirs under the distinguished editorship of the late David Farrer. I have been equally lucky in that Rivers Scott and Gloria Ferris, who were Caryl's last literary agents, have introduced me to Prudence Fay who has been patient, firm, imaginative, and encouraging. I am very grateful to her.

Ned Sherrin

Champneys
Tring
Hertfordshire

September 1985

Foreword

NS Caryl Brahms left a mass of autobiographical notes when she died in 1982. Some were elegantly and painstakingly crafted after innumerable revisions – her usual habit. Others were reworkings of previous critical articles. Many were free-ranging, unconnected jottings which she stubbornly refused to arrange in a sequence which made it possible for a reader who did not know the nuances of an anecdote to understand why she had chosen to include it. Always an innovator, particularly in the brilliant comic novels which she wrote with S. J. Simon, she clung with increasing determination to the idea of breaking rules for the sake of breaking rules, and it has been my task in compiling this memoir to risk incurring her posthumous wrath by unknitting the deliberately tangled web, and adding a chronological commentary. I have reassured myself that she would have preferred her reminiscences to be published in this form rather than not published at all.

Caryl contemplated several titles for her autobiographical book. One was *Failed LRAM* – a reference to her inglorious career at the Royal Academy of Music. A second was *Tables and Liberties* – a phrase remembered from her schooldays when a hated headmistress had trumpeted in assembly: 'Girls, girls, you take tables and liberties and never put them back.' *Too dirty for the Windmill* was the one she favoured; but she reckoned that she would never get it past a publisher. While she worked on the book over a period of two or three years, she always referred to it as *Fred*. Intensely competitive, she refused to attack such a book for a long time and she kept to that resolve until Weidenfeld and Nicolson commissioned me to write my own autobiography in 1979. As soon as they had done that she began to pester visitors to New York to pack American yellow foolscap legal pads for her before they made their return journey (she held that they were easier on her eyes), and she covered reams of paper with her spidery, much scored-through hand.

Her *first* idea for a title was *A Sufficient Magic*.

CB I feel, sometimes, that my entire life has been spent in search of a sufficient magic. It started when I was around a wondering three years of age. My father had a golden sovereign purse. He would tell me to blow on it and up would pop a gold coin. Hindsight suggests he pressed a spring. However, that was my earliest sufficient magic.

NS She was never confident of her ability to hold the reader's interest in her unique Edwardian childhood; or even whether she could remember it accurately.

CB Researching for the lunatic novels which stand history on its head, some written with that genius among humorists, S. J. Simon, some with my second long-time collaborator Ned Sherrin, and some by myself, has created its own problems when it comes to thinking back through the years.

    Do I really remember the London of the clip-clop clipper-clopper horse-drawn carriages as in, for instance, *Trottie True* (Brahms-Simon), or the street vendors, 'like supers in a late-night market scene', as in *Rappel 1910* (Brahms-Sherrin), or the growlers full of their large Victorian families (many of them already howling) as in *Away Went Polly* (Brahms-solo)? Or is it just that I have read about them?

NS In encouraging her to write about the scenes of her childhood, which I found exotic and fascinating, I met a great deal of resistance. It was characteristic of her to be more interested in today and tomorrow than in yesterday. Although nostalgia had its appeal for her, the challenge of contemporary events was irresistible. The beginning of her life was cushioned and comfortable. By the end of it she had lived fully, given generously, and often spent rashly. She was frequently hard-up. For a long time her name, along with those of Cyril Beaumont and Arnold Haskell, was synonymous with ballet criticism, and this again rep-resented a past period, a closed book which she had to be encouraged to prise open.

CB Long ago I fell in love with the ballet, together with the writing of the Sitwells, Osbert, Edith and Sacheverell, which was to have a prime influence on my own writing. Later there would come the discipline and pseudo-naïvety of Rupert Brooke, the stories of Beatrix Potter and Katherine Mansfield, and much later still, the theatre critiques of James Agate. A writer could have worse mentors. Indeed, now that I come to consider it, my life's work has been little more than a spreading patchwork of the influence of other writers. And then there have been people – S. J. Simon who was Skid to one and all, Ned Sherrin, and the close companion of the moment, whoever he may have been. I have been vastly lucky in the people who have shared my life and my laughter.

NS   Without wishing to indulge in amateur psychology, it seems to me that her delight in working with a fellow writer sprang from the lonely childhood which she describes so vividly and which provoked her search for the companionship of a collaborator. Working in tandem, as she did for nearly fifty years, gave her great skill in drawing out from another person insights which were peculiar to them but would probably never have surfaced had she not fished, encouraged and sometimes stormed to such good purpose. However, much of her best and most evocative writing was achieved alone.

She was never an unselfconscious person, but paradoxically she often behaved with a total lack of concern for the effect she was making – admittedly on other occasions her outrageousness was keenly calculated. In a profile written in 1981, Maureen Cleave included the perceptive observation, 'Ned was making tea. Miss Brahms was making the most of the situation to behave badly.'

Her friends will remember this side of her character as well as they will recall her energy, her courage, her attention to detail (particularly when she was ministering to the needs of someone in trouble) or her imperious manner on the telephone – a naked 'Do I know you?' was often her reply to a simple statement of a name. Equally abruptly she would replace the receiver without finishing a sentence. Her mind was probably on the next problem, the current one having been dealt with. Another close friend holds that she eschewed the word 'Goodbye' because of the sad possibility of finality which it carried with it.

Caryl's carefully stated inspiration for recording her memories she ascribes to a paragraph in R. A. Butler's *The Art of Memory*.

CB   I came across a passage on Chips Channon which brought me to a sharp halt. 'Chips examined himself with admirable candour,' Lord Butler reported. "Sometimes I think I have an unusual character, able but trivial. I have flair, intuition, great good taste

[xvi]

and only second-rate ambition. I am highly susceptible to flattery. I am riveted by lust, furniture, glamour, society and jewels, I am an excellent organizer and have a will of iron . . ."'

So I decided to take stock of myself. I have a gift for discovering talent. No personal ambition whatever, just a wish to write better. I am content in conversation to appreciate wit in others, reserving my own for my writing. My clothes seem to have little communication with my body and I wear them badly – or do I? I love flowers, jewels, music, the drama, laughter, wit and Greenwich . . .

Inventing Caryl Brahms
(an Edwardian childhood)

NS Caryl Brahms was born on 8 December 1901, a fact which she thought
she had kept a closely guarded secret, certainly for the last forty years
of her life. She would have been furious to know that after her death,
although many of her friends were surprised by her great age, all the
newspapers were within three days of getting it right. She died on 5
December 1982, three days before her eighty-first birthday and they
put her down as eighty-one. To policemen, officials, form-fillers and
other inquisitives, she was 'over twenty-one'. I had sneaked a look at her
passport some twenty years earlier while taking her through Kennedy
Airport (or Idlewild, as it then was); but I did not let on.

She claimed an unconventional great-uncle who was a surgeon to
the Sultan of Turkey, and that her grandmother, the surgeon's sister,
a Miss da Silva, who lived there too, was courted and won by a
businessman based in London, Moses Levi. The Levi family had
moved to Turkey from Spain in the fifteenth century when many
Spanish Jews were expelled in 1492 and taken in by the Sultan. A Levi
bank still exists in Istanbul. Miss da Silva's given name was Sultana.
Many of her descendants are called Tana. A rough English contemporary equivalent would, I suppose, be 'Queenie'.

After her marriage, Sultana remained in Constantinople, visited once
a year by her husband who, in a deal of travelling, divided his years
roughly between London and Constantinople. On each of these annual
visits she conceived another child.

Moses Levi had, in fact, been born in Turkey and was the first
person to import brass bedsteads into that country – a practical line of
business for a prolific parent. He was a naturalized British subject and
later he was made Freeman of the City of London. He died – of
Spanish flu – in the early months of the First World War, some ten
years before his wife who lived until 1924.

In the 1960s, when Caryl used often to eat at a section of the Lyons

Corner House at the corner of Oxford Street and the Tottenham Court Road called 'The Restful Tray', she took an interest in a young Turkish waiter. She was always concerned for waiters and cloakroom attendants and usherettes, and imaginative in her kindness to strangers. As the friendship developed she talked of her delight in her grandmother's rose-petal jelly, and very soon pots of rose-petal jelly began to arrive from Turkey. Finally she explained one day – a little grandly – that 'my great-uncle was surgeon to the Sultan'. The waiter was delighted, but not impressed. Rising just above the Restful Tray which it was his job to push, he said, 'My great-grandmother was wife to Sultan.' They stayed friends until he and the Restful Tray disappeared.

The time came (it was probably in 1873) when Grandmamma Sultana in Constantinople grew dissatisfied with her husband's annual visits. According to another grand-daughter, Tana Lowe, she 'eventually got fed up', collected up her surviving children – she had borne at least twenty-one by now, of whom Caryl's mother, Pearl, was one – took a coal boat to England and joined her hitherto patient, but then unsuspecting, spouse.

She landed in Liverpool with her brood after a long voyage for which they had packed their own bedding and food. The first that Moses knew of this dramatic step was a telegram from Liverpool which brought him hurrying to collect them.

I am indebted to Caryl's cousin, Professor Anthony Levi, for some additional, and occasionally conflicting, information about Moses and Sultana and their family. In the first chapter of his book *Changing Faith* he suggests that their oral history, passed on through at least twenty descendants, admits variation and inconsistency. More specifically, his father's birth certificate states that his grandmother was originally Sultana Jourado, not Da Silva. 'The given name is the same,' he writes, 'and since she cannot have been married before, I am inclined to believe in Jourado.'

Anthony, who never met his grandparents, 'although by all accounts they were a remarkable couple,' confirms that his father, on his own evidence, was the youngest of twenty-one children and that there were no twins. He reveals that Moses Levi also had a mistress in East London 'where he spent nine months of his life each year'. This part of the oral history appears to have been kept from the ears of the old man's female descendants, and neither retelling reveals if there were any illegitimate offspring or if Moses confined his procreative drive to Sultana. As well as carrying bedsteads to Turkey, he claimed to be the first commercial importer of Persian carpets to Britain. His principal client was Maples, and in Anthony's father's version it was on their doorstep that Sultana landed with her children and 'demanded to know where her husband was living. Maples was indiscreet, or over-awed, or clever enough to tell her.' Whether she had got wind of her rival is not recorded: but the existence of the other lady certainly makes sense of Moses's hurry to establish his family in a large house on the other side of London. In official documents Moses was described as an 'indigo merchant', a term which covered anyone who dealt in coloured cloths, including carpets. His telephone number was 'London' followed by three figures only.

If we assume that the tally of children was twenty-one, ten seem to have survived to make the journey. Tana Lowe thought that an eleventh, Isaac, stayed in Constantinople where he died of TB. According to Anthony Levi's father, Isaac was the eldest surviving son. He suffered from asthma and settled in Italy on account of this, where he practised as a photographer.

Of the English contingent, Nissim Hyam (Nissim means 'miracle of life') was the senior son. Known as Uncle Ned, he became a carpet importer and specialized in Oriental carpets and rugs, returning at one point to Constantinople. Known there as 'the Mad Englishman', he was the first man to ride a bicycle in Turkey and took a barge laden with beer up the Nile to the British troops at the battle of Omdurman in 1898. He was also present at the Constantinople earthquake and the massacre of the Armenians. In 1898 or 1899 he married Lettice Elizabeth Anderson. They lived on Canvey Island, then in London, and finally in Poole until 1945. She died in May of that year and he died in the same week.

Pearl's other brothers were Lionel – later President of the Antique Dealers' Association – and Lewis and Bert, both of whom dealt in retail carpets; the boys were all educated in a London Jewish school. The six surviving sisters were Sally, Rebecca, Vicki, Laura, Rose and Pearl. Of the others, those who did not die at birth were lost in a typhoid epidemic. Caryl always insisted on her uncles' flamboyant eccentricity. The sight of a dubious impresario in urgent conference with a shifty entrepreneur invariably reminded her 'of my uncles'; but she wrote little about them. Anthony Levi sketches Nissim as 'delightfully paranoiac, owner of seven boats, half an island, a large house in Poole and a large stamp collection', and adds: 'He occasionally but undramatically reduced his expenditure by smoking filthy tobacco

[3]

and having sandwiches sent in for lunch.' There is a charming romantic aside: 'He used himself to remove fallen rose-petals from the lawn because they so upset his wife.' Uncle Lewis incurred disapproval when he 'started to leave the city at three to play bridge in his West End club, to which he was driven in his Rolls-Royce by his white-gloved chauffeur'. Anthony's own father's career had included planting rubber in Malaya where he 'kept a pet elephant and once escaped from a tiger by feigning death'.

In a letter to me, Anthony writes: 'The thing about the uncles' businesses needs unravelling.' I fear that this is not the place, nor am I the economist, to do the job. At one time they all appear to have been partners in one another's businesses. Apart from carpets and furniture these also included selling the chassis of Rolls-Royce cars when the carriage-work was custom built, and running a theatrical agency which went broke. At one point Sultana was required to sell most of her jewels, managing to hold on to her engagement ring, 'an enormous diamond of not very high quality, set in gold filigree studded by some fifty brilliants'. After their fiascos with the motor chassis and the theatrical bodies, the brothers consolidated their efforts on the central importing business, dividing some responsibilities. Nissim, who had the most children, specialized in the lucrative carpet-repair operation. Much of his work came in from insurance companies who still found it cheaper to repair rather than replace damaged carpets. The other branches were shared until Nissim's death. Then, after much agitated activity by accountants, a split was made. Lionel took over the antique side of the business in Duke Street, eventually specializing in French furniture of the seventeenth and eighteenth centuries. Lewis had the retail and contract side, opening 'Lewis's' in Victoria Street, and Bert, Anthony's father, diversified the wholesale importing and carpet factoring business into furniture coverings.

These were the vivid brothers into whose family Caryl's father, Henry Abrahams, married. Pearl, his bride, was still living at home in Park Hill Rise, Croydon, in the large house that Moses had found for her and her family. Caryl's visits there were plainly some of her happiest childhood memories. She enjoyed quoting her grandmother's oft repeated, quaintly accented statement: 'I am a *pair*fect English lady, and I know *too* much!' In fact Sultana never mastered English.

Caryl's mother's engagement to her father, Henry Abrahams, is described as stormy in Caryl's memoirs – the storms came from her grandmother.

CB For some reason never very clear to me, my petite, poker-backed Grandmamma, whom I adored, turned my Mamma out of doors when she became engaged to marry my father; and this my Grandmamma did in the most public manner. I have lived with the legend, which I believe implicitly, that my irate grandmother, attended by my Aunt Sarah, ascended awfully to my mother's bedroom, flung open the window – it gave on to my grandparents' back garden – and bundled out a trunk. This was followed by my Mamma's entire wardrobe, piece by piece, while my meek Mamma waited in the garden below to stow away her belongings. First, some highly blushworthy underclothes, flannel combinations, corsets, bloomers, petticoats, stockings, shoes – the list seems endless.

When it was the turn of my Mamma's best nightdress my Grandmamma changed her mind mid-air. The dialogue went something like this: 'Go immediately down to the garden, Sarah, and tell your disobedient sister, Pearla, that I want the nightdress back for your sister Laura – it is her best nightdress and Laura shall wear it when she visits your married sister Rebecca (or was it Victoria?) who lives in Coburg.'

When they came to my Mamma's dresses there were many more such journeys for my poor Aunt Sarah: 'This spotted foularde, now would it become Nissim's wife, or . . .', she turns the spotted foularde over. 'No,' she decides, 'there is a bad stain on the back, Pearla can keep it . . . much good may it do her!' Sniff.

NS Eventually, everyone calmed down and bride and groom set up home on Canvey Island, from which their only child, Doris Caroline, would sometimes be sent back to Croydon to stay with her grandparents.

CB I looked forward to the visits I would be sent on with my detestable governesses – tell-tale sneaks to a woman – although my grandfather, who might have served as a model for Job, frightened me. I was staying with them one year when he had a birthday, an occasion when my governess and I sallied forth for the penny bazaar, where for threepence – half my worldly wealth – I bought him an impressive cigar. This he hid behind an ornament on the chimneypiece, to my chagrin. Why didn't he smoke it? He smoked those he bought himself in the cedarwood box from a colourful place called Havana. I was allowed to tear off the picture of Havana when the sweet-smelling box was emptied.

[5]

There was one house, on those walks I was taken on when staying with my grandparents, from which my governess and I were under strict orders to avert our gaze. It was, I have since been told, the establishment of a charitable organization. Nothing very wrong about that, one might well have supposed. The sinister thing about it in my grandparents' eyes was that it was a Church of England establishment and in it lived she whose name must never be spoken. The sinner was my never-to-be-seen Aunt Rosa who had changed her religion and dwelt therein. I still have her Bible with the page past which I must not read on, the great divide between the Old and New Testaments, though how I came by it I do not know. I had a twist of golden unspun silk to mark the great divide.

Aunt Rosa, clearly a woman who had her own lights and acted by them, played a mysterious role in the family saga. Every now and then my father, by now fully accepted into the family, and one or other of my mother's brothers known in their tribal collectivity as 'the Uncles', divine beings whose word was law and must never be questioned, would be summoned by Aunt Rosa's Superior. It would seem that Sister Rosa had done it again – 'it' being helping herself to the contents of the poor box, but only in order to give it to some more – in her eyes – deserving cause. My father and the Uncles would then put matters right by paying back the money plus a generous contribution to some charity of the Mother Superior's choice – nothing if not ecumenical, I like to think it could have been a Mission to the Jews.

NS   The community on Canvey Island consisted of some 200 people, which included Nissim and Lettice, and a Catholic priest, Father Gregory, who celebrated Mass, courtesy of the Levis, in the lounge of Nissim's home, Kismet, until Nissim arranged for a shed and then a church to be built for him – an ecumenical gesture echoed by Caryl's later interest in Christian forms of worship. Caryl described her father, in interviews she gave late in life, as a jewellery designer and as a jeweller. Her friend Max Landau, who knew Henry Abrahams over some twenty years, writes that he had a 'wholesale fancy-goods business opposite the Houndsditch warehouse'. Caryl was always interested in and knowledgeable about jewellery, antiques and carpets. Her favourite ring, an enormous amethyst, had belonged to Edith Sitwell and Caryl lost it on New Year's Eve 1980, coming away from dinner at her friends', the Lacys', restaurant. After that, whenever she saw a large ring decorating

[6]

the hand of a television presenter, she would get close to the screen to make sure it was not hers. On one occasion I was being interviewed by Sue Cook on 'Nationwide', and was given strict instructions to check her hands. Alas, her ring, though undoubtedly large, was a different shape and decorated with a different stone.

Contemporaries describe Caryl's father as small and excitable but much dominated by his very positive wife. Caryl was clearly more attached to her father than her mother, with whom she fought constantly. Her espousal of the Sephardim side of the family seems to stem from the lively Levis – though the details of religious observances which she gives appear to owe more to her Ashkenazi father than to her Levi relations. None of her Levi contemporaries remembers a comparable religious discipline in their own households.

CB Organized religion was, in the main, the province of my father, though my mother would often chip in with unfair moral improvisations such as 'Remember, you are one of God's Chosen People,' from which I deduced I'd better eat up my endless slices of bread-and-butter, or finish my heartily detested sago-and-milk pudding, or I would be letting my creator down. I was dreadfully shocked each time my cousin Tana, the eldest daughter of a mixed marriage, chanted Hilaire Belloc's observation:

How odd
Of God
To choose
The Jews.

One day when I was three, nudging four, I was being more than usually recalcitrant about my good plain nursery fare, preferring the unsuitable dishes the grown-ups were enjoying. I pushed aside my plate.

'Now that's very naughty of you. Finish up all your nice greens and potatoes or God will be disappointed in you. He is watching and you are grieving him.'

'But God's in synagogue.'

'God is everywhere, and He sees everything.'

'Is He in the garden?'

'Yes.'

'And in the dining-room?'

[7]

My mother pointed piously aloft to the ceiling. It had a crack in it.

'Yes.'

I abandoned my cooling slops. Thereafter God, to me, was the crack in the ceiling. And nosy with it.

NS Caryl was reminded by *Proofs of Affection*, a novel given to her by the author Rosemary Friedman, that one could tell the changing of the seasons in the Jewish calendar . . .

CB . . . by the hats of my own attire for the autumn high festivals when I was a child. I always wore a new black beaver hat with a wreath of holly berries on the brim, new shiny patent-leather strap shoes – how they pinched – which made a sound as of blocks on a board as I peacocked along the pavements (a limping peacock perhaps), white woollen gloves (the scarlet wool were for every day) which made my hands feel dry. '*Mais, mon enfant,*' Mam'selle would say, '*il faut souffrir pour être . . .*' she looked at my face puckered with distaste and my permanently askew steel-rimmed spectacles; the word *belle* choked her . . . '*pour être bien mise,*' she substituted. These high-festival accoutrements were accompanied by a new navy-blue reefer coat with underneath a *vieux rose* velveteen dress or one of saxe blue, and, final touch, my very own dark-blue Singer's prayer-book – the one item that was not new every year.

It was a proud moment when my parents and I reached our special pew. It had a mahogany door that gave it an air of an aproned-off hansom cab – for all the congregation (who were not too busy praying or donning their *taleisim* in the case of the males – females did not count unless they happened to be *la Maman*, who must never be questioned and always obeyed) to see. Our pew was directly opposite a probably terrible stained-glass window which depicted Eve, her apple, the trees of the knowledge of good and evil, the fruits of which Man was forbidden to eat, and her serpent Lillith, in segments of sapphire and ruby and emerald glass, the fantasia being executed in the manner of *l'art nouveau*. In the words of the song:

It was beautiful
Beautiful to mine eyes.

It could only have been a few weeks after I had been introduced to

[8]

the Almighty that I became acquainted with Death. The meeting
took place in the garden on my way back from some expedition with
my Mamma and attendant governess. The latter, with eyes
habitually on stalks for imperfections, noticed the pathetic remains
of a sparrow left on the path by a cat. 'Poor thing,' she said, as she
pitched it over a hedge, 'it's dead. The cat's been at it.'

'Has it gone to its Mummy?' I asked hopefully, since being away
from my own was the worst thing I could possibly imagine at that age.

This prompted Mamma to go into one of her most dramatic
improvisations. Up went that index finger skywards. 'No, my child,
not to its Mamma but to heaven to live with God.'

God again! This time it was too much to bear. I broke into dismal
howls and could be neither comforted nor bribed. Even the terrible
threat 'your father shall hear of this tonight,' failed to quell my sobs
and hiccoughs.

As I grew up I began to notice that my Mamma was less observing
of the Jewish dietary laws than my father, and only rarely accompanied
us to synagogue. But when I was around four nudging five I had no
such puzzlements. I remember particularly one morning awakening to
the sight of a tent which had sprouted in the night with all manner
of fruit and flowers and vegetables. 'This,' said my father, 'is a
Succott. It stands for a festival of rejoicing. For seven days we eat
in the Succott and take our ease.'

'Lovely,' I said.

My father chanted grace before and after the evening meal on
Fridays at sundown, and walked me three miles to synagogue and
back on Saturday mornings, and saw to it that the high festivals
were decently observed, and that no ham or shell-fish entered the
house. On Friday night and Saturday morning our menu was
reasonably fixed. On Friday night he broke bread and salt and we
drank home-made raisin wine – I was allowed to chop the raisins
but not trusted to add the cinnamon. Cold fried fish and hot
spaghetti was the main course – and at the weekend the feasting
was crowned by luscious grapes. Saturday dining consisted of
chicken cooked à la Sephardim in tomato sauce, with at least three
vegetables, the routine four afters (of which one could count on
chocolate blancmange blessed with fresh thick cream), the cheese
board and fruit; and I was given claret diluted with lemonade to drink.

But one day – I must have been about four – human fallibility
raised its ugly head. This happened at a party. It cost me my faith in

orthodox religion and orthodox Jewish religion. Among many dietary
rules made in the interests of good health in hot countries was the law
forbidding the eating of shell-fish. My friend Monica was C of E.
She attended morning prayers in Assembly which were prohibited to
me, straining my ears from the lobby to catch those
exciting-because-forbidden words before I was allowed into Hall
to answer the school register. Seven or so beautifully kempt little
maids from school were invited to Monica's birthday tea-party –
the usual tempting jellies and glamorous pink blancmanges. But
first, deliciously thin paste sandwiches. I took one in each podgy hand.
The plate came round a second time. Observing my relish the
hostess plied me with more. The woman tempted me and I did
eat. 'Won't you have another shrimp-paste sandwich?'
    Shrimp! I looked at the ground in a panic. I expected the earth to
open before me and that I would be consumed. I wasn't. It failed to
part like the Red Sea and swallow me. Not even a rain of thunderbolts
was hurled at me from the avenging heavens. I was relieved, if shaken.
Sin set in. From now on it was but a step to dancing class on the
Sabbath and being turned out of Hebrew class at my finishing
school. I was on the gentle slope towards oysters, going to theatres
on Friday night and eating on Yom Kippur.

NS   In later life Caryl always insisted that she suffered all the pangs of
hunger and headache on the Day of Atonement that she would be
feeling 'had I fasted with my brothers and sisters in Israel.'

CB   The most I can claim is a perception of some purpose in my life,
and that sometimes, more often indeed than I have deserved, the
Purpose has relented. I call that Purpose God.
    On the matter of Jesus Christ my father was most helpful: 'You
will hear, my dear, a lot about Jesus Christ. Christians believe he
was the son of God. Jewish people do not. Think of him as the
best man who ever lived and never forget he was a Jew,' which,
for a reasonably observing Orthodox Jew, was ecumenical to
a degree.
    My father handed down to me, his only daughter, two rules which
act on me as the Ten Commandments act on other people:

1. Never lend – give.
2. Never make a threat you are not prepared to implement.

[10]

But, of course, parental guidance was by no means confined to Papa in his wisdom. Mamma would weigh in regularly with, 'Wasting your time again reading a book! Go tidy your bureau drawers like your cousin Pearl,' or, almost equally annoying, 'I can see you there under the dining-room table (*con molto expressivo*) reading again!'

'Your father will be told about this,' was a phrase frequently on my mother's lips – often followed by, 'Why can't you be more like your cousin Pearl? When your Uncle Ned took her out from her convent school in Namur the only thing she wanted him to buy was silk underclothes.' How I hated my cousin Pearl at that time. I adore her now!

NS Caryl's cousins Pearl (Welch) and Tana (Lowe), both of whom died shortly after Caryl, were the only close friends of her childhood –

CB in the brief interludes when my Mamma and her sister-in-law, my favourite Aunt Lettice, were on speaking terms; for the two sisters-in-law were apt to fall out. There was, for instance, the history of the bathing-hut erected for our families to share, and for a happy, salty, sunny six weeks all went merrily as the bells of Holy Russia. But two forces, compounded of the differing temperaments of the hut's two chatelaines, proved abrasive, and a dividing wall was put up in the summer shanty, only to be removed a few weeks later when the two ladies had made up their differences. That dark-green corrugated iron wall was put up and pulled down as often as an umbrella on an April day. Out came my mother's flower-sprigged china when the skies were clear, and we children could all swim together. But back went the pretty flowered pieces and out came the plain, thick, kitchen crocks when the sky was overcast, and we cousins were directed to swim between different breakwaters. I have digressed this time in an effort to show what a terrifying but intoxicating treat company – any company – was to me, at that time.

NS The picture which emerges is of a lonely child, with a strong mother and a dominated father who occasionally let fly in a burst of exasperated rebellion.

CB He was a very gentle man, so gentle that on the only occasion when he spanked me, he was every bit as upset as I. Officially it was for lying. What made the whole horrifying incident so unfair was that I had been telling the truth as I understood it. This was, of course, not my first brush with grown-up injustice but it was the occasion that most hit home, as it were. Vividly I remember some irresponsible remark of my mother's touching the morals of an elder sister of one of my friends – an observation not intended for childish and uncomprehending ears, which I repeated to my friend in a spirit of scientific enquiry:

'What do you think it was your sister did?'

'I'll ask her.'

There was no room for doubt about what her sister did next. She threatened to bring an action for slander! So my parents found it expedient to declare to me that I was lying. What a bewildering world it was outside the schoolroom for the scientific enquirer.

NS Henry Abrahams was devoted to light music – a Gilbert and Sullivan fan *par excellence*. Caryl preferred to hear his baritone issuing through the bathroom door than in the comparatively public setting of the drawing-room, where he would perform for friends, 'You should see me dance the polka,' and she would not know where to look in her embarrassment; or 'Onaway, awake, beloved' with its chorus of

> *'Does not all the blood within me*
> *Leap to meet thee, leap to meet thee?'*

Less embarrassing was his enthusiasm for the pianola on which his daughter was not allowed to play.

CB The rolls were very different from those made, I am told, by the master pianists of today. He would sit for hours playing away, 'putting in the expression' and turning to my Mamma when he had rattled off some rendering: 'My love, did I not play "The Arcadians" (or, say, "The Chaminade") particularly well?' To which I would like to think my mother would reply, 'You always do, dear.'

NS Henry Abrahams was not the only close relative with musical aspirations.

CB I was all of four years of age, or so I have been told – for what follows has passed into the family saga – when my father's cousin,

Aunt Dinah, came to luncheon, announcing on arrival that she must
leave at four o'clock. As the afternoon wore on, Mamma seated
herself at the piano. I particularly admired the tucked amber silk
behind the walnut façade of fretwork, for it was a 'drawing-room
upright', and wondered why Mamma took off her several rings,
flexed her fingers and tossed off the 'Minute' waltz. Mamma's way
with a piano was a lively hit or miss affair. 'Do sing one of those
pretty songs, my dear Di, which I'm sure you've got tucked away
in that music case.'

No sooner said than done. Off went the two ladies *con brio*. Cousin
Dinah sang a wobbly soprano, very flat:

'Under the deodah,
Under the deodah,
Over the sea,
Dear heart to me,
Under the deodah.'

So warbled my father's Cousin Di with my spirited Mamma dashing
off the chorus. Spirited, yes; but to the unforgiving ears of a musical
four-year-old, an ordeal not to be endured. Off I toddled to the
guest-room where lay Cousin Dinah's bonnet, a resplendent affair in
claret-coloured velvet, a nest of flowers and a twirling of feathers
and, most admired of all, a long swathe of claret-coloured satin
ribbons for tying under the chin. I seized this millinery marvel and,
holding on to one ribbon, dragged it off to its owner who had
progressed to 'The Indian Love Lyric' and was assuring me that
she was less than the dust beneath my chariot wheels.

'Cousin Di . . . Cousin Di . . . It's four o'clock – time you went!'
Bed again. No supper again. It wasn't fair again.
But once a critic, always a critic.

NS Caryl's memories of the physical comforts in her home were as vivid
as her recollections of childhood set-backs.

CB The parties! Those quivering, clouded, pink blancmanges, those
café-noir biscuits with domestic animals outlined in white sugar,
the bright clear jellies, the long table in the hall laden with all kinds
of coloured edible delights. But after the feasting, sure as the Day of
Judgement, the ordeal of the party piece – a recitation punctuated

by promptings. One's own turn coming nearer, ever nearer. Of no avail to hide one's head in an alien nanny's skirt.

My Mamma made me recite to visitors, poor wretches, the ballad that begins 'There's a breathless hush in the Close tonight,' and I, an earnest little girl in white socks, all corkscrew curls and steel-rimmed spectacles permanently askew, even at that early age felt there could be something wrong with the great Henry Newbolt's philosophy. It was an embarrassment too, when my Sephardic Mamma insisted that I should don my ballet shoes and dance *sur pointe* for the delectation of the visiting Rabbi or 'Haham', as Sephardim say.

Magical reminders of my childhood were scents and smells, and one that has spoilt me for almost all others was the scent of the Benfleet blacksmith's forge when we had driven Jennie in the dog-cart over to get shod and waited while some great dray-horse was having red-hot horseshoes applied to its thrashing hooves, which gave off a delicious and very singeing smell – my nose still wrinkles at the thought of it. Sweet-peas have a nostalgic scent that takes me right back to escape for the lonely only child, to my Auntie Lett's garden and all the cousins' company into which I could thrust myself. The scent of wallflowers, too, is wonderfully evocative of the tennis afternoons of my teens. Mignonette, with its muskiness, summons sunny afternoons and sessions of sweet silent thought in the tiny little gardens which were the scenes of highly competitive gardening wrought by my two cousins, Tana and Pearl.

NS One basic difference between Caryl and her mother was their attitude to money.

CB I have always had decided views on money ever since, with my hair in pigtails, I was suddenly given ten shillings a week for hair-ribbons and dress allowance. Money I held, and still hold, is for spending. I would rush off with mine to buy a book and let my clothes take care of themselves. Money is for spending. My Mamma had other views. So lavish with puddings – she would have been ashamed to have fewer than four on a Friday night, the great Jewish sit-in night – she thought that money was for saving. She went to extravagant lengths to save money. She once gave my father a cretonne sofa-cover for the guest-room for his birthday present, poor, unprotesting, gentle man . . .

S Visits to the theatre were highlights of Caryl's childhood, as they are for most children. From her solitary perspective they seemed even more momentous than usual.

B My long-time live-in affairs with the theatre started when I was four or five. Little did my parents realize what a deep-rooted climbing creeper had been planted when my Mamma was given two stalls for the pantomime at the Theatre Royal, Drury Lane, by her friend Ella Lindow, a theatre journalist with the imperishable pen-name of Gabrielle Wodnil. Miss Wodnil floated, bursting at the seams, through life, composed of so much generosity and romance and bosom – the poor man's Mrs Patrick Campbell, only a giver rather than a taker. They had put me into my scarlet Red Riding Hood cloak over my party dress – I could swear it was, of all unlikely garments, a sky-blue satin creation . . . or have I confused it with that of the Kinema-coloured child-heroine of the first moving picture I was taken to see? (Actually the picture didn't move much and was probably more of a series of coloured magic lantern slides.) But as it seems to me now, there was I in sky-blue satin with – dear God! – my hair in poker curls, my feet imprisoned in single strapped shiny patent-leather slippers, which no doubt pinched; and there was my Mamma in a much-admired – at least by me – cinnamon gown that accorded with her coiffure, piped with turquoise-blue velvet ribbon; and off we set, my mother and I, not in a horse-drawn carriage or clarence, not in that elegant 'gondola of the London streets', a hansom cab, but, of all conveyances, the snorting, vibrating, new-fangled, highly chancy, but no doubt cheaper, motor-bus. Whatever can have induced my mother to board this evil dragon I cannot imagine, unless it was her passion for economy. Certainly it can have been no surprise to her when it started to belch out a cloud of smelly black smoke and the passengers were ordered to abandon bus before it combusted. Like so many hopeful female economies, it cost more than it saved. I was taken straight back home by a passing horse-drawn vehicle. The enthralment of a lifetime had been postponed.

The next time, my departure for Drury Lane was presided over by that floppy-petalled over-blown poppy, Miss Gabrielle Wodnil, in person. This time to travel hopefully was to arrive; for we were wafted there by clip-clop, clipper-clopper, fly-blown Dobbin-drawn hackney cab.

That year the entertainment was illumined by Little Rene Meyer, a child star, playing a captivating Puck – don't ask what Shakespeare's spirit was doing cocking a perky nose at a towering, fee-fi-fo-fum Ogre. When at long length the walk-down, from brokers' men to stars, was ended and the crimson curtain came down, not to rise again until tomorrow's matinée, Miss Wodnil, in a hat with an over-generous and floppy brim, fastened to her head with at least half a dozen blue butterfly-wing hat pins, took me, her timorous small guest, by the hand and led me backstage to Little Rene Meyer's dressing room, so crowning my first visit to Drury Lane with my first Star. Who could foretell what will o' the wisp this prancing Puck was to cast into my life? Best of all, Rene showed me her Tuppence-Coloured Theatre. It must have been a first-night present. That its tiny safety curtain had warped did not abate its magic. At all events, this pantomime was to turn an only child's solitude – that forlorn loneliness that I can only liken to that of a batsman dismissed early in his innings, and doomed to the long trudge from wicket to pavilion – into a many-peopled harlequinade.

NS By now the child was old enough to feel embarrassment as well as loneliness.

CB The next time I remember being taken to a matinée, it was by my father. I must have been about ten, an earnest introvert still in steel-rimmed spectacles which never would stay straight. By now I had taken to collecting books with suede covers and, what was worse, reading them. Worse, that is, in my mother's eyes, for she held that reading was a waste of time which would be better employed in embroidery on my tambour, 'like your cousins'. At times like this I hated cousins almost as much as I hated sewing. Going out with my father was a rare treat, even though somehow it always included a shaming lecture which made me turn scarlet and prickle with embarrassment. I used to await it with dread. On this particular day the *plat du matinée* at the Lane consisted of some torrid tale of Eastern passion which did nothing to ease my wary attitude, or deflect the wrath of God which I knew must be well on the way. Clearly the Day of Judgement was about to take place at the first convenient moment.

We adjourned to the nearest Fuller's tea-shop and a silence

descended so resonant you could have punctured it with a wafer. It so happened that one of my treasured suede books contained the aphorisms of Oscar Wilde. I thought them wise, funny, and gloriously grown-up. What, it seemed, had been my undoing was the underlining with a meticulously sharpened pencil of those passages I considered remarkably perceptive and adult. Some sneak had pried into my suede book and taken it to my father. Normally he was a gentle and patient man, with a chirpy sense of humour that I considered quite good – for a parent. But this was no normal occasion . . . At length my father – could he have been embarrassed too? – addressed himself to the tea-shop ceiling. 'About Oscar Wilde,' he announced. 'You know, my dear, no-one takes the fellow seriously.'

NS Caryl recalls various servants in the comfortable house on Canvey Island – called Riverside: Mabel, a nursery maid, Martha, cook-general, 'from whom I learned the gourmet joys of hot dripping toast and treacle tart'.

CB We also had a butler – though how this portly personage consented to deploy his grandiose deportment in our modest establishment I shall never know (clearly he was my mother's method of keeping one ahead of 'your Aunt Letty'); and, circling in his stately orbit, one nursery-maid, one cook-general, one dressmaker who was so often with us as practically to be a member of the staff, and one groom-gardener. Butler was so helpful with whispered instructions upon which of the many brightly shining spoons and forks to use, until one day we returned early in the dog-cart to catch the poor pompous gentleman turning joyous cartwheels on the lawn. Exit my solemn instructor on the benefit of putting a bit of h'elbow grease into silver-polishing.

A constant stream of governesses, English and French, began to babble by. The English ladies were hot on posture and elocution (*'Shoot if you must this old grey head, But spare your country's flag,'* she said). The French contingent had a cold in the nose all the year round, and began to inculcate in me a schoolgirl French which availed me little when – much later – I was faced with translating the *risqué* situations, and esoteric and occasionally rude *argot* of the farces of Feydeau.

NS Collectively the governesses – French and English – added up to a threat:

CB – a depressing chain of genteel wardresses standing eagle-eyed between me and my attempts to deviate; swift to report my short-fallings to my mother, who in turn would tot up the scarlet sins for my father on pocket-money day.

My teenie school, a village affair but none the less fervent for that, tried hard to make me conform like the other girls, but to no avail. Still, if I did not master, at least I had a bash at, French conjugations here, and was almost persuaded that *bail, corail, email* and *vitrail* do or do not favour *aux* in their plural form. I learned, too, the Highland Fling ('Out, behind, before, behind – put some *go* into it, little girls').

After teenie school there came a tutor, a patriotic and military-minded gentleman, who taught me and two girl cousins, a little apprehensively, to 'about turn and form-er-threes'. So I was prepared to defend my country in the first of the wars to end wars.

NS Caryl's cousin, Tana Lowe, recalls this period as their attempt to found a Scout Troop, mounted on seaside donkeys: 'Tana was the Colonel, Caryl the Lieutenant and Pearl the Private.'

From her earliest years, Caryl had been passionate about music and dancing, and in her memoirs she implied that she was taken away from dancing-class when it looked as if she was going to be good.

CB For my introduction to the ballet I was wrapped in a woollen shawl which covered my mouth and satisfactorily muffled the bronchial wheezes that were the bane of my childhood. Thus I was taken to my very first dancing-class. It took place at the grandiose, parquet-floored Masonic Rooms situated above a pastry-cook's in the tea-salons to which it was *de rigueur* for the Young Ladies of Madame La Jardinière's School of Dancing to descend for restoring cream-buns and suitably weak tea. A whole new brightly coloured world beckoned the companion-hungry only child, too delicate to go to school, guarded by a depressing trail of governesses, with a gaggle of intimidating extrovert and healthy cousins as companions, and these in the summer only.

However, when I got home from my first dancing-class, wheezing

and congested as a jukebox, it was with despair that I heard my mother
say to my French governess, 'Put the child's dancing slippers away,
Ma'moiselle,' and, turning to me, 'You will not be needing them
again this term.' I knew full well that I was about to be abandoned
to the burning-hot poultices of bran and linseed oil which were
the barbarous treatment of the day for bronchitis; thereafter I was
forced to wear 'protectors' back and front, of ginger-coloured
thermogene wool, of which the only good thing to be said was that
when all the poulticing and the burning of asthma-cure powder
was done and I was adjudged well enough to sit by the fire in the
day nursery, 'not too near that nasty draughty window,' I was permitted
to pull away small segments of the wool every day – strong proof
that some day I would return to my world, which in this case was the
dancing-class.

I did indeed return.

Back to the Masonic Hall on Wednesdays; and Wednesday lit my
week. To arrive at my dancing-class I had to travel to a seaside
town by donkey-cart, row-boat and by train. And it was worth the
wait at the ferry, the wait at the station, and the heavy shopping baskets
that had to be lugged home later. It was even worth the flat feeling
when dancing-class was over – the journey back in the dark by
train and stepping-stone (for the ferry was tidal and land-locked)
and donkey-cart. And how very deflated a person can feel when they
have done badly at the thing they most love doing. But when I had
done well, when my arabesque had contrived to become
arrow-straight, my *entrechat* was taken high and strongly cut, and
my *porte-de-bras* crowned with a 'Queenly, dear girlie' by Madame La
Jardinière – why then I walked, waited and drove through the night
on air – dark, squelchy, easterly, Essex air. Usually I returned
deflated.

Looking back to those high ecstasies and black defeats, I realize
I was formulating a philosophy that still upholds me: next week would
bring another Wednesday. Next Wednesday I would do better. I
lived for Wednesdays – happy when I was practising, furious if the
weekly shopping which had to be done on the same trip to town
caused me to miss one thump of the thump-tinkle-tinkle of the
classroom piano, one thud of the thud-thud-thud of the dancers,
or one sniff of the glorious smell of ballet-shoes and rosin. Most
of the other girls were taken to class by their mothers; splendid
ladies in firm hats who would wait and watch and tap proud toes

to the irresistible thump-tinkle-tinkle, and smile encouragingly at
their dedicated daughters and wipe their brows with an
eau-de-cologne sprinkled handkerchief during the breaks. But my
own mother was almost always ailing, and I was escorted by
Martha who had been with my mother longer than I had and did,
and was, everything to us both. Martha would sit by herself, not
tapping, not smiling, but – oh, the bitter burning shame – nodding
off to sleep with her mouth open. Thump-tinkle-tinkle went the piano;
thud-thud-thud – that was us on the shiny parquet floor; and
Martha, strongly, steadily, almost thirstily and quite understandably,
snored. Ah, well – next week would come, and with it Wednesday.
And next Wednesday perhaps Martha would stay awake.

In spite of fatigue brought on by the excitement, the long, cold,
and often wet journey, and the weekly shopping, I would work like a
fiend in class. All that effort and vigour could do to make a future
ballerina out of one destined, instead, to become a future critic
of ballerinas, went into my magic Wednesday hour. But I must have
made some hard-fought progress because one day I found myself
transferred to Madame La Jardinière's Professional and Perfection
Class.

Now I had to work with girls who had private lessons and were
given a solo to dance at the yearly display at the local hospital for the
benefit of patients who had come through worse than this. We were,
or so we thought, a talented lot. We had our Margot Fonteyn –
her name was Fanny Gibbs. Fanny, the only girl in real silk tights,
dazzled her classmates with all of two turns on the *pointe*. Our
Antoinette Sibley was Polly Jones, a scraggy girl who never missed
her 'Queenly, dear girlie', and later married a curate. Our Makarova
was an up-and-coming five-year-old ('a second Fanny Gibbs,' the
mothers said) who kicked off a toe shoe at the hospital display and
had to be carried screaming out of the ward.

But I, too, had my moment of glory before boarding-school
claimed my Wednesdays and 'ballroom' became the order of the
dancing-class day, when, a very wobbly swan in a very prickly white
tutu, I danced with my huntsman – a fine sonsy girl in scarlet
sateen – on the hospital lawn before the gracious lady (I suspect on
this occasion she may have been a 'good gracious!' lady) who was to
become the Princess Royal.

Far away and long ago, they may seem tame to you, those
Wednesdays which lit my week. But I look back gratefully now to the

portly, somehow majestic figure of Madame La Jardinière in her short black gym tunic, with her 'and *one* – two – three – *one* – two – three – *smile* – two – three – *smile* – two – three'; to the pianist in the large black hat that was as much a part of the music she played for us as her crisp rolled arpeggios, and the cold in her nose; to the stretching, bending, bracing, holding that is the classroom routine of the dancer; and to that ineffable smell of ballet-shoes and rosin.

They were my Wednesdays. Nothing can take them from me.

NS At home Caryl was able to persevere with her education as a pianist.

CB When I was still so small that my white-socked feet could not reach the pedals, I used to attempt to play a duet on the pianoforte with my mother. I played the treble; she the bass; and it always ended in tears. The wretched opus was entitled *The Robin's Return*. It opened merrily enough, and I could rattle off the first few measures with considerable éclat, for they were in unison in my part which enabled me to keep up wth my bravura Mamma. But before long my hands were required to go different ways. I went to pieces invariably at this point. My chubby knees turned to jelly and I dissolved into tears. The same thing happened when I tried my luck solo at 'Christians Awake'.

Christians awake,
Salute the happy morn,
Whereon the Saviour of the world was born . . .

was a triumph, with both hands pounding the same notes an octave apart. But thereafter the beastly staves divided, and I was at their mercy. Practice did not make perfect.

NS The safe, cushioned, if lonely life at Riverside was eventually interrupted by school, as Caryl's somewhat haphazard education continued.

CB I went unwillingly to school, next, as a weekly boarder. The establishment was presided over by two middle-aged ladies whom hindsight has taught me might best be described as 'close friends'. I ended an essay on Holidays, for the less butch of the pair, with: 'And if you should be thinking of spending your honeymoon on a punt, my advice to you is "don't".' This early literary exercise netted me one hundred lines for 'impertinence'.

After that came Crowstone House, shamelessly proclaiming itself 'A School for the Daughters of Gentlemen' on the front gate. Here, in a week of crises brought about by a wave of Asian influenza, I cooked what I could (fried fish and raisin wine) for the boarders.

NS In a letter dated 11 November 1980, Caryl replied to Thelma Chadwick who had written to her asking for information for a book on Jewish girls' public schools. In the letter and in some subsequent postcards she added extra observations on her next place of education, Minerva College:

CB Do I remember Minerva? The very thought of it brought me out in a rash. Miss Whaplate standing in the door of our four-bedroomed dormitory in the middle of the night saying, 'Girls, girls, it is not friendship that you feel for one another it is passion.' I was left wondering what she was on about since we had all been peacefully asleep before her eruption . . . Cherry in those tasteful knitted jumpers and a drip on the end of her nose because of her perpetual cold. Miss Edith (Hart) from whose unspeakable Hebrew classes my father refused to release me, but thank heavens I knew what I must do – get expelled from them, which I did forthwith.

The 'education' one received at Minerva College was, to all practical considerations, non-existent. Never mind, researching my curious views of history has filled in many gaps.

Was I happy at Minerva? I still dream that I am back having my hair searched for lice and not on the bath list.

Sincerely, Caryl Brahms.

PS: On the rare occasions when my work in the theatre takes me to Leicester, I grip my driving-wheel and feel terribly sick until I'm out of it.

PPS: What about hockey?

NS In Caryl's considered memories of 'Minerva College' the same themes recur.

CB Boarding school was a bad dream.

Minerva College was in the village of Stonygate near Leicester, and even now I can hardly bear to write the name of Leicester for the shut-away feeling it brings back to me. Horrible hockey matches. Smells. Lemon between inter-school sets of lawn tennis, and being made to pay for the slices consumed at the end of the week. Hunger. The Brahms-Haydn *Variations*, mechanical and regular, going on in cold bedrooms overhead. French at meals: 'Passez-moi le bread-plate.'

Tetrazzini at the de Montfort Hall. Elocution in the conservatory. Outbursts of laughter in the dormitory. And always, every minute of the day, homesickness.

Then there was the Principal, Miss Whaplate, a cottage-loaf of a lady who suffered from shortness of breath and had been heard to say: 'Girls, girls, you've had a choice of fish and 'ash!' She is forever locked in my memory for a tirade which asserted: 'Girls, girls, you've taken tables and liberties and not put them back!' I was, to my utter dismay, always put in the fiendish hockey team because in my blind panic I hit that ghastly ball as hard and as far away from me as I could. To instil a love of literature to her somnolent class came weekly to Minerva College Miss Elgood, a sandy-haired, squirrel-tippeted former Cambridge don. 'When reading aloud Shakespeare, an effect can be made by underlining the pronouns vocally.' An effect indeed that might better be defined as disastrous: '*Her* father lov'd *me*; oft invited *me*'.

NS The bad dream of Minerva never left Caryl. She described it in painful detail.

CB The bad dream was one which, long after I had left, I kept on dreaming. In it I was back at my detested boarding-school, but grown up. As a grown up I was on no bath list. However, I was subject to the dread Test by Toothcomb. This was a torture dreamed up to ruin whatever was left of Sunday evening after the school walk – in crocodile. Miss Liebermilch, a German lady, with that thoroughness which is a national characteristic, would assemble the school in a red-flannel dressing-gown roll-call and a huge – or so it seemed to our anguished apprehension – toothcomb. Legend had it that some wretched girl had once been found with visitants in her hair, and terror swept through the ranks. In this nightmare of a nightmare, I was not able to leave the school buildings, and I would wake up sweating with a scream stifled in my throat.

Time passed: not so the terror of that dream. Believe it or not, I, having by now acquired some small distinction as a ballet critic – also a fiancé who was aware of the strength of the horror that these dreams held for me – was asked back to give away the prizes. The richest girlie in the school, being academically incapable of winning a prize for any subject whatsoever, was given a gilt-edged, tooled-leather volume for being 'the girlie with the highest ideals in the school'. How could they possibly know? By what measure could they compare one schoolgirl's ideals with another's?

Why, the reader will be asking, did I agree to go back to Nightmare Abbey? It seemed ungracious to refuse. So I provided myself with an old school chum – shall we call her Astarte? – and together we rattled down through the misty-moisty Midlands in my ancient jalopy. After all, we consoled each other, we would be spending the night at an hotel.

No sooner had we driven down the drive of Nightmare Abbey when a thick fog descended on us.

'Now, girlies,' said Miss Whaplate, 'there is to be no question of your going to an hotel tonight.'

'None,' said Fraulein Liebermilch.

'I,' said Miss Whaplate, 'stand in *loco parentis* to you both.'

'But I'm a married girlie,' Astarte pointed out.

'And I am an engaged girlie,' I bleated.

But they would not listen.

At last, we wrung from them their slow consent to Astarte's telephoning her husband, and me my fiancé.

'Do something,' I begged. 'It's happened. The Nightmare. The Midlands are enveloped in fog and I'm beleaguered because of the car, and I'm not on a bath list!'

That night Astarte and I slept side by side in a dormitory.

'Tomorrow night I'm sleeping with my husband,' she hissed.

'No talking after lights out,' ordered the prefect.

NS In an interview with Sheridan Morley for the *Radio Times*, Caryl explained that her mother was an invalid and her parents had decided that Caryl, in early adult life, would make her a good companion. To another interviewer she described her upbringing as 'disgraceful' – explaining that she was conditioned to assume that a life of leisure awaited her. When her mother became ill, they moved to the South of France, 'living like pampered gypsies, surrounded by servants, moving from Villefranche to Monte Carlo and back.' She had developed from a

CB   countrified and, of course, steel-bespectacled child awaiting each Friday with its argosy of the comic paper *Puck*, which for some reason was held to be suitable literature after the kindling of the Sabbath candles, the ceremonial tasting of a morsel of bread and salt, and the draining to the dregs of the delicious raisin 'wine'

NS   into a more independent and rebellious teenager – though she was still closely observed.

CB   For a long time I was not allowed to go to a *thé dansant*, or any other social gathering for that matter, unless the boy who lived two roads away was of the party, even though my hair would have been half-up in a door-knocker – the pleated plait ending in a broad ribbon that announced the transition. However, one day my mother descended with hat-boxes and dresses. I was about, it seemed, to 'come out'. I had no say in the dresses and hats. To protest would have been an enormity.

NS   She confesses to another obsession:

CB   I thought about the first kiss constantly. Would it change everything? Would I look different? Who would he be? Nothing prepared me for what actually happened. I had a toffee in my mouth. I discussed it afterwards with a friend.

    'Do you think he knew?' I asked.

    'I expect so.'

    Some time later I was dancing with a medical student, rather a dashing South African. He cupped my breast with his hand.

    'Did he know he was doing this?'

    'I expect so.'

    I was very slow to develop. It might be thought in some circles that I have made up for it since.

NS   From her 'just-past-chaperone-time' Caryl recalled two 'farcical engagements'. One was to a South African (the same?) who sought to clinch his case with the ultimate persuasion, 'God, Caryl, you'll love the *bundu*!'; one crept up on her when she was on a visit to Wales, and received a proposal from an amateur boxer. 'As we were standing outside the door in the rain at the time, I thought it wise to say "Yes" in order to stay dry.' His proposal accepted, the ecstatic young man rushed inside to tell his parents. The telephones buzzed, and Caryl's mother arrived by the first available train to deliver her from the misalliance.

Caryl, not surprisingly, had different ideas of a career from those of her parents. After finishing school she won a place at the Royal Academy of Music. ('What were my parents to do with this lump of a girl?') She was studying the piano, but found she had to give it up.

CB My sense of criticism was too developed. I simply could not stand the sound I made when I practised on it. The Royal Academy of Music was understandably somewhat hesitant about my enrolment. Here I learned a rich variety of Lifemanship and to take my Harmony exercise to the hall porter, an ex-Kneller Hall Bandsman, to deal with. From this establishment I emerged with a bronze medal.

NS However, two things happened in her enjoyable student years before she failed her LRAM. She started writing light verse for the Academy's magazine and discovered that it was something she could enjoy in private. She also found that she was good at it. At that time – she was now in her twenties – she could do nothing so bold as leave home; but here was work which could be done without her parents' knowledge. Her simple verses were much in the manner of Robert Louis Stevenson. To have published her work under her own name, Doris Caroline Abrahams, would have given the game away, so she shorted 'Abrahams' to 'Brahms' and amended 'Caroline' to 'Caryl', choosing a version which would leave editors in an unenlightened age in some doubt as to whether she was a man or a woman.

2

Ballet beginnings

NS Having invented herself, Caryl Brahms started to put herself to work against the backdrop of the 'twenties which she entered at the age of nineteen.

CB The Young Things had officially become Bright. The high-pitched gaiety that had swept their dancing mothers through war engulfed them on their return from it. Armed with personal bottles of gin, the Bright Young things betook themselves to endless parties – pyjama parties, bottle parties, treasure-hunt parties, gate-crashing parties, midnight-bathing parties, coming-out parties costing thousands, and surprise parties that did not cost their hosts a bean. Dressed by bright young dressmakers, be-publicized by bright young photographers, the Bright Young Things with bored young faces were making up to themselves for the past, perhaps, or comforting themselves for the future.

NS Later, in *You Were There*, the last novel she was to start with S. J. Simon, she recalled an incident during the General Strike.

CB A luxurious Rolls-Royce, travelling in the direction of the site where Grosvenor House was one day to rise, pulled up in the Finchley Road before a bus stop where a shy but observant Jewess was standing, hoping for a lift. The owner of the Rolls had given generously to charity. He had given a country house to England's prime ministers. In fact, giving things had become quite a habit with him. He gave the little Jewess a lift. His passenger installed, her temporary host leant forward.

'Have you ever driven in a Rolls-Royce before?' he asked in a kind voice.

Equally kind, the little Jewess hated to disappoint him. She said, 'No.'

'Ah!' said the owner, 'then you can always remember that Lord Lee of Fareham gave you a lift in the General Strike.'

He sank back against the accustomed comfort of his corner, well pleased.

NS Then she added the lethal footnote, 'And Caryl Brahms has not forgotten.' She described her early journalism thus:

CB My first 'paid' work (if we do not count my Auntie Lett's caterpillar teas, at which my cousins and I were rewarded with salmon and anchovy paste sandwiches for collecting green caterpillars) was at the handsome rate of fourpence a line for poems for children in Raphael Tuck's *Annual*. With luck, I'd earn as much as six shillings and eightpence for an eight-line poem, printed with a byline. But you can't keep a good girl down, and my next income bracket was reached on the Home Page of the *Evening Standard* where I was paid three guineas – guineas, mark you – for a set of verses irrespective of lines, on a weekly contract. Literary agents took note of my byline and began asking me out to lunch. Soon my fee rose to the giddy heights of five pounds a week – every week.

NS From occasional verse to regular ballet criticism was a change of emphasis which she was at some pains to explain.

CB The ballet held its place in the roundabout of my life for many a year, imparting its sophistication to my early unformed taste, teaching me to discriminate, bearing me on its strong currents from Chaminade to Stravinsky. Music became my world's foundation – the extended line of the dancer was the poetry in this pilgrim's unpredicted progress. When the Diaghilev Ballet left London at the end of a six or eight weeks' season, I grieved; but each winter my parents went to the South of France in search of sunshine to lessen my mother's asthma, where I would join them for the hols.

It had been here that my mother first took me to see the Diaghilev Ballet at the Casino. Someone with a difficult Russian name was appearing in a ballet called by a difficult French name. I was terribly disappointed. It wasn't at all like my dancing-class. Fortunately they were dancing *Les Sylphides* on my next visit, which did much to

restore Diaghilev to my favour. I felt that this ballet of tulle-clad
dancers floating in the moonlight was a bit more like the Masonic
Rooms – and in the Shades I see the pale faces of the great Diaghilev
and the genius Fokine wince. When, in the first two decades of the
century, Diaghilev brought his Ballets Russes to London they
became instant, if unlikely, arbiters of fashion. The London
sitting-rooms broke out in rash of jade, violet, sapphire and cerise
adjuncts from the palette of Bakst, and of course where London led
the great country houses were to follow. Limp silken Pierrots Lunaire
sprawled across loose covers on which previously roses and eglantine
had reigned unchallenged, and stylistically irreproachable neo-Tudor
paisley cushions reflected new and exotic shades. We all sported
silk scarves in batik which challenged the rainbow.

On one of my family visits to the South of France, a dark and
very secret cloud had obscured the Riviera's gaiety for me; I needed
more than my pocket money – ten shillings a week was no longer
sufficient – for the ballet and the books which were the breath of life
to me. How was I, magnificently unprepared as I was, to earn? I sat
back and took financial stock. What did I know more about than other
people? Madame La Jardinière's dancing-class came instantly to
mind. The message was unmistakable. Thus equipped, I could
write about the ballet.

NS She took to haunting the pit queue at the Princes – now the Shaftesbury
Theatre. Her first exercise in criticism was a notice written, rewritten
and re-rewritten, of the Satie-Massine ballet, *Mercure*. She sent it, in
longhand, to Lady Rhonda's *Time and Tide*. An assistant editor, Margaret West ('Blessed Margaret West'), sent it back with a note saying that
she would keep the embryo critic in mind should a suitable opportunity
arise. A year later the summons came. It was to review, not a ballet,
but a play. Five hundred and fifty words were required. The deadline
was a week away. Caryl remembered the address of *Time and Tide*
vividly (32 Bloomsbury Street), but not the name of the play. She
posted her critique and sat back to await immortality and, more urgently,
cash. On press day she got a frantic call from *Time and Tide*. Where
was her copy? The memory of the re-rewrite had to be hastily re-re-
rewritten and taken to Bloomsbury Street. The flurry of activity yielded
two guineas.

However, she had a foothold in *Time and Tide*, and used it to write
about the ballet, the opera and the theatre – which at that time ran a

bad third. Late in life, when going to the opera became too expensive for her, she missed it cruelly. She recalled then her first visit to Glyndebourne, in its second season. She had gone on behalf of *Time and Tide*, and John Christie, the founder, had been the object of the sceptical young journalist's investigation:

CB He took me round every inch, the grounds, the dining-halls, the scene-painting sheds, the practice rooms, the kitchens, the dressing-rooms and, adjoining each, the lavatories. 'Lavatories!' John Christie gloated, 'built especially wide to accommodate crinolines. Mind you,' he said, suddenly stricken, 'they ought not to be wearing them in here.'

NS In spite of her forays into opera, ballet continued to be Caryl's principal subject.

CB Those were the days when ballet was not the *plat du jour* at Covent Garden, but a seasonal toy. I saw the captivating Pavlova once only, and then she was past her prime. At the end, news of her death in Holland reached us. It was rumoured that her arms had gone through the movements of the Dying Swan, the simple choreographic poem Fokine had created for her and which she had charged with her own magic. I wrote a short story for the *Lady*, setting out her death in counterpoint with the death of a pickpocket, in which both ballerina and thief, in their last moments, went through the customary motions of their profession – Pavlova sketching the final fluttering of a swan; the pickpocket, light-fingered to the last, ending by filching his doctor's watch.

Anton Dolin, inspired showman that he has always been, organized an evening of ballet in celebration of Anna Pavlova's life in art. In it he played, on an empty, blue-lit stage, the music Saint-Saëns wrote for the Swan who, dying, sings. That empty stage was our *ave atque vale*, and I do not think there could have been a throat in that packed house that did not have a lump in it. On the day before the sale of Pavlova's worldly goods, I went to Ivy House on Hampstead Heath and was brought very near to tears by a roomful of limp-limbed pierrot dolls – they were the high fashion of the times – and long tulle-skirted ballerinas, and dolls dressed as the traditional Russian brides, all of them gifts from her adoring public. Most eloquent of all, I found a singe on her silverwood dressing-table stool where she had rested a cigarette. And as I looked out to the little lake set in her grounds, I saw a floating of swans – her symbol.

Caryl's favourite Pavlova story was, of course, less poetic. All her life Caryl preferred international ballet, danced by artists picked from all over the world and presented by international creators, over the parochial homegrown product – unless the British performer was unquestionably musical. She cherished the memory of an aggressively English girl – plain, technically accurate, and tactless, who was standing in the wings at the Palace Theatre one night when the orchestra struck up Pavlova's introduction to *The Dying Swan*. 'Suddenly,' she told Caryl, 'inspiration seized me and I sailed out on to the stage before Madame could make her entrance ...' Madame was waiting when she came off. 'And, do you know?' said the usurper, 'Madame Pavlova sacked me!'

Caryl did not see Nijinsky dance, and only glimpsed him when 'he was an emptied shell of a man' who had been taken to a box at the Princes Theatre on the instructions of his doctor, who felt that the experience might bring to life the impish spirit which he was sure still lurked near the surface. Nijinsky was sitting there, 'his face as grey as his hair. I hardly liked to look at him for it seemed such an intrusion.'

From much the pre-war period she remembered Woizikovsky, 'the most eloquent Petrushka of them all', and Lydia Sokolova the great English ballerina, both of whom 'were absorbed into Anna Pavlova's eternally rotating company, at odds in the alien corn of its drawing-room repertoire'.

The absorption was the result of Diaghilev's death, of which Caryl read in the now defunct *Evening News*, on top of a bus. 'Desolation! My bright world, caught by catastrophe, had vanished, it looked like forever, into the wings.'

However, she had seen Karsavina once, 'as the dreaming girl in *Spectre de la Rose*, with Anton Dolin in the role Nijinsky created. The great ballerina must have been in her late forties or early fifties, yet one did not for a moment doubt her youth in this romantic ballet.' She also saw Lydia Lopokova, who married Maynard Keynes: 'Loppie was the perfect example of what the French call *jolie laide*, with her saucer blue eyes and her flippant nose, her dancing inspired by the *faux-naïveté* which was the high mode of the day. In the '80s we would find it tiresome but the ballet-goer of the '20s recognized it as a part of her unique talent. To tease her, Diaghilev renamed *The Sleeping Beauty* and called it *The Sleeping Princess* when she danced it, because he said that Lopokova was no beauty.'

CB 1933 dawned, and with it Colonel Wassili de Basil and his 'Baby Ballerinas' – Baronova, Toumanova and Riabouchinska; and somewhere along the line we discovered that we had developed a ballet of our own, a resident ballet moulded by de Valois, featuring Alicia Markova and Anton Dolin, promoting Freddie Ashton and eventually producing our own baby ballerina, Margot Fonteyn.

NS Caryl's canvassing for the 'international' in ballet was as wholehearted as her mistrust of the choreographer who could not hear a symphony without longing to interpret it in the terms of his own art – The Dance. These and other strongly held views produced a certain tension over the years with dancers:

CB On one occasion I was coasting through the Crush Bar at Covent Garden when I saw Alicia Markova's back and advanced to greet her. She was talking to the outstanding American dramatic ballerina, Nora Kaye, whom I heard, as I neared the group say, in the clearest cut-glass tones, 'Don't turn around, Alicia, here comes that terrible Caryl Brahms.'
   '*Hello*, Judy darling,' said Alicia. (Judy was Caryl's name in Markova's family, who had known her since they were children and she was in her late teens.)

NS And with choreographers:

CB At a first night at the Lyric, Hammersmith, I spotted – across a not very crowded bar – Robert Helpmann, whose new ballet, *Adam Zero*, I had noticed unfavourably that morning. What is more, I had said it baldly, roundly, and less than kindly. The next thing I saw was a purposeful Helpmann bearing down on me, looking livid, pursued by his concerned friend, Michael Benthall, keen to avert trouble. However, Helpmann was too quick for him. 'Caryl,' he opened haughtily, 'I never read my notices myself, but my mother, who is sensitive to criticism . . .'

NS Occasionally Caryl strikes a more whimsical note – especially lamenting

[32]

Ashton's absence during the War when he was called up to be a censor, a job for which she doubted he was as well qualified as he was to make ballets. 'I'm exhausted,' he said to her one night in the foyer of the New Theatre where the Sadler's Wells Company was playing, 'I've been making decisions all day long.' Later, he begged her not to write a book about him which a publisher wanted to commission. 'Perhaps,' she explained, 'he read the book I wrote on Helpmann.'

Another, less distinguished, choreographer was Keith Lester, who did a lot of work for the Windmill Theatre and, among other things, a ballet for the Markova-Dolin Company, *David & Jonathan*, 'a ballet in which he danced David, or was it Jonathan, with Dolin dancing Jonathan, or was it David? [For the record, Dolin danced David.] Keith asked me what I considered the most important ingredient of any ballet. "Music," was my instant answer. "Wrong," said Keith with undisguised delight. "It's the voids – the spaces between the dancers."'

CB A76 and A77 were to be the numbers of my seats in the stalls circle of the Royal Opera House at Covent Garden. I called one of the books I was to write about ballet after them. It has a delicately traced, beautiful *eau-de-Nil* dust wrapper by that fine stage designer Oliver Messel, whose work, taste and palette influenced many of the designers of his day. I defined my function in *A Seat at the Ballet* as 'to act as a kind of Man from Cooks to the moderately new ballet-goer' – that blissful being who knows what he likes without knowing why he likes it and is willing to go back and see it any number of times.

When I sat there for one of my papers, not clapping, not paying for my programme, always in despair because in my heart I knew that I should never quite capture the moment, the palms of my hands were clammy for fear I might not find the words at all. When I went as a private person, I was free to frown or applaud, or even to comment in what is probably the most piercing hiss of the century – it must be, judging from the number of times the sentiments thus confided were repeated back to me (though in those days the hisses were usually ascribed to Arnold Haskell). When I was a paper I was deeply concerned if the ballet-goer was not getting money's worth – for whatever reason: bad ballet building, bad dancing, bad lighting or bad orchestral playing. When I am myself, I detach the nearest member of the management and announce the fact – a method I strongly recommend.

[33]

NS *A Seat at the Ballet* was published after the war. During the late '20s and the '30s, Caryl's income from ballet criticism was supplemented by small sums for verses for children on the *Evening Standard*'s Home Page, and occasional general journalism. In later life she was a little embarrassed by her child verse: 'I live in dread that nice simple people who write to me about those verses about children should come across the Brahms-Simon books with their crass gags and their lack of reticence.'

A more threatening embarrassment nearly overtook her in those early days. John Byron (the dancer and actor, who was a great friend at the time) reports a spectacular *lacuna* in Caryl's nursery repertoire over one of those early child verses. Apparently she was faced with a deadline and sitting at a table trying vainly to meet it. From the bathroom she heard what she would have described as 'my current young man' pom-pomming as he soaped himself in the bath. 'The hot's so hot and the cold's so cold,' he was improvising. 'That's rather good,' Caryl thought, and down it went. She embroidered it, completed it, and submitted it in all innocence. In all ignorance, the paper printed it – to have an irate A. A. Milne on their tail in no time at all. The innocent intent of the plagiarism was finally settled, but the skirmish was nearly expensive.

However, at the end of the '20s she published a collection of her child verse under the title *The Moon On My Left* – indeed, she published much the same book twice. The earlier edition was by Hodder and Stoughton. I can find no evidence that it was issued. Hodder's, who suffered a blitz on stock and records during the war, have no memory of it. It is undated and the illustrator is not credited. There are thirty-seven poems. Gollancz brought out another edition with forty-one verses in 1930, whose more sophisticated illustrations, by Anna Zinkeisen, included a moon on the title page with a face reminiscent of the young Caryl Brahms as the woman in the moon. There is a charming dedication common to both which concludes:

'The Editor of the Home Page of the *Evening Standard* has extended the hospitality of his columns to so many of the verses that it looked for a long time as though the book would belong to him; then the title was borrowed from Mr Hilaire Belloc, a Poet, and it seemed right that the book should be offered to him, because of this poem:

[34]

The Moon on the one hand, the dawn on the other;
The Moon is my sister, the dawn is my brother.
The Moon on my left and the dawn on my right,
My brother, good morning – my sister, good night.

But, when the book was finished, I knew that it belonged to my Mother and my Father, because they were my First Friends.'

The most popular poem in the book, 'Any Boy To Any Ship', was later set to music by Arthur Baynon and was sung at Caryl's memorial service by Robert Meadmore.

Any Boy To Any Ship

Do you need a cabin boy,
Ship in the harbour?
Do you need a cabin boy,
Ship on the sea?

I want to go to Africa,
India and China;
So if you're off to foreign parts,
Please take me!

I'm pretty good at polishing,
Ship in the harbour,
And quick at running messages,
Ship on the sea,
It's all right here for ladies,
Little girls and babies;
But if it's cabin boys you want,
Do take me!

I'm tired of the things I know,
Ship in the harbour,
I'm tired of the street I know,
Ship on the sea;
I don't like shoes with laces,
Collars, ties and braces;
So if you're off to foreign parts,
Do take me!

[35]

I'm tired of stupid places
And people's ugly faces
And if you're off to round-the-world
Please take me.

Meanwhile, *Time and Tide* used to send her on the occasional journal-istic foray, like the one she remembered in later life under the title, 'On Not Taking Tea with T.E.':

CB As I emerged from the Reading Room of the British Museum on a damp and foggy afternoon, I raced the rest of Great Russell Street and Tottenham Court Road, pray-and-dashed across Oxford Circus and right on along Oxford Street almost as far as Marble Arch. Bumpus's Bookshop, the best browsery in London, was to be found there. I browsed. My rush had paid off. There was time, and to spare. I was there to see the Tuppence-Coloured Victorian Juvenile Theatre, which was giving two afternoon performances of *The Merry Miller and His Men*, or *Sweeney Todd – The Demon Barber of Fleet Street*, or '*My name is Norval/on the Grampian Hills/I tend my father's sheep*'. The young man who worked the models and spoke the lines and raised and lowered the painted crimson curtain turned out to be called Speaight. Any relation? Yes. Robert Speaight, the actor, was his elder brother. There must have been some mention of *Murder in the Cathedral*.

    The man in the raincoat had an open-air look to him. He was shortish. His fairish hair was shortish. And he moved so quickly and lightly that I do not think I knew that he had joined us that afternoon at Bumpus the Bookshop. Norval was silent. He had already done his slotted cardboard nut on those Grampians; and the ancient music-box, there to sprinkle the air with the overture and play the house back to the bookshelves, was silent. There would be a longish interval for browsing and buying before the second house. I asked the younger Mr Speaight to play the musical-box. He said Mr Wilson would not allow it between shows. And to make quite sure of this, Mr Wilson kept the key. Bumpus was a bookshop, not a toy shop; not Queen's Hall. So there it was – until the man in the raincoat spoke. He may have been there all the time.

NS Caryl first told me this story when we went to see Alec Guinness in Terence Rattigan's play, *Ross*.

[36]

CB He did not look unlike Sir Alec Guinness: more often and longer
in the open air, maybe, and even more detached; more sturdy than
was Sir Alec in those days and more compact than he is now. Not
perhaps a man of fun, but evidently a man of impulse. 'Give my
compliments to Mr Wilson, and tell him I would like to see it
work.'

Was there a shade of emphasis on 'I'? Even so, he did not speak
as meticulously, beautifully, definitively as Sir Alec. But his voice had
a sufficient authority. The younger Mr Speaight sped off: I suppose
I said something vague and civil and quite unmemorable to the man
in the raincoat. He must have made some polite and unremarkable
reply. I may even have told him I was there to see the Juvenile
Theatre for my paper, for I was very green and loyal and proud of
being what was probably the worst young critic ever worn by a
weekly – *Time and Tide* – that was, before they fired me. That was,
before they reinstated me. That was, before they fired me again.
Thinking back, I realize that I richly deserved the sudden painful
severance. But that is a story for some other time.

The younger Mr Speaight came speeding back. He brought with
him a king-sized key. Wheels whirred, cogs cogged, the musical-box
ground out its silver tune, and the entire shop was filled with a
resounding tinkle. Heads came up out of books, looked vaguely round,
buried themselves again. 'Interesting the way these old things work,'
said the man in the raincoat. 'You understand the principle? Well, let
me explain – you see that roller there . . .'

I went into the daze which is my defence when anything of any
kind is explained to me. Long years of resisting 'I was holding three
to the knave of hearts' has given me a certain perspicacity in sensing
salient points and nodding as though registering them. I decided
that the man in the raincoat must be a teacher; probably a born
teacher. He could make springs and ratchets sound like sense –
at a distance through a cushioning of haze. But at heart I knew I
hadn't registered at all – I was just a convenient pupil on whom
to hang a lesson in mechanics.

And then the tinkle and the lesson were at an end. And still the
crimson curtain of the toy theatre stayed down and people who
had drifted over, drawn by the music, drifted away to prowl about
the shelves and bookstalls. I hope I had the manners to thank the
man in the raincoat for his cogent *exposition raisonnée* of how the
wheels go round.

Maybe I hadn't taken him in for a minute. Maybe he felt secure because I was so very green and foolish and so clearly hadn't the shadow of an idea who he was. Maybe he felt in a mood for teaching and I was the nearest to hand. Perhaps he was just being kind. He said: 'I'm going to have some tea now. What are you doing?'

'I'm staying to see the show – for my paper.' I was going to add proudly *Time and Tide* (a paper can always use a new reader), but lightly, quickly, suddenly, he had gone and the younger Mr Speaight was looking at me.

'You don't know who that was, do you?' There was condescension, almost pity in the way he spoke – he was a very young, younger Mr Speaight. And because it was true, the accusation stung me.

'I seem to know that face,' I said. I was lying, of course.

'It was only tea with Lawrence of Arabia you've just turned down,' said the younger Mr Speaight with maddening superiority.

Lawrence of Arabia, who had no time for journalists; and no time for women; and as for women journalists . . .

NS While she was at the Royal Academy, Caryl lived at a students' home run by a friend of her mother's in the Finchley Road. Max Landau recalls that her parents also had a house in Brondesbury Park at this time, and remembers her twenty-first birthday party, a big, bustling affair with a marquee in the garden. The Abrahams moved around quite a lot. They lived for a time at Westcliff; at another time they had a chalet on Stevens Eyot near Kingston, complete with launch and canoe. However, it was at the boarding-house in the Finchley Road that Caryl met S. J. Simon, a fellow-lodger who was to become her great collaborator. A White Russian, born in 1904 in Harbin, Manchuria, he was working part-time as the host at a bridge club and 'like all Russians, was studying forestry'. (Shades of Chekov's doctor in *Uncle Vanya*, one of Caryl's favourite plays.) His name was Secha (or Simon) Jascha Skidelsky – known as Skid – and together they arrived at his *nom de plume*, S. J. Simon. When the Home Page of the *Standard* found an extra chore for her, the professional coupling of Brahms with Simon began.

CB In the '30s, the *Standard* had the rights to some drawings by David Low of a dog whom he had created to scamper among the manic Hitlers and frog-like Mussolinis. I wrote the words to go with them.

At first we called the dog Mussolini, but then the Italian Embassy complained to our editor, so we changed it to 'Musso': 'Musso – the Home Page Dog'. After a while, I found it impossible to think of something new for Musso each day, so I roped in Skid.

3

Brahms and Simon

NS Two months before she died, Caryl embarked on her character study of S. J. Simon. It was the passage in her book about which she was most self-conscious, the assessment she was most anxious to get right. She chose to write it as a double portrait – 'look here, upon this picture and on this'. Her second sketch was of me – her other regular collaborator. A month later she produced another draft. She did not show me either section; but she did tell me, rather severely, that she thought she might have been too hard on me the first time and had decided to let me off more lightly. In redrafting she closely intertwined the two accounts, and I have decided not to separate them since she brings Simon so vividly to life. I place them here because so much of what follows depends on understanding something of the unique, anarchic humour of Simon, whom I never met.

CB S. J. Simon and E. G. Sherrin: Skid and Ned. Two sides of the Caryl Brahms coin. Alike only in that both have worked with me, who bears in some measure the imprint of them both, and could be said to be the metal between, and who is jolly fortunate to have worked with both.

People have called me a wit, but I don't think this is true – more the bounced-off cause of wit in others. Auguste or Fall Guy who has tumbled flat on his back while over his appreciative body the sparks fly – those sparks he has lit in others, the cause – maybe even the first cause – of wit in others.

Skid and Ned: Ned and Skid: Skid with nothing about which to be secret, withholding nothing; Ned the schizophrene, grappling to himself his secret or secrets, yet changing as the wind changes of a March day, a child of sunshine and considerable charm. But beware the Ide, Caryl; oh, beware the Ide.

[40]

Skid working in my mind and I in his, in a creative kind of ESP – it was a very barren day indeed if I had to turn to Skid or he to me to say, 'Now we should bring on Stroganoff,' or Disraeli or Trottie. Ned, withholding what he writes so that I can at most act as a kind of corrective governess, embellishing his work. Often Ned and I have furious arguments, but, as with Skid, never over money; always on the placing or replacing of words, or occasionally on a point of creative wit. I carry as a truepenny Skid's pejorative, 'That's not humour, it's wit: OUT!' – by which he divided humour that bubbles up from the diaphragm – or at least, *my* diaphragm – from wit, which is a mental exercise. Skid was a clown by birthright. Ned is a wit – at times a disturbingly arch wit. I am a pendulum – or should it be a chameleon? – borrowing my colour from both: Skid and Ned and also Caryl – the Chameleon.

Even in appearance they could not have been more set up to the north and south of one another. Skid with his shock of straight black hair surmounting a face of white dough with blackcurrants for eyes to blink at objects around him, round full red succulent lips, mostly with a cigarette spilling over with ash tilted between them, and a couple of chins, generous in mould as in nature. Ned with close-cropped hair somewhere between red and brown (well, say sandy, like his mother's, a delightful country lady), steady, piercing eyes, pale thin lips, not unlike an egg in a bitter mood, making a biting and shrewd assessment of his peers; except where he resembles an refulgent egg, basking in a sunny social climate in which wine, wit and conversation flow. Not a whip-cracking ringmaster but a gag-master, he can supply his own one-liners which he delivers with a timing second only to my own. Yet, when first I met him there was no bitterness discernible in him, only a happy, friendly, eager ambience. Life is always a matter of mountain tops and deep valleys to Ned, just as, in a way, it mostly is to me; but my achievement rises to no such heights and I drop less harshly, only to pick myself up, dust myself down and start all over again. Ned is, as Skid was, a man of very real compassion, far greater than mine; even though Skid's compassion was accompanied by mirth. Skid was less able but more secure than Ned, whose insecurity takes the form of never admitting to being in the wrong. Only once in all the years I have worked with him have I heard Ned say, 'That was my fault.' And that was not admitted to me. My failure, in a way, I think. He is lucky in that he soon starts believing his own lies, and this I find

[41]

half-infuriating and half-touching. Skid saw no necessity to lie.*
His whole world was filled with bridge, work with me, dog-racing (the
instinct to gamble being markedly a characteristic of so many White
Russians†), 'wenching', and singing 'Otchi Chernia', his favourite
song.

Ned has led my work into many fascinating paths, but in the
beginning was the word and the word was laughter – Skid's kind of
laughter. And after all, no one could be kinder, sunnier, funnier
than Ned when the sun shines in his personal sky.

Work with Skid meant, in the main, writing the wildly inventive,
if insufficiently dragooned, Brahms-Simon novels and a certain
amount of fictional journalism. I took no part in his bridge books,
he took no part in my ballet and drama criticism. We sweated blood
to keep our songs in the Ambassador's Revue, we turned *Bullet* and
Dizzy into radio plays, and we waged inglorious war to the death in
the lost cause of staging *A Bullet in the Ballet*, the history of which,
viewed in the perspective which hindsight in its mercy bestows, was
lunatic and lost from the outset.

Skid and I laughed our way through a world war and in so doing
forged our reputation.

Work with Ned leads me into many fields of endeavour way above
my station – I would not have found myself writing lyrics for the
Dankworths or mounting *No Bed for Bacon* at the Bristol Old Vic or
working on 'That Was The Week That Was'; and while it is
conceivable that I might, though less enjoyably, have written *Beecham*
without him, never would I have written *The Mitford Girls* without him
or *I Gotta Shoe* (our all-black version of Cinderella) or won the Ivor
Novello Award for the best screen song of that particular year. Still,
it could be argued, I would not have dropped that bronze figurine
on my toe and put wearing a shoe out of the question for eighteen
months.

Really the range of activity and achievement working with Ned
has been a mystery which turned my work into my career – for I had
not thought of my writing in this manner until Ned, at his most
lordly, invented it for me and dropped 'That'll be good for your
career, Caryl,' into a conversation. And me? I work and learn all the

* Why bother? Shrug.

† Once we overheard someone say, 'A man has *no right* to call himself a gambler if
he dare not take a risk.' We both thought anyone using the word gambler in any way
that was not pejorative was comical, and to boast of it wildly funny.

time. For instance, only recently I worked on a perfectly true short story with *Punch* in mind. It was about a crimper, for whom I invented the name Fred Thribb. In himself he was a kind man, always helpful and generous. But a rich client descended from his stars, promising to make him her heir. My story was to show Fred's change from permissible optimism to totally unacceptable greed.

I worked it over and over, this sordid little tale. Humour bubbled out of it, I made myself laugh aloud two or three times. But the more I wrote the more anti-semitic it became and the uglier Fred Thribb's greed. Now I have abandoned it, with the reflection that all is not grist that comes from the mill of real life.

Wasted endeavour? No, just a belated lesson.

Perhaps I have drawn only one face of the many-faceted Ned, and only as I see him, at that. For Ned has at least seven Neds jockeying for position under his skull, which must put him at permanent pressure.

As I write Ned is coming up to fifty-two, good-looking in a paunchy way and narcissistically brimming over with confidence. However, there is, I think, a price to be paid by the over-confident. Can it be only the thin ice covering the dark waters of self-knowledge beneath? Ned is fortunate in that his mind has never been more widely open to trend, his wit never more keenly honed. He has reached what should be his ripest hour. Do the seven Neds equate with one happy man? Only Ned can answer this one, and it's all Lombard Street to a China orange that he will tell himself firmly that, in the words of William Blake, joy is his name. Being Ned, he will profoundly believe himself. Certainly where money is concerned, he is the most generous man imaginable. Compared to Ned, Midas would be Scrooge.

Skid was an open book for all to read; Ned is an island under an April sky; a sphinx – I wish I had the understanding to solve his riddle and to help him in the way that he helps me.

Whatever work Ned attempts soon gets a professional polish on it. Take cooking. Time was when I was served steaks of leather-and-wood by this impetuous chef, for Ned would hurl himself at his cuisine – did I say himself? I mean, of course, his seven selves. He still hurls, but now to some purpose. I am never allowed to penetrate to his cooker while he prepares elaborate sauces and goes balding-headed at his stoves. This method may be

[43]

seen to dominate his work. Speed is of the essence in his sevenfold working fury. I like to select and, as it were, taste my words: Ned's sevenfold demons drive him on torrent-wise.

A Bullet in the Ballet, the first book I was to write with Skid, came about quite by chance.

4

A Bullet in the Ballet

NS The chance which led to *A Bullet in the Ballet* occurred in 1936.

CB Arnold Haskell, the popular ballet critic, writing at the time for the *Daily Telegraph*, went, at the drop of a hat (three-cornered, no doubt) to Australia, forgetting in his haste to let his paper know he would be absent, so the *Telegraph* invited me to cover the ballet until his return. It was during my tenure that Lawson, the Managing Editor, sent for me.

Panic-stricken, I tried to reason this terrible, mystifying thing out. Of course, I told myself, it couldn't be the sack. I only rated the office boy or someone equally lowly to fire me. But did I believe my rationalizing? No.

NS The Brahms-Simon partnership on the Home Page of the *Evening Standard* was by now firmly established and Caryl took Simon along to Fleet Street with her for moral support – 'somewhat absent-minded moral support'. Her neurosis got them to the *Daily Telegraph* an hour early and they waited in the Kardomah Café a few doors away.

CB To pass the inexorable time we started plotting a detective novel in which, initially, Arnold Haskell was to be tossed flies-high in a blanket, like the Corregidor in *The Three-Cornered Hat* and found to be dead, on landing back in the blanket; and when that failed to ring true we changed the ballet to *Petroushka* and invented the victim.

NS Using the Brahms-Simon formula of loud laughter followed by immediate dismissal of an idea – 'not funny!' – they worked out the hour of waiting, and Caryl went off for her interview.

[45]

CB When, finally, I got myself across the vast expanse of parquet that spread like a golden sea before my careful feet, the man sitting on the other side of a terrific desk looked the very image of my uncle Lionel. All I was to be asked was whether or not the Royal Academy of Music should be encouraged to move to new premises. Reflectively, of one of the ballerinas, Lawson said, 'It's a pity she's such a stupid little girl.' I remember wondering if she was stupid or just scared out of her wits, as I was at that very moment.

NS As a result of the Kardomah session, Caryl and Simon arranged to meet on the following Wednesday to start writing their murder mystery:

CB 'Eleven o'clock,' he confirmed sleepily.
   'Sharp,' I said.
   Skid yawned luxuriously.
   Wednesday dawned and eleven o'clock arrived. Not so Skid. At a quarter to twelve I telephoned. Where the hell was he?
   'In bed, my dear sir,' he said. I was always 'My dear Sir' to Skid, and in moments of high approval, 'My Caryl'.

NS Two favourite catch-phrases were born early on. Simon's initial tardi-ness provoked the speculation which, in the book, always preceded the rumoured arrival of the designer, Benois: 'On Wednesday – if 'e come.' At this time Simon's fortunes were at a low ebb, 'a Skid constant at any point', and he was acting as host at a bridge club (not the Acol, which was his haunt). Caryl tracked him down there one afternoon to confirm a programme for work. While they were discussing it, a tall Central European came in. He looked around. 'You schange schmall scheque?' he asked hopefully – giving immediate life to their modern choreographer, Nevajno.

CB In *Bullet* the Brahms-Simon mix was all too apparent. Skid took over the detection and the love scenes, and I did the ballet bits. Together we wrote the narrative. Thereafter we were to write all of our novels together save for the occasional descriptive passage which I would write. The work progressed bumpily, punctuated by Woodbine cigarettes and frequent cups of tea, amid storms of wild laughter. Inevitably, Skid being Skid, it started late. It was like a long, laughing, wrangling conversation with both of us jumping

[46]

Moses and Sultana Levi, Caryl's grandparents

Contemporary silhouettes of
Henry and Pearl Abrahams, Caryl's parents

Caryl with her cousin
Tana, and dog

The infant Caryl with her
mother, Pearl

The comfortable house on Canvey Island

The Canvey Island community, including Fr Gregory (back row)

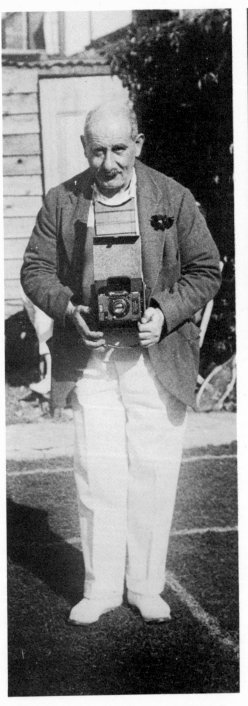

Three of the uncles: Ned
(Nissim) (left); Lewis (above);
Bert (below)

Opposite: Henry Abrahams:
'small and excitable', and close
Caryl than her mother

The child Caryl: 'steel-rimmed spectacles and corkscrew curls'

Studio portrait of Caryl aged about 12

Pearl and Henry Abrahams with car (and chauffeur, centre)

This family group includes Pearl (third from left), Ned (standing),
Ned's wife Lettice (seated, centre) and Henry (second from right)

Caryl aged 18: the picture is inscribed on the back:
To dearest Mumsy and Daddy from their affectionate daughter Doris

in on one another. We would speak lines to each other and laugh at our own jokes until one of us stopped and said 'out'.

Every time their invention faltered they set up another murder victim. As they began to lose confidence in this easy answer, they sought advice. Caryl took their work in progress to a fellow writer, Ernest Elmore, who had actually had a crime book accepted under the pseudonym of John Bude. 'You'll never get this thing published,' he said; 'go back to writing little child-verses.' However, he did offer a helpful device 'for which I bless him to this day': 'When you get a block try changing the scene, or finding a blood-soaked handkerchief.' 'Schange schmall schene,' said Simon, happily. They persevered.

Before they found their eventual publisher there was a false start. After Caryl's death I found a letter among her papers from Lovat Dickson, publishers. It is dated 6 January 1937 and she has scrawled '*Bullet in the Ballet*' across it. It would appear that she had submitted part of the manuscript to them since Mr Dickson ends his letter: 'We would like to see the complete manuscript. Will you let us do that? If so, you can be sure that we shall give it careful and sympathetic consideration, for we are anxious to hold on to you as an author, and would be unhappy to see you go somewhere else.'

His main reason for rejection is interesting:

Dear Miss Brahms,
I have read your very intriguingly entitled MS and I have also asked someone else who advises us, as it happens, both on books concerned with the Ballet and on thrillers, to give us his opinion of it. [NS: *it is not hard to imagine the mixture of curiosity and fury with which Brahms and Simon would have speculated on the identity of their uniquely versatile anonymous judge – especially after reading what follows.*] His opinion and mine coincide. It is a jovial book, which is an original thing in a thriller, and it is based on an excellent theme. We both feel, however, that as a thriller – and this is where it must succeed – it does not come up to form, our chief objection being that insanity is never considered a good *raison d'être* for a crime novel . . .

The letter was sent to 32 Ascot Court in Grove End Road, to which Caryl had moved by 1936. Max Landau remembers various addresses in the years immediately before this. Certainly there were other flats in Gloucester Place and in Albany Street. She had been in Albany

Street in 1930 when Max, still a medical student, dealt with her mail for a month. His sketch of her at this time suggests a busy, but not a fashionable, social life: 'I once partnered her at the Acol Bridge Club; on frequent Sunday afternoons we met and attempted the Torquemada crossword in the *Observer*, with her friend Kahn she was involved in jigsaw puzzles and formed a Jigsaw Club. On some Sundays music was played, and on occasions there were visits to the Palladium for Sunday afternoon concerts conducted by Landon Ronald.' (Landon Ronald's name always amused Caryl because of the incident at Drury Lane when he conducted the orchestra in front of a spectacular production which featured a desert scene. On the first night wind-machines malfunctioned and the orchestra was covered in sand. The word went round London – 'Have you seen the Sandon Ronald?')

Max also remembers her driving a Salmson Weyman saloon through London during these years. He comments, 'Very fast!', but I am not sure if he refers to the speed of the car at the time, or to Caryl's lifestyle, which he also thought a little racy. He confirms that she was living at Ascot Court by 1 October 1936, having occasion to remember it because that was his wedding day and he and his bride drank champagne there with her.

It must have been from Ascot Court, since Caryl did all the administrative work in the collaboration, that *A Bullet in the Ballet* was dispatched to its publisher.

CB Our novel, in Skid's – shall we settle for erratic? – typescript plus my heavily inked-in corrections, at last complete, we sent it to Michael Joseph, once my literary agent, but, by the time we'd scattered our novel with a multitude of schanged scenes and blood-stained handkerchiefs, a publisher. 'It's dangerously two-stoolish,' he wrote, and instead of paying the customary £50 advance – between us – he offered us £30 – between us.

'Done!' we agreed ecstatically.

How to celebrate? We were broke. I went to a theatre I was covering for my paper. Skid shot off to the Acol Bridge Club.

Publication week. Reviews began to trickle through. They were what optimistic authors call mixed, with the emphasis on the bad side. Indeed, *A Bullet in the Ballet* established a pattern of mixed reviews, so that they took on the nature of foregone conclusions as we added to the novels Skid and I wrote together and, save for *Don't, Mr Disraeli* which became the *Evening Standard* Book of the Month,

[48]

and *Trottie True*, the frosty notices took on the similarity of rosebuds on a cottage wallpaper. We cherished the good notices, and carried them about with us until they crumbled away; and we laughed at the bad notices and took them to read aloud to our friends. When our first printing – a meagre 1,000 copies – was sold out, which was unexpectedly soon, our publisher declined to order another printing – we remained 'two-stoolish' for many years, in his eyes, anyway.

NS The good reviews included *The Times Literary Supplement*, the *News Chronicle* and Howard Spring in the *Evening Standard* who congratulated 'Messrs Brahms and Simon'. They followed it with *Casino for Sale* – another, but more contrived, murder story set in a decaying resort in the South of France; and *The Elephant in White*, in which the Ballet Stroganoff was almost relegated to the wings. Caryl later referred to it in a diary note as 'a comedy of character – the first of the crazy Russian books'.

Meanwhile the success of *A Bullet in the Ballet* was producing some curious film offers.

CB One day, with the war looming nearer and nearer, we had a letter from a film producer, Walter Forde. He wanted the rights in *Bullet* and offered us £100 for them. We knew that as an offer for a film this was a bad joke – worse than any we had perpetrated in our book. But we accepted it in the belief that it would at least serve to show us what a film script should look like. £50 each had to be better than sevenpence ha'penny, ten shillings, three guineas, five guineas, or fifteen guineas, the individual earnings of our partnership to date, and our publisher (the old two-stooler) seemed to share much the same view of our work. War clouds were gathering overhead – we ignored them. One at least had a silver lining in the shimmering shape of a trip to Paris to advise with our expertise on *Petroushka*, which was to be recreated in the film by Nijinska, the sister of the great Nijinsky. We scampered round Paris for two carefree, luxurious days, during which time our counsel was sought once only.

'What's the difference between Russian and English music?' we were asked. There was only one answer.

'Russian's louder,' we said.

NS The visit to Paris did not advance the movie, but rumours of production of *Bullet* continued to reach them. The rights changed hands many times. The initial sale which robbed them of their interest in the property had been achieved with the connivance of one of their agents, who later turned out to be part-purchaser. Eventually, it moved on via Ealing, who cancelled production plans a week before war broke out, to MGM for £10,000; the film company held on to it until the '70s when an English group bought it back for the same amount. At one early stage, Caryl met a Central European 'of sallow complexion, Sergei something', who had been asked to write a treatment for the film. 'You will be delighted,' he assured her. 'I have taken out all the stupid jokes.' In Regent's Park one day a little man with a neatly trimmed Van Dyck beard stopped her. 'I hear you are casting *A Bullet in the Ballet* – would you consider me for the role of the conductor?'

'Er . . .,' she said cautiously.

'You see, I am a conductor.'

Later she learned from a friend that it was his nightly habit to don a black velvet jacket, go down to an empty dining-room, lay out a score, rap the table with a baton and say into the emptiness, 'Silence, gentlemen, please, I must have silence!'

Her wartime diary carries echoes of her pre-war life. 'Before the war I used to say that it was worth being born into this age because of Diaghilev, Leon Goossens, Bea Lillie and Donald Duck. I see no reason to alter this opinion. It's not an easy age, but it's the only age.'

Her journalism now embraced the *Standard*, *Lilliput* and an Odhams publication, *Mother*, for whom she wrote a monthly feature.

CB When they were naming *Mother* the personnel used to try it out, thumping themselves on the chest when they passed one another in the corridors, saying in anguished voices, 'Mother! Mother! Does it do something to you (thump) here?'

NS Meanwhile, as Simon trotted obsessively to the Acol:

CB Skid and I are both in the *Daily Telegraph*'s obituary files. Skid is very hurt because he is only there as an author, not as a bridge player. He played for England at the Hague. There hasn't been any international bridge since. I wish the *Telegraph* would let me polish us up – authors ought to be commissioned to write their own obituaries. I've thought of several good cracks to enliven the copy a bit.

[50]

NS Caryl was pursuing her career as a ballet critic and enthusiast.

CB To the dress rehearsal of *Apparitions* with Anthony Asquith. We thought they would never be able to get the ballet on. They were still rehearsing an hour and a half before they were due to ring up, with, naturally, some of the costumes yet to come.

A radiant first performance with Margot Fonteyn taking her first major creation and taking it brilliantly.

NS An attempt to help found a ballet company (still-born) with Dennis Van Thal (some-time composer, now an agent) was backed by the wife of a famous self-raising flour merchant, and called, by the personnel, 'The Self-Raising Ballet'.

But she threw her theatrical net wider than the ballet, collecting a tale of Mr Webber of the Webber-Douglas theatre school.

CB Mr Webber, who was famous for having cut the Queen of Norway dead in Bond Street by mistake, was once asked to transpose something down for an insufficiently tenor singer. 'My dear fellow,' he replied, 'I know of a way to make a bass into an alto, but there is no method known to man of reversing the process.'

NS She and Simon also happened on one of their favourite stories at this time: 'Skid and I adore it. We worked it up into a chapter for *Envoy on Excursion*, we toned it down for a story in *Lilliput*. We tried it as a sketch for a revue, and whenever we felt miserable we told it to one another and roared as at a freshly coined masterpiece.'

It concerned one Rabinovitch, an Armenian who addresses a close friend:

CB 'You see that restaurant across the way? The proprietor was very rude to me last night. So I'm going right in. I'm going to take his customers, one by one, and throw them out into the street. You can stand outside and count them as they land on the mat.'

So the pair crossed over and into the restaurant Rabinovitch went, leaving his friend all set to count the flying figures. There was a terrific sound of breaking china. A form came flying through the air, all arms, all legs, and landed on the mat.

'Vone,' counted his friend.

'Shtop counting – it's me!'

[51]

NS The story continued to be an obsession. It was also brought into service in a pre-war BBC Radio revue. The newly fashionable writers assembled 'the first strip cartoon ever projected on the air'. The format was a mock newsreel, produced by Frederick Piffard with music by Dennis Van Thal.

CB We wrote Newsreel seven times for Maestro Piffard, but when the agony was forgotten, all we remembered was a 'mix' of the Queen's Hall Applause Record and the applause from a Variety Record which they kindly played for our show. I hasten to add that as it was sent out to the Empire and had to be done at 1 a.m., we couldn't have an audience to do the clapping for us. We especially liked being asked to supplement this grand sound-effect by laughing loudly at our own jokes in the direction of the mike.

NS By now Caryl had become friendly with Jack Bergel. She fails at this stage in her diary to disclose how close their relationship was; and that they were contemplating marriage. 'The Bergel did theatre criticism, as well as everything else in sight, for the *Evening News* in between war years ... A grand journalist. A brilliant companion. The Bergel is quick and perceptive and gloriously glum. And I like his faults.' When war broke out he became a ferry pilot, 'blissfully happy playing around in high-speed fighting planes'. After war had been declared, a visit they made to the Albert Hall inspired memories of the last months of peace.

CB I was reminded of a late afternoon in the summer that ended in war, when I had driven Alicia Markova on from a party at Anton Dolin's to a rehearsal – *corps de ballet* 200 – of a charity show that she was giving at the Albert Hall that night. The girls were wearing cloudy ballet frocks, and Alicia, at the other end of the great building, spun round the stage (*déboulée* or *manège*, as Legat used to term the brilliant knife-edged turns) a small, black, determined travelling-top.
   And then I thought of the hall brimming, as I have seen it for Menuhin. And full of movement, when I covered the English Folk Dance Society Festival for the *Daily Telegraph*. [One of those folk dancers was another close friend of her youth, Harold Kahn.] And how I picked out Harold's dark head and Massine-like brows in the moving sea of dancers.

NS When war broke out she was still living in a top flat at Ascot Court,

CB opposite Sir Thomas Beecham, or so I thought until I started to write a play about him with Ned and found his dapper descents to the pavement most mornings were from the flat of a *chère amie* – not the spouse of his marital couch.

It was at Ascot Court that I stood one warm day at dusk and heard the voice of Neville Chamberlain on the radio, questioning if we must go to war for a small nation far away just because we had signed a treaty. Words inconceivable from an English Prime Minister. Years later I saw newsreel film of Chamberlain, the jaunty little man, stepping on to an aeroplane along with his furled umbrella and proclaiming 'Peace in our time,' knowing he had played bluff with Hitler and won another year of partial preparedness for poor peeled-eyed us. In 1938 *Punch* published a poem of mine which summed up my speculations on War and Peace:

It's peace

It's peace!
We're building up the barricades;
It's peace!
Where did we put those hand-grenades?
When tired from digging trenches, at last we seek our bed
We cannot get to sleep for airplanes zooming overhead;
There's a siren in the cellar and searchlight on the shed.
It's peace! It's peace!

We're never going to fight again
Our statesmen all assure us;
Four men and one interpreter –
That's all we need to cure us.
So we really cannot understand why Lloyds will not insure us.
It's peace! It's peace!

It's peace!
The gas masks are distributed;
It's peace!
Ten millions are contributed.
We've dug up lots of trenches in everybody's garden
We've commandeered the Underground without your leave or pardon;

Dad's with a balloon-barrage, Mum's an air-raid warden.
It's peace! It's peace!

We're going to use diplomacy
For every strained relation
We're going to live on friendly terms
With each and every nation –

And we've just completed all our plans for swift evacuation,
It's peace! It's peace!

5

It's war!

NS Although Brahms and Simon had quickly followed *A Bullet in the Ballet* with three other books, none of them had had the same impact. In *Casino for Sale*, another Stroganoff book, the plotting creaked. *The Elephant is White*, published in August 1939, was more successful – another witty animadversion on a group of Russian *émigrés* inspired by an unlikely source, *Ecclesiastes 10*: 'By much slothfulness the building decayeth; and through idleness of the hands the house droppeth through. A feast is made for laughter, and wine maketh merry: but money answereth all things.' The White Elephants, stranded in Paris, form themselves into a club to support one another in their determination to avoid work, to encourage a reclining posture, and to protect members from people who wish to lecture them for their own good.

Next the collaborators started a new novel, which they considered to be a part of their war effort. *Envoy on Excursion* is dedicated to Walter Forde, who was still hoping to film *A Bullet in the Ballet*, and 'whose optimism we hope will some day be rewarded'. In their efforts to make their readers laugh, they flung in everything, including the Ballets Stroganoff, a nonsensical plot, and innumerable 'funny' names. Senior Centime, Stung and Bauldstock, and King Hannibal the Hothead, jostled with Ribbentrop, Mussolini, Goebbels and Hitler. In a diary entry in 1944, Caryl's verdict on the book was succinct: 'Stinko – film rights couldn't be more available.' She added:

CB The only notable thing about that Brahms-Simon vol. is that it appeared on the day Hitler marched into Holland, so relegating the Maginot line to lavender and making us out of date before the copies reached the shops. Harold Kahn, who was a very special influence on my life, had, while his regiment was at Lille, just received an early copy, and marched into Belgium with it. It kept right on retreating with him till the order came through to the BEF to make for the coast. It looked as though Harold would be taken prisoner, together with the greater part of the BEF, and he didn't think a Brahms-Simon book would make the right impression on the Nazis. So, three-quarters through, he scuttled *Envoy*. He was furious at having to leave the tale unfinished and almost the first thing he asked, when he arrived in England after twenty-four hours on the beaches at Dunkirk, was how *Envoy* ended. 'I had to get back to find out,' he told me.

NS Kahn also provided Caryl with another piece of early wartime gossip.

CB It was Harold who let me into a closely guarded defence secret. Poole Harbour, where my uncle Ned lived and my father's Gibbs-built motor launch, soon to become a war casualty, was moored, was being guarded as a likely German invasion port, by a gun brought back from Dunkirk – an incomplete gun. It could not be fired and was just a piece of window dressing. After that piece of information my knees really did knock, and my stomach turned. But apart from Poole Harbour, the threatened invasion was not a very real incident to me. It was mainly symbolized by a tin of lobster soup which I called Invasion Soup. I bought it against the moment of catastrophe and never opened it. I reckoned I would need something to hearten me if ever the day dawned.

I think with pride of the letters I received about the Brahms-Simon books. Later we learned that both a Japanese prisoner-of-war camp and a Stalag in Germany had established a waiting-list ahead of publication. One letter came on a half-sheet of lined paper from prison, such being man's inhumanity to homosexuals in those days. It was about a copy of the Penguin edition of *A Bullet in the Ballet*. I had fought a hard fight with Trusty Lusty and insisted on his releasing *Bullet* for paperback (sixpence a copy, in those days) as a part of the Brahms-Simon war effort. Another letter, sent by a friend, told me that he came upon a copy of *Bullet* 'poised surrealistically' in the sand of the desert, and after he had read it, he buried it in the sand, 'lest it made someone else feel as homesick as it has me.'

Yet another letter came from an unknown reader whose plane had come down in a jungle. Having crawled through it for two days he came upon a hut and in it were some books. 'One was *Don't, Mr Disraeli* – I felt that a friend had taken me by the hand.' Later I was to meet Ronald Searle, the cartoonist, on the very first night of the very first production of *Oliver!* – Lionel Bart's musical blockbuster. Searle had suffered a long incarceration in a Japanese prisoner-of-war camp. He told me that there was a queue of prisoners-of-war asking for the latest Brahms-Simon novel and he showed me, too, the prisoners' hand-written news sheet which they kept up until they had no more strength left.

Less poignantly, an old lady of eighty wrote claiming to remember clearly an incident which the authors of *Don't, Mr Disraeli* had invented.

Caryl continued to attend and write about the ballet regularly, for various papers, and Simon played and wrote about bridge, publishing his still much-read and admired classic, *Why You Lose At Bridge*. As a fashionable new pair of writers, they began to be wooed as revue and theatre contributors, to discuss with grave men from the BBC the new and mysterious art of radio comedy. They were even solicited by Vivian Van Damm to write a sketch for the Windmill. Caryl remained inordinately proud of the severe rejection – 'Too dirty for the Windmill, Miss Brahms.' And they embarked on their first 'historical' novel, *Don't, Mr Disraeli*, 'not a novel set in the Victorian age; but a novel set in its literature'. They and their admirers found the form at which they arrived difficult to define. 'Lampoon? Farce? Pantomime? Crazy revue? Extravaganza?' asked the *Evening Standard*, finally settling for 'master-piece of wit'. For Frank Swinnerton in the *Observer* the word was 'phantasmagoria'. They limited their period to 1800–1900: 'This device has enabled the authors to prolong the life of some famous men and women, and allow others to live before they have yet been born.' Disney, Beecham, Gielgud and Coward rubbed shoulders with Lady Caroline Lamb, Disraeli, Lewis Carroll and the Marx Brothers.

Their flippant description of their work method has, however, a ring of truth. 'It will be seen that the proper execution of the novel required a great deal of research. Brahms left it to Simon. Simon left it to Brahms. Eventually they read aloud to each other.' They supply a meticulous bibliography, embracing E. F. Benson, E. M. Delafield, Philip Guedalla, André Maurois, Peter Quennell, Edith Sitwell, Lytton Strachey, Angela Thirkell, Queen Victoria, A Lady of her Court, William Shakespeare (the peg of a plot is *Romeo and Juliet*) and Mrs Braddon's *Lady Audley's Secret*. But, they added, 'since in our own story, time has taken a little too much Madeira, it did not seem fair to associate their names with these libations in our narrative.'

In fact, their disappointment in their own work on *Envoy on Excursion* brought a new and unfamiliar application to their approach to *Don't, Mr Disraeli*. Although the anarchic, the sportive and the preposterous are there in liberal quantities, the book's 250-odd pages are put together deftly and lightly, without apparent strain. Publication, the excellent notices, and the *Evening Standard* Book of the Month accolade, were a profound relief.

CB I shall never get used to having books come out on me and Sunday papers pronouncing on them, even though I've done years and years of pronouncing in the press myself. The Bergel came back from Fleet Street with a copy of the paper for me. 'Seen what they call you?' he asked with disgust. *'Lunatics of Genius!'*

It wasn't so very blitzy as we made our way to the Cumberland Grill, for my autumn and winter were bounded by my sector and its neighbouring sectors [she was by now an air-raid warden] and we had a very grand meal on me and a lot of wine on him and it was great fun. And I didn't care if they did call me a lunatic, for I was celebrating the publication of a book that we had finished in the middle of a war, and that was quite a thing to have been given time to do.

NS They had then just survived the worst of the 1940-41 bombing, and she was very conscious of the extra gamble involved in starting a book which one collaborator or the other might not live to finish. Later, she recalled the aftermath of a bomb-raid on the City of London.

CB I went to see the City on the Sunday after the fire. It was a cold, clear day. The Christmas tree on the steps of St Paul's still bore its coloured lights, and snow was falling very finely on the shoulders of the endless procession of Londoners out to see what had been done to their city.

The traffic had been halted at the top of Fleet Street and the only sounds that could be heard were voices, the tread of feet, and the axes of the demolition squads.

Through St Paul's churchyard, the only way that was left open, past the stone that commemorated the last time the City was burnt out in 1663; and along devastated Watling Street, fantastically void, where Pepys had seen the Lord Mayor of London running without his wig, and been sent by him to the King at Whitehall to tell him that the fire burned so swiftly that they could not pull down the houses in time to stem it, and asking him to send the army out to help the fire-fighters. And then, up to the Guildhall – roofless, surrounded by coils of hose, with the Union Jack flying.

The City had been burnt out again. I was upheld and consoled by a sense of the continuity of history . . .

NS In 1941, Caryl began, at the prompting of a Cambridge don (she was in Cambridge on an unlikely mission to house Central European refugees), to keep a diary. She started it in 1941, and much later she wrote:

CB I have come upon a part of that diary written by me in the Blitz.
Hard to decide whether to include some parts in this book. The truth, the whole truth and nothing but the truth is that some of it is so well written that I fear comparison with what I write herein.

NS She called her journal *Palookas in Peril*: 'Palooka: n. An enthusiastic amateur. One who aspires to greater things. An object with all the charm of the home-made. *Brahms-Simon Dictionary*.'

This was the only entry ever conjured up for the *Brahms-Simon Dictionary*, but 'palooka' was a favourite Brahms-Simon word, and although it now appears in the *OED* its etymology is not recorded there. It seems to have been commandeered by Simon from the Russian. The collaborators used it first in *A Bullet for the Ballet* – modified to provide a surname for Anton Palook, one of the murdered dancers. It was a word they never abandoned.

Caryl was not immediately convinced that she should start a diary.

CB In my room I thought the matter over. It seemed a terrifically
self-indulgent thing to do. It would involve going out and buying one of the lovely exercise-books that you could only obtain in Oxford or Cambridge in those days. It meant writing about all the people I liked best and recording the things they said about their strange new wartime jobs. Everyone of us palookas – energetic amateurs in flying, sailing, shooting and the care-taking business. Everyone of us in peril. And everyone of us faintly disbelieving in our own activities.

May 11th – I bought my exercise book.

NS In recalling the early years of the war, Caryl drew heavily on her detailed account in the diary – especially memories of the work which she and Simon put in as air-raid wardens in the area east of the Edgware and south of the Marylebone Roads. Throughout the war her anxieties were increased by the fact that her mother was too ill to be moved and her father stayed with her in Vichy France.

CB I spent the war like a pendulum swinging between terror, well-disguised I hope, and relief. Terror was the animal instinct to take cover however inadequate. Relief took the form of laughter as one scrambled out from under. Skid and I laughed so much in the Blitz that one night, walking home through the blackout, a bodiless voice from the other side of the street called out : 'That's Caryl and Skid – I recognize you from that laughter.'

My very dear young man, a ferry pilot, Jack Bergel, killed in action in 1941, was my mentor in most things. He was the drama critic of the *Evening News*, and I was with him on the occasion of my first bomb, which mercifully fell far away. I was determined to behave decently. 'Want to go down to the air-raid shelter?' he asked.

'Certainly not. But I wouldn't mind a small brandy,' I said, firming my knees.

Later I was to join the ARP and become an air-raid warden, and, later still, I was on telephone duty in the midnight to 7 a.m. shift in the Blitz when a bomb hit a church two streets away. Furzecroft, the block of flats to which I had moved [NS: the flat she was living in had been lent to her by John Byron for 'the duration of the war'] and where the ARP Post F-for-Ferdie Four was situated for a time, seemed to try to lift from its foundations and its walls seemed to concertina. Then all was dust and silence. As I scrambled up from under the desk, I observed, 'Local bomb makes good!' The Bergel said, when I told him, that from that moment on he would have no more fears for me; I was obviously of the stuff of survivors.

NS There came the brief move to Cambridge to help transplant German refugees into new jobs and new accommodation in a permitted zone outside London.

CB I scooped up Skid and my German housekeeper and crammed them into my silver Singer Coupé jalopy, along with my portable gramophone, some favourite recordings and whichever of the Brahms-Simon books was in progress.

NS   They arrived in Cambridge:

CB   My German refugee housekeeper was a Brünnhilde-like figure, formerly an opera singer, who would shatter the peace of my awakening in the slow run-up to Armageddon by frenetically brandishing my early morning tea, demanding, 'When are the British going to bomb Berlin?' One such morning she surprised me sharing my couch with a blond young man, the pair of us entwined and asleep. Brünnhilde waved the teapot and gave us her Brangäne. Comparable only to my discomfort when my father sang, for the delight of my parents' guests, the words which intimated that they should see him dance the polka, was my acute embarrassment when my Brünnhilde insisted in singing her Aida at me in a small room over a paraffin stove (the kind that used to throw a broderie-anglaise-like pattern on the ceiling in my country childhood) and, addressing herself to her audience of one, not only belted out the aria but flung herself on her knees at my feet by way of a bonus.

NS   Caryl's colleague in sorting out her refugees and finding them jobs – usually domestic – was Margaret Braithwaite, wife of Richard Braithwaite, an eighth-generation Quaker and a philosophy don at King's. The operation was run by a formidable Quaker lady, somewhere between seventy and eighty.

CB   One of my cases which I remember with total clarity was the wife of a German refugee professor – pure routine – a little lady with a face that shut in her feelings, whom I drove out some twenty or thirty miles to an English country house that must have taken considerable upkeep. We toiled a distant but resonant bell and were admitted to the ancestral hall. The professor's wife emitted a warning sniff, but before I could jump in with some comforting gospel the Lady of the House had descended on us. I gave the *curriculum vitae* thoughtfully handed me by the head Quaker, an old campaigner in the placing of German refugees. The Lady of the English Country House, meanwhile, had switched the unblinking searchlight of her gaze on to my refugee. Her scrutiny concluded, she addressed herself to me. 'Well, all things considered she had better start next Monday – early!'

But here the professor's wife asserted herself. 'Is much silver to clean?' she enquired.

The chatelaine's response was crisp: 'We're not afraid of a little hard work, are we?'

'Jawohl!' said my refugee. 'Me, I am afraid of work!'

'In that case . . .'

The interview was closed.

Back we drove to the Quaker lady. She preserved her customary silence. Not so Margaret Braithwaite. 'Caryl Brahms,' she said, sternly, 'you have ruined the Frau Professor's chance!'

NS After a month of lugging mattresses and refugees and their belongings, coaxing European professors' wives to take jobs as domestics, and coping with the Braithwaites' eccentric conversational requirements (Richard Braithwaite had on one occasion absconded from a fire-watching patrol just when a German bomb fell. Missing him, his fellow wardens searched for his mangled corpse. Later he admitted, somewhere between airy pride and schoolboy guilt, 'I had just nipped home to take Margaret in my arms'), Caryl felt that she had had enough of Cambridge. Simon agreed. He was missing his current girlfriend – one of his more pressing reasons for leaving London in a hurry.

CB Skid had been dallying away one afternoon with his inamorata and at length tore himself away to board a homebound bus. By chance he found himself face to face with the inamorata's husband, who was getting off it.

'Funny,' observed the husband, 'I've got a tie just like yours at home!'

He hadn't, of course. Nothing if not absent-minded, short-sighted, languorous Skid had stretched out a reluctant hand and donned the wronged husband's tie, leaving his inamorata to explain away as best she could the frayed, soup-stained, ash-bespattered remnant of a tie which had inexplicably usurped its place.

NS On his return, Simon notched up a new, and again not entirely satisfactory, romance.

CB He had persuaded a regulation tobacconist-kiosk's Hebe to come home and see his etchings. I gathered she, like one of Madame Marie Rambert's English ballerinas, 'had Streatham in her soul' and took a lot of persuading. Skid, however, who turned everything save bridge and the dogs to laughter, coaxed her clothes off, petal by petal, until the last petal peeled off. Skid blinked at her finally revealed breasts. 'Where did you get those pretty things from?' Then, the habit of laughter proving too much for him, 'Woolworth's?'

'Sweetie,' he said to me wryly afterwards, 'you never would have thought from the time she took to undress that she could have got them all back on so quickly.'

NS Before going to Cambridge they had discussed their new book with their publisher. The suggestion was that they should write another 'just like *Don't, Mr Disraeli*'. Michael Joseph himself was away, 'fighting the war to end wars'; his deputy was Robert Lusty, now Sir Robert, always Trusty Lusty to Brahms and Simon. ('Later,' Caryl wrote in 1981, 'Trusty was nearly to end my span as a writer altogether, but that story is for another, sadder day'.*) To write a book exactly like the last was anathema to the collaborators. What they produced was a warmer, richer book, but one which in its playful rearrangement of history revealed higher truths of character and event. And it bore a family resemblance.

CB We settled for a novel about Shakespeare. Our theme, if ever we could be said to have such a thing, was that Bacon wanted a bed that Queen Elizabeth had slept on to leave to his children's children's children as a gilt-edged investment. This was the fixed purpose of which fate was always robbing him. 'Centuries from now,' says Master Bacon, 'people will come from all over the world and pay good money on 5-groat days to see a bed Gloriana has slept upon.' We flung in a girl-boy player and took part of the plot of *Twelfth Night* for good measure. When we had finished we took the result to Trusty Lusty, who said we were ten thousand words too short.

NS Before they began the novel they tested the Cambridge temperature with Margaret Masterman. 'I know,' Caryl wrote to her, with a charac- teristic *faux-naïveté* designed to provoke encouragement and, more particularly, the help she needed, 'that there must have been many books written about Shakespeare. But would there be any serious objection from Cambridge were we to write a fun book about him, and

* Chapter 6.

[63]

would it be possible to get a spine of books to research him at the University Library?'

Brahms-Simon research had a quality all its own:

CB While initially innocent of the fact that Burleigh was the Lord Chancellor of England, I read in Nicoll's *Progresses* that Lady Burleigh had given Gloriana 23 silver buttons, one broken. Hey Presto! Burleigh, clearly, was a mean man.

NS Caryl stored the fruits of her own research in the form of headings on a series of index cards. Simon's 'research' consisted of 'carrying round Black's *History of the Elizabethan Age*', which she vowed he never opened. The collaboration was nearly interrupted before the first chapter could be started.

CB What with Skid's short-sightedness, and what with the presumably flat-footed shuffle by which he progressed to the nearest traffic light, in front of which he would stand blinking and singing 'Otchi Chernia', we took it for granted that Skid would not be conscripted, until one afternoon he telephoned. 'That you, sweetie? They've passed me fit for the Army.'

'But Skid – you've got flat feet!'

'Not at all, my dear sir,' said Skid, as haughtily as it was in his amiable nature to speak; 'too much trouble to lift them.'

NS Caryl was never precise about how Simon's wartime activities were diverted from part- to full-time work as an air-warden, but somehow they were; and both operated in the same district, conspiring to baffle the District Warden under whom they served.

CB He was deeply mystified by Skid, his idiosyncrasies, for which the portmanteau word was 'Bohemian', and the messages we left for one another in the official log-book. They had nothing to do with the geography of incidents or calling for ambulances, so far as he could see. I was bombarded with disgruntled notes from the baffled District Warden:

Miss Brahms, please see that Warden Skidelsky does up his flies. Miss Brahms, Warden Skidelsky must close the door of the WC when he sits on it. There have been complaints.

[64]

Miss Brahms, what does the following entry in the log-book for
F-for-Ferdinand Four, initialled S.S. mean?

It was, of course, a message left for me about the work in progress,
since Skid and I did Box and Cox on the night shifts – I would
be on duty from 6 to 12 one night, and Skid would do 12 to 6 at
any of several posts in the district. The message was perfectly
obvious to me. It ran simply, '*Glib, Glab, Glob.*' It was clear (but not
to the Chief Warden) that Skid was making suggestions for the naming
of the theatre, to be called the Globe, where Shakespeare was
working*.

Skid would be sent out on patrol too. I recall with great affection
the time he attended his first fire incident. 'The flames looked so
pretty, Sweetie,' he said next day. 'And there was Senior [Senior
Warden] with a bucketful of water – a *pail* of water' – he spoke
with the nearest approach to awe I ever saw on his face – 'and half
the street was alight!'

NS In their short story, 'F-For-Ferdinand 4', published in *Lilliput,* they
gave a thumbnail sketch of life at the post:

CB The telephone rang.

Miss Bragg looked at it, laid aside her Proust and stretched out
a nicotine-stained finger. 'F-for-Ferdinand Four,' she said
toughly. The three air-raid wardens lolling in their deckchairs
reached vaguely for their steel helmets. Limbs were still relaxed
but they were ready to stiffen at any moment.

'That,' announced Miss Bragg, in some disgust, 'was Report and
Control checking the line again.'

The wardens relaxed. Miss Bragg noted the time, 04.27, and
returned to her Proust. Warden's Post F-for-Ferdinand Four in
the Borough of St Michael's and All Angels resumed its normal
aspect. It was in fact in the basement of a block of luxury flats.

NS In the 1890s Caryl assembled her most vivid memories of the Blitz..

CB I waged my share of the war, always with laughter, sometimes with

---

* Peter Levi points out that this is also a quotation from a Russian poem onomato-
poeically suggesting the sound of horses' hoofs. Obviously Simon never told his collaborator.

anger, and more than once with tears. My own preoccupation in
the Blitz was entirely concerned with trying to wedge my tin hat on
my head and keep it there. In the wartime stories we wrote about
it, Skid and I called one post F-for-Ferdie Four.

Hindsight suggests that I did take on one fairly brave task –
'hindsight' because, of course, when it was happening there was no
time for heroics; indeed, it seemed the most natural thing in the
world. We had an Incident just outside F-for-Ferdie Four. An
almighty bang outside and pitch black inside. Our lighting system
had gone. Almost simultaneously our block of flats [Furzecroft]
seemed to rise, the walls concertina'd inwards, then expanded, our
mouths filled with the, by now, routine dust. We felt for our regulation
electric torches and crawled to our emergency lighting system. It
too had gone.

Someone had to go through the Blitz for paraffin. The bomb that
had caused so much havoc had pierced a gas main, and a column
of fire like the highest column of flame in the world was spurting
between Ferdie Four and the paraffin and lamp critical to manning
the telephone to summon ambulances, which normally would have
been one of my jobs. The Post Warden called for a volunteer. I
volunteered. I pointed out that I had no children, no dependants. I
was the obvious choice. What was more, I had my tin hat jammed
on and thought if I carried my head at an angle I might well be able
to keep it on, my one obsession.

So off I went. Going was easy. Comparatively. That is to say, my
tin hat stayed on. Coming back was quite another matter, with
the highly ignitable paraffin and a paraffin lamp, past the column of
fire which I tried to keep the heat off by reminding myself that the
Children of Israel progressed through the wilderness steering by
the sun by day and a column of fire by night. I got back to the post,
manned the telephones, and ordered out the ambulances. It was
later that I learned that two dear young wardens of F-for-Ferdie
Four, pretty girls in their late teens, sisters, had been killed in that
Incident. Rest, rest, perturbéd spirits.

One of those wretched, lonely, wartime Christmases. It was around
4 a.m. There was the usual earthquake. Out of bed. One and a half
minutes to hurl on some clothes. My tin hat wedged on. Through
to Ferdie Four, where Report and Control informed me that a small
homemade bakery had been hit while baking Christmas cakes: how

many ambulances should I be likely to need? A small bakery that was doing nobody any harm reduced to rubble, and probably all the houses in the street a'swing with blast. I wept hot, angry tears for all to see and wrote, 'Bloody hell!' in the log book.

NS One of Caryl's wartime colleagues was Valerie Hovenden, who introduced her to her war work, and who after the war formed one of the first 'fringe' theatres. Her married name then was Wolf-Flanagan.

CB I had a very special friend at the Marylebone Town Hall ARP Recruitment Centre, a handsome woman called Flan, short for Mrs Wolf-Flanagan. She had a darling roly-poly husband at Ferdie Four called Flan Two and about sixty years of age; if ever a man was a whimsical twinkle of fun it was he. Every morning at lunchtime I would go to the town hall for an hour to relieve Flan One to do her shopping or whatever, until it dawned on someone that I had never taken the warden's examination. So Flan One decided that my only chance of passing and continuing to relieve her at snack-time was for me to be examined privately at her flat by the highest-up warden at Report and Control – a rough diamond, but a willing aider and abetter. He had his method. Every time I came up with the wrong answer he would say, 'No, girl – you don't *mean* that, now do you? You mean . . . , don't you?' Which is how I got my credentials for membership of the very tough little band at Ferdie Four.

I remember once swaying with fatigue – fatigue I swear – and picking my way down a street strewn with glass to meet Skid for breakfast – which when I got there, I was too tired to touch – and a work-session at the Marble Arch sister to Piccadilly's Regent Palace. There was a Blitz-time ritual for meeting people. We used to say we'd meet at a certain destination, adding, 'And if that's down we'll meet at . . .' – some other designated venue. Well, a high-up seeing me toddling through the glass decided I was altogether too exhausted and gave me two weeks' leave – and what's more, Ferdie Four ganged up against me and insisted I should take it. On my way to Liverpool Street Station I passed through the blitzed City of London. When I returned by the same route I said to my driver, 'Thank heavens I live in a safe area – compared to the City the Marble Arch district is a picnic site!'

To come back to Flan One, Druce's Stores on the corner of Baker
Street was on fire. Flan One had been up all the night before with
another Ferdie incident, but she staggered over. They created her
Incident Officer, which meant that she had to be hung all over
with blue net and to hold a banner like a trident with 'Incident
Officer' written clearly for all to read. She was required to answer any
questions the wardens might put to her, such as where was the
nearest water hydrant – that sort of thing. Someone, probably
Flan Two, obligingly got out an armchair from the blazing store for
her to sit on and, what with the heat, the hissing of the flames,
the soft sound of water from the fireman's hose, and sheer
human dead-beatness, she fell asleep. She woke up, blue net,
banner and all, to find a fatherly policeman bending over her
solicitously. 'And 'oo do you think you are, dear,' he asked,
'Casabianca?'

Several funny episodes come bubbling up. Skid got conked on the
head in the blackout and the ten-shilling note which was to have lasted
him to the end of the week was pinched. It happened only a Molotov
throw away from Ferdie Four. After this I confessed to Skid that I
was apprehensive when I had to walk alone through the blackout.
'Palooka!' he said. 'All you have to do is to say out loud, "How
silently you walk in the blackout since you joined the Commandos,
Colonel." That'll scare them off.'

One day, towards the end of the Blitz, I was walking down
Bloomsbury Street, where Skid and I would celebrate the odd
publication day by going to a shop on the corner of Bloomsbury and
Oxford Street, mount an ancient staircase, and delight ourselves with
red caviare sandwiches – real caviare, none of your caviare-type –
at a cost of about six shillings. There was one terrible celebration day
when we were skint and I pawned a gold cigarette-case for the price
of a seat at the cinema (I knew I could recover it because it was
pawned for so little) and Skid went off to the Acol Club to win
money from someone else. That day – it was a sunny spring
morning – the workmen on the scaffolding of a bombsite were
whistling and calling to one another. I was wearing my new scarlet
suit – new, because a reader unknown to me, soon to join the army,
sent me all his civilian coupons, I can only suppose in a moment of
inebriation, to thank me for the books; and along I swung at a

spanking rate until the whistling turned into wolf-whistles. 'Where are you off to, Miss – the fire-engine?'

In addition to our work with the warden service, which neither of us thought of as our proper war-effort, Skid and I took our work of laughter-making in novels and short stories as our real contribution to winning the war. When the Blitz was contained in London we wrote our novels, but after one terrible night when, to our astonishment, London had no alerts, our bones told us that our peace must be at the expense of some other place and we saw clearly that we must write a series of short stories to hearten cities like Bristol and Liverpool by showing them that laughter could abound in Blitzen. It was our creed. It was what we were sent into this world to create. Nation shall laugh unto Nation. Laughter, the truly classless communication. So we went on writing at our ARP posts between Blitzen, or in one or other of our flats, even on bus journeys – anywhere and all the time, and laughing aloud as we composed sentences. Dear Skid, with his avoidance of wit: 'That's not funny,' he would admonish me, and I see, now, what he meant. His shock of straight, inky-black hair. His white fleshy face. One sock coming down. Smoking a Woodbine because we could not afford a more ambitious cigarette. He used to say we would both write so much better if we could afford a dozen oysters and a glass of champagne every morning at eleven.

Caryl's summing-up recalled 'the weariness of it all. A weariness that caused me to sit on an electric fire and put me *hors de combat* for a fortnight.' There are nearly 600 pages of *Palookas in Peril*, and Caryl *had* decided to include extracts from them in her memoirs before she died. She had not chosen the passages. Picking moments from such a manuscript is a complicated business, for part of the charm of a diary is the way in which themes and characters announce themselves, disappear, and crop up again, as the slowly unfolding narrative casts its spell. The effect is very nearly a series of running gags, or, as Brahms and Simon called them, 'ti-tums'. Villains and heroes, optimism and frustration, surface and submerge between isolated incidents and bouts of meditation. Taking the responsibility of selection, I have tried to extract from the book certain story-lines which give some idea of the hectic nature of Brahms-Simon activity during the war years, some reflection of the odd, optimistic bundle of schemes in which Caryl was engaged, and some of her thoughts about the Blitz, her colleagues and her friends – as well as her embattled instincts when working with theatrical collaborators – especially composers. In order to do this I have had, reluctantly, to write some short, linking passages. The first major thread I have chosen to pick up is the way in which the collaborators wrote *No Bed For Bacon*. It gives a half an answer to the question Brahms and Simon were always asked: 'How do you write together?' The success of *Don't, Mr Disraeli* had made them more conscious of their responsibility to their readers.

On 16 May 1941, Caryl returned to London from Cambridge. 'London had a fire blitz while I was away. The House of Commons and Queen's Hall.' Simon had a new anecdote – a man had tried to borrow a copy of *Don't, Mr Disraeli* for his brother. He opened with, 'My brother tells me you write tripe – well, of course, I don't mean tripe, but light sort of trash.' He closed with the revealing phrase, 'My brother reads a lot of books.' An American review from the Macon, Ga., *Telegraph* struck a sobering note. '*It is highly probable that persons who subscribe to* Punch *found this book howlingly funny. As to this reviewer, she* Don't, Mr Disraeli.' Caryl, however, was unabashed. 'I met a girl at Oxford,' she goes on, 'who was reading history and had been directed by her professor to read *Don't, Mr Disraeli* in order to acquire "elasticity".' This was bettered by a professor of music at the university of St Louis, USA who directed his class to read our *Bullet in the Ballet* for its "cultural background".' Even the Army showed enthusiasm. A gushing friend wrote, 'Dumpy's Colonel is a *Don't Dizzy* fan. When he heard she knew you, she was nearly made a Major at once!'

When Evelyn Waugh's *Sword of Honour* trilogy came out – books, which like all Waugh's work, Caryl admired greatly – she was delighted to come upon a description of soldiers reading *Disraeli* with enjoyment. At the end of her life she was pleased to find Waugh's own approval of it confirmed, on the publication of his letters.

Her diary records that *No Bed For Bacon* nearly started with a setback.

CB *May 18th* – I learn that Michael Joseph (our publisher) lost his entire stock of paper when his printer got blitzed at Plymouth . . . The Ministry of Supply has seen the light and given him some more. So our new book is provided for. But I wouldn't be a first novelist for anything in the world – excepting, possibly, a gallant gesture.

NS At Cambridge Caryl had met Margaret Masterman's cousin Ted, a seventy-year-old monk from Mirfield. He delighted her with a story of an Irish priest who preached on the text, *And Enoch walked with God*, and, having repeated it, opened: 'Brethren, let us consider this eminent pedestrian.' On 22 May he wrote to tell her that the only book on the monastery shelf devoted to light literature was '*Oh No, Mr Disraeli!*' (sic). It suggested a new Brahms-Simon advertising slogan: 'No monk can put them down.'

26 May found Caryl in despair. 'There is so much we cannot capture in *No Bed For Bacon*. So much that lies outside the scope of a comic book. So much that is forbidden to Brahms-Simon.'

To lift her spirits she went to the ballet with Jack Bergel: *Les Sylphides*, *The Prospect Before Us* and *The Wanderer*, 'a choreo-catastrophe!' 'In the RAF,' said Bergel, as they did the first lovely lift from the wings in the *pas de deux valse* of *Sylphides*, 'they call that an assisted take off.' 'Another of my moments gone for ever,' wrote Caryl. (Crass remarks by ballet philistines always irritated her: I remember being told sharply at Covent Garden, when I muttered 'Sitting duck' as prince pointed arrow at swan, that it was about the twenty-first time she had heard it.) On the occasion of this *Sylphides* they found the romantic ruin of a backcloth depressing – 'it reminded us of bomb damage' – and Caryl reflected that 'no company remembers the way to dance *Sylphides* any more!' However, there were compensations: 'In Margot Fonteyn they have a young Nemchinova. Helpmann is a good dancer and a very fine actor.' She lamented the effect the war might have on promising dancers. 'Once a dancer stops dancing he cannot go back to being a dancer again.'

At the beginning of her diary – the whole book is subtitled *1. The Lull* – Caryl was carrying on an uncharacteristic conversation with the BBC. It is not quite clear in what capacity they might have employed her.

CB *May 27th, 1941* – Up for an interview with the BBC . . . 'What, no Russian?' . . . Half-way through I felt impelled to ask just what the appointment was that they seemed to think I was applying to fill. I think it must have been one for which all concerned had already decided I was unsuited. Some months ago they had set me a simple general knowledge test and subsequently they notified me that I was no longer being considered for the post. I awfully liked the White

[71]

Queen feeling of losing the job first and being interviewed for it afterwards.

NS At Oxford, before the war, she had begun a lifelong friendship with Christopher Fry. A letter from him was some consolation:

'*From Christopher Fry: A Private (97002837) in a non-combatant force.* At last the cold wind has stopped blowing. I've been waiting for this moment for months and today I've come out into the sun like a snail coming out into the rain. We changed our billet the day after I got back from leave ("we" equals my section) and moved down to the race course which had concrete floors and a few doubtful oil-lamps for lighting and so many draughts that we might have been esquimaux using a colander instead of an igloo ... Responsibilities begin to pile themselves on my shoulders, i.e. a squad I have to take to work every day – under Bredon Hill. Under my own three-years-ago eyes, looking down from the Vicarage Garden at Bredon ...'

NS Caryl records one other event for that day: 'Today the *Bismarck* went down.'

Her assumption of rejection by the BBC was premature:

CB *May 28th* – The BBC, elaborately unconcerned, phoned me today. Will I present myself for interview tomorrow? This time it's the News Department, so may be I am about to be turned down by the right people at last.

NS That evening she heard a piece of hot wartime gossip at the ARP Post.

CB Reception is an interesting job, as ARP jobs go. One of my great regrets is that I was not there the other day when Godfrey Winn dropped in on Flan:
'Are you Mrs Flanagan? Well, my friends keep nagging me to drive a car for the ARP, so I thought I'd better drop in and talk to you about it.' Finding that Flan had nothing very suitable to suggest, he rose to go. 'You might tell my friends that I have offered,' he said. 'The name's Winn, Godfrey Winn.'
'How do you spell it?' asked Flan.
May 29th – My interview at Broadcasting House went almost too

smoothly this afternoon. Easily the most intimidating thing was the calming manner that lays you out at the reception desk. No Harley Street specialist could pronounce a death sentence more soothingly than the infinitely refined voice that requires you to fill in a form and follow the boy. We got a bit bogged down on my bronze medal at the RAM, so I don't think I shall be offered the job, particularly as, when asked why I considered myself to be suitable to write about Foreign Affairs, I heard myself saying, 'I'm so adaptable.' Oh dear!

is On the same day she dined with one of her agents, Herbert Van Thal (of whom she was later to tell the story of a rupture in his friendship with Sonia Dresdel, who was acting at the Oxford Playhouse at the time. The parting was violent: 'She kicked him in the Woodstock Road.') The surprise on 29 May was literary: she told Van Thal she was doing a journal, strictly for publication by Michael Joseph. 'I couldn't be more interested, Caryl,' he said. They toasted the journal and drank to it.

Caryl spotted a slab of manuscript only half concealed under Van Thal's napkin. 'As a matter of fact it's *my* journal,' he confessed.

'What fun,' she said, in a hollow voice. 'Where are you sending yours?'

'I thought,' he replied, 'of taking it to Michael Joseph.'

The proliferation of wartime journals is a recurring theme in the diary. A few months later, Caryl borrowed £5 from 'my beloved Bergel' and invited him to take her to Simpsons. 'He is now the only man living to have dined at Simpsons in two journals written by two women in the same war. The other journal – not nearly so good of course – is written by Naomi Royd-Smith.'

The next month Bergel crops up in a third book, Agate's *Ego*; and Caryl complains of Agate's selective editing of an encounter with her in his *Express and Admirable*. She had offered him four seats for Toscanini concerts to induce him to reply to a questionnaire for a theatre book she was editing. He reported the offer with glee; but not the fact that he had taken it up.

In November Caryl discovered that Michael Joseph himself had embarked on a journal.

:B I awfully like the aspect of the Lull that shows all the professional writers madly doing diaries, snatching one another's stories, and ecstatically committing themselves to forestalling one another for the rest of the war.

NS On 30 May she recorded her mother's birthday in exile and a visit to *The God's Go A'begging*, 'villainously played by two young women at the pianos,' which were the staple accompaniment of ersatz wartime ballet; and a new Gluck ballet on the Orpheus legend by Ninette de Valois. 'At the end of the work a voice behind me was heard to observe: "Ah well, London can take it!"' She added her own note of advice to choreographers: 'The thing about scope in ballet is that much should be allowed to remain outside it.'

On 1 June she heard the news that clothes were to be rationed. 'The answer is, I suppose, to wear a uniform.' She and Simon spent the day with Shakespeare and Burbage naming the Globe Theatre. In the evening he took her to see *Major Barbara*. 'When we got back from the cinema we were told that we had lost Crete! There is nothing like the news of a defeat to make you stop caring about the clothes ration.' The only compensation was the first of a series of heavy-breathing phone calls on which she later loved to dwell. The ardent inquirer always used the same formula, with an authentic period ring to it, 'Is that you, Muriel darling? Will you be wearing your cami-knicks tonight?'

Reginald Pound, the Editor of the BBC department which had interviewed her, wrote to tell her that he could not choose his own staff, so for the moment her BBC staff career was at an end.

CB *June 4th* – Today Skid arrived for work earlier than I expected and straight from his advanced gas exam. 'Could have been here ten minutes earlier,' he announced, 'but I didn't want to finish too quickly and be conspicuous.' As his usual mode of progress is to lumber through the streets, hair in the wind, feet a'shuffle, blinking blindly at whatever presents itself to his consciousness, and singing 'Otchi Chernia' at the top of his voice, with both socks coming down, it seemed an unusual consideration for him to harbour.
Will Shakespeare chose a Boy Player in our work session today, and took Master Bacon down a peg or two. He was a nasty piece of work, but by God! a stylist.
The Kaiser – pathetic villain of my youth – died today at Doorn.

NS While they were writing *No Bed For Bacon*, Brahms and Simon were juggling with three stage projects. The composer, Leslie Julian Jones, was having a success at the Comedy Theatre with his revue *Rise Above It* which starred Hermione Baddeley and Hermione Gingold. Another revue was being assembled for the Ambassador's Theatre and together with the composer of that show, Tim (H. Temple) Abady, Brahms and Simon were trying to insert some numbers. At the same time they worked on a stage version of *Don't, Mr Disraeli* with Julian Jones; and, later in the year with Abady they started to plan a Russian extravaganza. All these enterprises produced a good deal of energy and some heat.

On 5 June they had an ultimatum from Lusty demanding *No Bed* at no fewer than 75,000 words by the second week in August. 'I've sworn to do it, Weakling! ... Bacon gave Shakespeare a few lessons in stagecraft in today's session. We laughed a lot but I'm not at all sure that we're being funny.' In the evening they went to the first night of Leslie Julian Jones's review, *Rise Above It*. 'Hermione Baddeley has only to say a line and it becomes a riot . . . the large, good-humoured house was tremendously pleased to find itself there.'

B *June 6th* – Started the day well by picking Skid up in a taxi. After frenzied consultation inside cab we found Skid had 1s 9d and I had three half-pennies. We went into the matter of making up the tip with four Woodbines, but decided against. Undignified we felt, so we stopped the taxi and started to walk. 'Onward, the millionaires,' said Skid.

Frantic work session. First we went over the plan of the book, trying to invent plot for 75,000 words. We worked out that we have to do a minimum of 7,000 words a week – impossible in collaborated humour, more than ever since we can only do an hour's work every other day, when Skid is on ARP duty.

s At the ballet that evening, Margot Fonteyn got a pat on the back for her work in the Mazurka in *Sylphides*. 'That tiny degree more of control will give her ballerina-dom! That little more!'

The next day spirits were higher. 'Dined with Skid at *L'Ecu de France*. Journal do not blink. True, it was but yesterday that you saw us debating the taxi-driver's tip. But a pound (Skid's) on a lucky dog . . .'

They reckoned that by now they had written some 25,000 of their 75,000 words. They were beginning to feel the pressure. 'A hard ungrateful session. 600 words. But we've finished building the Globe Theatre and got an Elizabethan audience into it. The play, *Hal 8*, is now under way. Tomorrow we burn it down. The fun writers have!'

The next day they had to lunch Kaye Webb, the editor of *Lilliput*, to tell her they could not write any more pieces for her until they had delivered their book. 'This must be the first time on record that contributors have lunched an editor in order *not* to sell her anything.' To stiffen their resolve, Trusty Lusty sent them a contract 'meanly inserting the date clause. Can foil this in sleep.' But, having set light to the Globe and 'left it burning', they were unable to resist a request from Pemberton, the manager of the Ambassador's Theatre, to write some numbers for his new revue. Caryl, always fascinated by backstage politics, hastened to St Martin's Lane.

CB At the theatre, chaos, of course. But a quiet, clear girl called Anna Duse is to produce our material. Hermione Gingold does the rest – and I find Abady quick and easy which is a great help. As I supposed, we were called in to do last minute, dogsbody work. Opening number and Finale – which would be infuriating but that it gives us the chance to provide a few lines for Joan Swinstead and Ernest Thesiger. Two sentimental foxtrots to gay little tunes already written (can't help wondering who walked out and took their material with them!); and a point number I suggested to them, 'Left-behind Balletomane', to feature the line, '*I wonder how Massine likes Massachusetts?*', a nostalgic little song which I guess they'll scrap when they get down to Running Order . . .

Weakly agreed to do them all in spite of the Shakespeare book. Threw a temperature afterwards, wondering what Skid would say when I told him I had committed us. What he said was, 'Urhur!' Trying hard to forget that I said that the last Gate Revue was home-made and heartless in equal parts. Some discussion over the title. A large blue-eyed man who I gather Has Money In The Show had prepared a surprise for Pemmie: he wants to call it *According to Plan*. But Pemberton thought it too much of a gift to make to the critics . . .

NS Dinner with Bergel at Coquille after the ballet yielded the news that Frederick Ashton was to be called up. 'This seems to be a crime against the very things we are fighting for.' They went home to play gramophone music and Caryl confessed that she had embarked on her journal. 'Oh well,' he said, 'it took the plague to make Defoe do a diary.'

CB *June 13th* – A cold in the head. Frightful row with Skid. Couldn't have hated him more. I mean to have a contract dawn up by my own solicitor the minute *No Bed For Bacon* gets itself finished, to restrain us from doing another book together for three years – Skid says five. It is to feature heavy indemnities for infringement.

IS Work on the revue had the perverse effect of speeding the progress of *No Bed*. 'We are having a lovely time with the poets at the Mermaid Tavern . . . another good work session . . . Shakespeare coming upon Ben Jonson writing his epitaph. Shakespeare read it, "Good," he said, "but untimely" . . . I wish one of us could do heroines.'

A couple of songs were delivered to the Ambassadors by Tim Abady. 'He says they like it. Made the opening a bit dirty but that was the only way to get a little character into it.' At cocktails at the Abadys', Caryl gleaned the news that Cyril Ritchard was to replace Gingold as director and that her composer, 'modern miracle, can write his own music down!'

CB *June 16th* – Completed Tim's 'Hey! Ho!' lyric. Couldn't like it less. Got in one line that pleased me, however. Following a lot of 'Sing Heys' and 'Hos' and everything else in sight:

'. . . *Sing bass or bust,*
Sing "Otchi Chernia", if you must!'

IS She was still on regular duty at Ferdie Four.

CB In the middle of the afternoon a postman appeared at my elbow and plonked a photo on my telephone desk. It was a photo of himself in evening dress and with his hair neat, and five small sons with their hair neat stooging shinily on either hand. Clearly this was 'An Act'.

'I'm only with the post office temporarily,' he explained. 'The White-eyed Kaffir was my Godfather and I was at dancing school with Charlie Chaplin when I was a boy. Never got 'is step-dancing right,' he said severely; 'kept turning 'is toes out.' (Small demonstration.) 'See? Now,' (another demonstration) 'that's the way to do it.'

Ferdie Four looked down its nose. One gathered that this was no way for a postman to behave. But Charlie Chaplin's schoolmate sensed my sympathetic ear. 'See these two lads,' he pointed to the sloe-eyed stooges staring at me from the log-book, 'my sons. Doing our Act.

Nippers they were then. This one,' he pointed, 'is in the Air Force.
I lost their mother six years ago. I'm a postman now, but my heart's
in the Act.'

One of the wardens, a decorative young woman whose husband
is in the RAF, listened to my postman disdainfully. She is the
only example of a stage-child I know who cannot bear even to go
to a theatre. Mother on the stage. Father on the stage. Theatrical
families on both sides. She eyed my postman grimly. She had seen
this kind of thing before.

'But he's so pathetic,' I said, as Charlie Chaplin's schoolmate tore
himself reluctantly – but so reluctantly – away.

'Aren't they all?' said the stage-child, laconically. And meant it.

The other warden on duty, Old Brownie, is one of my special
friends. He was a sailor before he was a butler before he was a warden.
Today he unbent so far as to tell me that his mother had been
personal maid for ten years to the Jersey Lily, 'Mrs Langtry . . .
as she was then.'

NS Caryl summed up the close wartime camaraderie of Ferdie Four in
two final paragraphs.

CB I have been reading recently about a wardens' post in, I think,
Kensington. The writer said they had on their personnel a colonel, an
ex-naval commander, a pianist, an actor, a chauffeur, an historian
and a novelist, and they all worked together with never a cross word.
My eyebrows went up so quickly they probably whistled! All I can
claim is that at Ferdie Four we have a company director, a Digger
from Gallipoli, an ex-sergeant major, a tea-planter, a cobbler, a
butler, a newspaper-shop proprietor, a Church Army Hyde Park
orator, a carmen's pull-up proprietor, a hall porter, a works foreman,
a civil servant, a jeweller, a cabinet-maker, a man who got his
German in the last war and has a medal to show for it (with the
sinking *Lusitania* on one side and a line of American tourists on
the other, standing outside a booking office, queueing up to take
their tickets from a skeleton), the daughter of an ex-editor of the
Evening News, a seamstress, a girl whose grandmother murdered a
man, the janitor of some almshouses, a variety of others, and me. And
we all quarrel like anything.

NS Caryl could never resist playing the casting game. At this stage she hoped to get Douglas Byng to play 'A Very High Personage Indeed' in the stage *Don't, Mr Disraeli* and Beatrice Lillie for Zaza, the Human Cannon Ball and Queen Victoria. 'Oh,' said one of her legal-minded friends, 'but you can't have Victoria on the stage unless she is standing still. And then,' he added hopefully, 'you can have her in the nude?'

She dined at the Café Royal with Jack Bergel, who explained in some excitement the thrill of starting a Hurricane for the first time. 'You know,' he said, 'how it is at a cinema, when the Wurlitzer has been playing "William Tell", and there comes a moment when the organist bends forward and pulls out every stop in sight – well, that's the way you start a Hurricane.' 'I can laugh a lot with the Bergel,' she wrote. 'And sometimes I can cry – and he doesn't mind a bit which it is, and either way he goes right on talking, which is helpful in a war.'

She was, however, disturbed by his attitude to stage *Dizzy*. 'The Bergel, who is so outrageously apt to be right, is awfully doubtful about the whole project. He maintains that (a) it couldn't be done and (b) it calls for a Cochran production if anything, (c) he thinks I'm crazy to ruin a property by letting it have a wartime production.'

Meanwhile, a new character, a principal backer of the Ambassador's Revue emerges:

B *June 17th* – The phone rang while I was still in bed this morning. It was The Man Who Has Money In The Show . . . He still wanted a title. Titles are easily the worst problem of a writer's life . . . maybe tomorrow. The Man Who Has Money In The Show has developed a name, Ted Hall. I shall call him Eddy. He was a racing driver before the war – got invalided out of the RASC after going through three days on the beaches at Dunkirk and coming back on the Isle of Man steamer. Now he makes binoculars for the army, owns the garage to which I owe six pounds, and has a daughter who skates and dances.

S Caryl suggested *Gathering Peasecods* and *London Pride* – before the Coward song. Neither was accepted. Nor was *Time Off*. She and Simon went back to a work session planning the Ceremonial Tasting of the First Potato in *No Bed For Bacon*.

B *June 18th* – Michael Joseph has been invalided out of the army. Skid and I are shattered at the cause – why couldn't it have been ordinary incompetence, a scandal and the retired list? – but delighted with the effect. It will be heaven to have him back in Bloomsbury Street, refusing to advertise us, vowing he's out when he hears the patter of our little feet on the stairs, and being amazed – but forthcoming – when it turns out that all we want is a fiver for the dairy. Clutched an extra week from Lusty for revisions of *No Bed For Bacon*. Even so, will be hard-pressed to deliver the manuscript by August 21st. And I don't – I never will – see 75,000 words.

NS However, they managed 1,000 words that day and heard a rumour of a new device which sounds like the birth of Radar.

CB News of a defensive weapon against night fighters. They call it Radio Location. The cloakroom attendant at the Cumberland Hotel was discussing it with the clerk at the Cable and Wireless Bureau, where, it being the forty-first anniversary of my parents' wedding, I was sending a cable to unoccupied France.

'Night bombers,' the girl was saying, 'nothing will keep them off. If they mean to come over, nothing will stop them.' She was nineteen. She wore a little bow in her hair. And she had no illusions about the night bomber . . .

Tomorrow I am to meet Cyril Ritchard, the new producer whom, I darkly suspect, will 'just want to alter one or two little things'.
June 19th – A painful day. The only thing that I care to record is the moment when Our Producer said to Our Leading Lady, 'All you've got to do is to be arch – just arch – from beginning to end.' And Our Leading Lady beamed . . .
June 20th – A pleasant lunch with Anna Duse, Tim Abady and Eddy Hall (The Man With Money In The Show) at Moulin d'Or . . . Tim brought the good news that our producer has now decided that he likes our 'Left-behind Balletomane'. It is to be done by Roberta Huby, who finds it a little difficult. Numbers go in and out of this revue so quickly that it's like supplying material for the famous Shell advertisement – 'That Was Shell That Was'! . . . Frenzied work session trying to get Our Leading Lady on in the Finale.

Dined with Jean Abady at the Café Royal . . . She told me our producer had called one of Tim's numbers 'academic'. 'How,' she demanded hotly, 'can you be academic in three-four time?' . . . Every time I open my address book I feel bereft. My friends. My special people. This *blasted* war.

June 21st – My hairdresser was talking of his golf-course in the middle of Hainault Forest. 'It's got everything,' he told me ecstatically. 'You can hear the cuckoo and the woodpecker, and cows mooing and the Home Guard doing a bit of practising with machine guns . . .'

The thing I like to remember most about today is our Producer saying to Our Leading Lady: 'Delightful, darling – but you don't even begin to get it.'

This afternoon, Leslie Julian Jones. He seems a little tired after the success of his show, *Rise Above It*. We planned a bit of stage *Dizzy* . . . Suggested cast is Vic Oliver for our Villain and Bea Lillie for everything in sight. Nina Tarakanova for the ballets, and Wendy Toye, who has a grand sense of fun, to arrange the ensembles . . . At midnight the fall of Damascus was announced . . . I thought of the agony of the fall of France. My personal anxiety for my parents, somewhere in the south, and the impersonal grief for an ally . . . Last week, I had a cable from my parents in Villefranche: '*Our forty-first wedding anniversary. We are very happy.*'

Almost no work on *No Bed For Bacon* today. Tomorrow we shall have to be teeming prodigies. And all next week.

June 22nd – Germany marches against Russia. I went my usual walk through the Park and back by the Bayswater Terraces, past the Chymist at the bottom of the street, before work session. They have a great bed of lupins at Lancaster Gate – not the deep blue lupins of my youth, clumps of hardy effective colour, but pale pink and pastel spires, more graceful but less convincing.

I remember walking to Lancaster Gate last year when dahlias were bedded out, in the middle of the September Blitzen. Skid and I had taken over the night telephone at Ferdie Four and by then we were just about rocking on our feet. I dragged myself out for my walk and after a bit I found I was standing in front of the dahlia bed which seemed to be brimming over with all the colours that had gone out of the world. I need hardly add that I was crying like anything.

Skid arrived today in boastful mood. He claims to have discovered a pub in his sector owned by a Mr Freshwater . . . The news is that our 'Madame will you Walk' is back in the Ambassador's Show again. I couldn't be more surprised. We did 800 words on the Shakespeare book.

June 23rd – Army anecdote overheard by John Byron at Army

lecture: 'There are 5 groups of Army pay. They are known as groups 1, 2, 3, 4 and 5.'

NS The same day Brahms and Simon heard that one of the actors (Hugh French) was leaving the *New Ambassador's Revue*: 'so I guess that two more of our numbers will come out'. She speculated that the billing would soon read, 'with no additional numbers by Brahms and Simon'. In the morning they heard that 'Madame will you Walk' was indeed out. Hard on the news came a call from a young actress, a friend of a friend. 'Do I know your work?' inquired Caryl.

'Well,' she said, very seriously, 'I come half-way between Frances Day and Beatrice Lillie.'

They were now approaching the half-way mark on the Shakespeare book – 34,800 words. 'First Potato tasted in today's work session.' On 26 June they were summoned by Jack de Leon, Leslie Julian Jones's producer for *Rise Above It*, to discuss *Don't, Mr Disraeli*. He liked the idea but wanted 'the modern element' stressed.

CB Leslie Jones delighted: 'We'll bring on the girls as nuns in cellophane . . .' So maybe I'll go quietly to Evesham. The BBC, evacuated there, has been stirring slightly once again.

NS The 'nuns in cellophane' were the tip of an irritating iceberg. Librettists and composer parted 'without the usual gestures of farewell'; and Caryl, when Julian Jones failed to telephone next morning, sat down to consider the pros and cons of dumping him. With a sense of drama never too far away from her confrontation of any crisis, she weighed the prospects of another Blitz, of an immediate invasion, and of attracting a new manager if de Leon was only interested in capitalizing on Leslie Julian Jones's success with *Rise Above It*. She summed up the possibilities as two – a production and cash in hand within eight weeks (an extraordinarily short time in which to write and mount a show) or 'Credit in the spring'. Before she had to make up her mind, her composer came to heel and telephoned. They agreed to work on a running order and present it to de Leon: 'a last chance for cellophane'. Later that day Brahms and Simon gave Burbage a father, 'of whom we are inordinately fond'. On the morrow, 'Shakespeare had a row with Bacon over *Twelfth Night* . . . "Mister Bacon," Shakespeare demanded, "did I write this play or did you?" Bacon look at him. He shrugged . . .'

The entry for 30 June is succinct. 'How in the world,' demanded

Skid, 'did you expect me to know that you were terrified when you merely looked truculent?'

CB *July 1st* – We sent Elizabeth on a Progress to Greenwich in today's work session. The book is going to be too short and too slow. In spite of all Elizabethan England, two fires, and Shakespeare at work in his theatre, it contrives to be about absolutely nothing at all. Why did we ever start it? Why did we ever suppose we were the people to do it? Why didn't our agent stop us? Tomorrow to Jack de Leon with re-planned *Dizzy*.

NS The visit to Jack de Leon established that they needed neither project themselves into 2041 nor bring on the girls as nuns in cellophane.

CB At least, I hope it is established . . . Narrowly averted Jessie Matthews and Sonny Hale. *Dizzy needs* Bea Lillie and Robert Helpmann. We are to take de Leon some more material on Saturday . . .

A guinea from *Lilliput* for a Gulliver paragraph; it being too little to pay my electricity bill, supplied Skid and self with delicious lobster lunch at de Hems today. We mean to tell Dowling, the editor, that if he uses two next month, we'll take him to luncheon with us . . .

NS The collaborators celebrated 4 July with a shattering row in the middle of a work session. 'I cried, but managed not to hiccough.'

CB *July 5th* – Skid, Leslie Jones and self presented our first batch of material to Jack de Leon at the Comedy Theatre today – a half-lit little huddle of intent people in an empty theatre. He liked our work and approved our lay-out for the Victorian music hall which is to be the finale for the first half, and in which we hope to present Bea Lillie as the Human Cannon Ball. De Leon says that if the rest of our material is as-good-as, he will present us . . . Leslie did a delicious little Schwanda-like polka for our Belinda Clutterwick number:

I have no little secret
In spite of all my hopes
Oh how I wish dear Archie
Had read his Marie Stopes!

Dined at the Moulin d'Or with the Bergel, and afterwards, it being a warm moonlit night, we sat in St James's Park and he tried to make me realize the speed of a Spitfire . . .

NS Leslie Julian Jones brought the news that the Ambassador's Revue had been postponed for a week. 'Felt a bit hurt at being told news of our show by a composer who wasn't doing anything for it.' By now Wendy Toye had joined the production team for *Don't, Mr Disraeli*. Together she and Caryl arranged with de Leon that the successful playwright, Rodney Acland, would collaborate on the book and that Joseph Karl, a busy and fashionable designer, would do the décor. However, when Brahms and Simon delivered their next batch of material, de Leon required it to be:

> '*Meatier,*
> *Stronger,*
> *Longer,*' and without any extra charge,
> '*Dirtier.*'

These demands were solemnly entered in Caryl's notebook, and the memorandum was to come in useful later.

Working on a scene in which Shakespeare coached Viola in the Willow Cabin speech for *No Bed*, Simon looked up as he typed out the blank verse with a look of awe on his face. 'You know, Caryl, this palooka can write.'

Elated, they went together to *Blithe Spirit* and marvelled at the lightness of Coward's touch.

Caryl lamented to her journal: 'my friends continue to fight the war while I continue to fight my collaborators.' She and Simon found an ally in Joseph Karl, whom she found 'quick and perceptive . . . what I want now is somebody like Guthrie or Gielgud to produce the words and Wendy to do the ensembles and movements. A great ambition has been born. Skid and I are waiting to hear Guthrie (or Gielgud) say to de Leon (or Leslie) "that line must come out, it's dirty!"'

Karl sounds like a character created by Brahms and Simon for one of their Stroganoff books. His favourite phrase was, 'What I demand of myself is: "Iz zis thing ze Offenbach?"' It was some time before Caryl realized that 'Offenbach' was his word for 'Victorian'. Karl wondered if de Leon's scene-painters would come up to his standards.

As far as he could remember they were more 'Kensington' than 'Offenbach'.

CB He quite won my heart by telling me that he would need time for 'research'. I began tentatively. 'I have some books, you'll find them in the foreword to *Dizzy*.' He waved them away: 'Those you quote I have already discarded.' . . . Borrowed ten shillings from the hall porter.

NS On 13 July, 'worked like two furies'. They wrote 3,000 words. 'A lot came from contemporary sources,' she admits, but Shakespeare's clowns worked out the business for throwing the first custard pie in *The Taming of the Shrew*.

CB *July 15th* – I have been in three theatres today. The first theatre was empty – the Comedy, where we waited for Jack de Leon to keep an appointment with us for three hours and ten minutes. The second was the Golders Green Hippodrome, bulging with an audience assembled to hear Bea Lillie. The greatest revue artist of her age. She did about six numbers – all with a clean, neat, intimate, deadly touch. Her wit is a steely flick. Her sense of fun is sweeping. Her handling of the audience is in the miracle class. She annihilated the space in the vast house while maintaining her aloofness and sophistication. Her numbers included a spoof Russian number and 'There are Fairies at the Bottom of my Garden'.
. . . The third theatre was the semi-empty Ambassador's where a lighting rehearsal was in progress. First night, Friday of this week.

NS Karl phoned on the 16th for more discussions, but Caryl was too involved with the revue to linger.

B Then Dennis Van Thal phoned. Bea Lillie – the pen stutters with excitement – has read *Dizzy*. She has asked to meet the authors of the book. We go down to talk to her on Friday, trailing the wretched Leslie who will have to sing and play the numbers. Small wonder that the man who had called to cut off the electricity was allowed to function unhindered by girlish pleas of the end-of-the-week variety, and indeed unnoticed until far too late.
We live in tremendous times . . .
The private dress rehearsal of the Ambassador's Revue. Betty

Ann Davies has great appeal, and Joan Swinstead will be dry and very deft when she eases herself into her effects. I may be partial but I thought that little Huby did very well in our 'Balletomane' number . . . Later our producer (Cyril Ritchard), an enquiring man, was heard asking at what I think must have been the top of his voice, 'Who the hell is Caryl Brahms?' I nearly went over and told him.

Later still I learnt, in the same manner, that an eminent contributor to the revue* had threatened to remove her material if the management did not cast Brahms-Simon out.

NS Caryl always insisted that the 'Balletomane' song stayed in because she owed The Man With The Money In The Show £6 at his garage and to keep her song in the revue was the only way he could see of getting it back. Meanwhile, she sat up with the choreographers 'suggesting cuts in other people's material – a soothing occupation and my last effort to save my own'.

At the public dress rehearsal it was still in – 'I could hear the stagehands through it beautifully.' But there was another hiccup.

CB They cut off my telephone. Blast! Out-going calls only. However, a blitz with Skid at work session this morning. A perfunctory row on both sides. Our hearts weren't in it . . . if only we had never started *No Bed For Bacon* we should not be in the awful position of having to get it finished by the middle of next month.

NS The 18th (first night) started badly. Bea Lillie postponed their meeting and outside the theatre they bumped into Tim Abady who broke the news that they had been cut.

CB We sunk miserably into a little French dive opposite . . . I said, 'I'd rather be told by Tim than anybody.' Skid said, 'It would have been awful to wait in suspense all through the first half.'

After a bit we stowed ourselves away in our stalls. People we knew started flowing in. Skid and I pressed ourselves hard against the back of our seats. We couldn't have felt worse. There was our number, printed on the programme, 'Balletomane', music by H. Temple Abady, lyric by Caryl Brahms and S. J. Simon. So our

* Diana Morgan. Ed.

tragedy would be plain to every pressman and lyricist in the blasted building.

After our opening had played to laughs, our part was over for the evening. We clapped Tim's numbers madly. We were beautifully behaved about the rest. In the middle of the sketch that came before the gap where our 'Balletomane' number should have been, I felt terrible. So did Skid. Then, after all, our number! The first-night audience took the points and laughed at '*I wonder how Massine likes Massachusetts*'. I deny that it was perceptible only to its authors. They stowed it away in front of the ballet, without any curtain for an applause point . . . not maybe a blaze of glory – it's certain to get pitched out tomorrow – but at least it's a beginning. If a line gets a laugh in a novel, the authors know nothing about it . . . if a line gets a laugh on the radio it's either the cast, which doesn't count, or a studio audience whipped to it by a man holding a 'Laugh Please' board. But there is a warm, personal element in a ripple passing over a house because a line has got home.

So for the rest of the evening Brahms-Simon were blissful. They took one another to the Café Royal and swanked like anything to their pet waiter.

NS During the next two days the papers were examined closely for reviews, which were lukewarm to moderately enthusiastic. The suspense built to James Agate's notice in the *Sunday Times*; but Agate waived it away till the next Sunday and wrote about Walt Disney in his theatre space. Ivor Brown's *Observer* notice was perfunctory. That Sunday the BBC dropped their practice of playing the National Anthems of the Allies before the 9 o'clock news ('I miss the pathetic heartening little cavalcade of the democracies'), but Brahms and Simon wrote a sketch for stage *Dizzy*, and for *No Bed* they 'polished off the Armada'. Eventually (30 July) their song got a notice from the drama critic of the *Spectator* ('Thank you, Graham Greene!'), and its authors continued to haunt the theatre to see how it was playing.

Caryl took a night off to see *Giselle* for the first time 'since the Massine Company presented Markova and Toumanova at Drury Lane in 1938. Fonteyn brings a touching simplicity to the mad scene, but she has neither the technique nor the poise for the wraith sequence.'

CB *23rd July* – With Leslie J. to Wigmore Studios to play our material to Bea Lillie. She was unassuming, interested, quick to take our points, very simple and very charming. She liked our Mlle Fifi, of the Café Chantant.

'*I gave you a glimpse*
Of what I show ze Prince!'

which the management had deemed insufficiently long, strong, meaty and dirty. She asked us to go and see her at Streatham Hill. We plan to go tomorrow, Civil Defence permitting.

Then to management to discuss plans.

Jack de Leon bounced on us a try-out in the provinces, while feelers as to the autumn Blitzen were put out. The Blitz hangs over stage *Dizzy* just as the war hung over film *Bullet* – till in the end it swept us all aside. No word of the Savoy Theatre, or the hitherto much discussed opening within a month of completion – Jack de Leon is fighting me step by step. Each move is treated as a separate campaign. Leslie Jones is more and more identifying himself with the management rather than with the production under offer.

NS Caryl's familiar irritation with composers who failed entirely to toe her line was growing:

CB *July 24th* – To the Ambassador's. Our 'Balletomane' number going very well. Afterwards on to the Moulin d'Or. Bobby Helpmann and Freddie Ashton with Rodney Acland and Emlyn Williams at the next table. Rodney was unable to come to a satisfactory arrangement with the management about stage *Dizzy* – will anyone, *ever?* . . . Bobby is to read the book with a view to doing the villain for us.

NS Next morning Leslie Julian Jones was back in the dog-house.

CB *July 25th* – Utter hell. Our morning work session broken four times by Dennis Van Thal in angry conclave with Leslie Jones or de Leon and back to us again. Brahms-Simon take a stand: either de Leon must take an option on the book, or we remove our material and hold ourselves free to take it to another management . . . it has dragged on for months and taken an absurd amount of everybody's time except Leslie Jones's.

NS Here her journal waits a week for a retrospective entry. There was a fire alert – the first in London since 10 May. 'Knee trouble, swung out of bed. Hated it.' The barrage was heavy and she got to her ARP post to go on telephone duty by 02.01. 'No fires reported, and our impression is that Jerry is on a return journey and just flying over the capital to jerk us out of our righteous slumbers. Enemy unpopular.' To add to her annoyance, she found that she had forgotten the locations of all the fire hydrants for which she was responsible, 'except that one outside Woolworths', and was 'definitely shaky on emergency 'phone numbers'.

The Bergel, on leave, took a look at her early diary entries and, 'couldn't have been less impressed. Says I make him sound sententious. This did little to make the party a riot.' And, 'stage *Dizzy* has thrown a large curdling cloud over our activities. Constant strife with the management, with our composer, with our joint agents.'

Another raid brought her on duty at 03.25: 'Fire reported in the City. 03.37. Made tea. 03.50. Sirens sounds "Raiders Passed". All wardens reported lights and insufficient blackouts as they came in from patrol. Ferdie Four definitely shocked. No one can call us a narrow-minded post, but . . . 03.57. Back to bed.'

Bergel took her to a Prom at the Albert Hall. 'The echo beat the drummer to it every time.'

CB Back through Hyde Park, where the grass was green and scented, and the trees calm sailing-ships and leafy green fountains, and the Serpentine a silver point. On the way we practically parted forever on the old subject of choreo-symphonies – this time slightly disguised as whether a ballerina should be judged by the way she dances her classics.

We expect to finish *No Bed For Bacon* by today week, with two weeks in hand for cutting and tightening and a week's grace of which I have kept poor Skid in complete ignorance.

July 26th – We lunched with Leslie Julian Jones by way of easing the situation. Afterwards we saw the Disney *Fantasia*, and our old friend the choreographic symphony reared its head again.

July 28th – Spent the afternoon tying ourselves and our agent up to Leslie Julian Jones for stage *Dizzy*, and deciding upon final terms to be put to Jack de Leon. Interview had terrific entertainment value and goes straight into our next book. At the close we were all three satisfied and our agent in a state of collapse.

July 29th – This morning Elizabeth of England refused the Earl of Essex the renewal of the Monopoly of Sweet Wines . . . Churchill sounded the first notes of what I feel sure is going to be a September Invasion Flap . . . As epilogue to frantic work-session, Skid promised to give me the Best Dinner in Streatham. (We were in Streatham to see Bea Lillie in a revue.) Marvellous how that man keeps his word. There was just one restaurant open . . .

Bea Lillie got round to saying she would like to come to the show . . . she continues to be simple and friendly. She told us that she went last week to her first Gilbert and Sullivan, *The Gondoliers*. Asked how she liked it, she said, a little doubtfully, 'Well, it's clean . . .'

NS On 30 July, the collaborators 'touched in a build-up for the Essex rebellion', luxuriated in their favourable mention in the *Spectator*, and read over their stage *Disraeli* contract. 'Our agents appear to have forgotten every word any of us said. Inexplicable!' Caryl 'zipped into the ballet to see *Sylphides* and found myself witnessing *Coppelia*. All three acts. And what is worse, liking it. Can I be losing my grip?'

On the last day of the month Brahms and Simon embarked on the last chapter of *No Bed For Bacon*, the Court performance of *Twelfth Night* given at the Temple Hall – which had recently been destroyed by the Blitz. That and a short epilogue would complete the book. 'I feel that I know less about this book than any I have ever written. Certainly it is not as good as it ought to be. But I am still too near to know why.'

With a sigh of relief at an end in sight, Caryl delivered herself of her considered statement on her pet hate – the choreographic symphony.

CB A symphony with its classical development and thematic treatment puts too great a strain on the idioms and the invention of the thing by which I have to stand or fall – good ballet. Moreover, no musician can really want to listen to his symphonies with their tempi dictated by the dancer or having his phrasing altered, his counterpoint underlined, by the choreographer.

I am always touched by the way that the same arguments put to me by so many different people as newly-minted coins that cannot fail

to convince, leave me touched but unmoved. The music is complete in itself and has no need of a visual line for its full perfection.
August 1st – Small work session. Shame on my head, for Skid was, for once, not entirely unwilling. But I was slow and submerged. We did the puddle and Sir Walter Raleigh's new cloak. It was raining. 'Elizabeth of England looked at him. A gleam came into her eyes. She beckoned . . .'

NS However, the next day the book was finished. 'While it is unlikely to be as bad as I think it is, there is a strong possibility that this time it may be even worse. The final stages were marked by my picking up an ashtray and emptying it over the wretched Simon. I have been wanting to do this for five years. The relief was exquisite.' They celebrated at L'Ecu de France.

CB In the midst of a dinner of unparalleled luxury, Skid remembered a pathetic story of an ancient White Russian restaurateur in Paris. It seems that he used to serve a very fine 10 franc dinner. Asked how he managed it, he admitted that he lost F1.50 on each meal he served. Asked why he did it, he replied with a sigh that if the dinner were not so good he would lose his clients . . .

NS With *No Bed* apparently out of the way, another project was broached. On 4 August Caryl had tea with the choreographer of the Ambassador's Revue, Anna Duse.

CB We decided to do an all-Russian Revue – a sort of *Chauve-Souris*, with a White Russian General for compère. We are to discuss the project with Tim Abady this week. And I have to break the news to Skid. It ought to be right down his Nevsky Prospekt.
   . . . Borrowed a pound from the hall porter.
   To the ballet . . . Young woman at *Sylphides* with tart accent: 'Well, I thought they were going to be first class. They aren't, you know.' Sniff. 'The one I like is the little dark one who's just cleared off.' Margot Fonteyn had been dancing the prelude.

NS Robert Helpmann was toying with the idea of playing the villain in *Don't, Mr Disraeli*; wild war rumours banged about ('Richard says he's heard some inside gossip of America taking over Ireland'); Bea Lillie claimed to like *Disraeli* more and more as she read more and more

('She must have mastered all of one chapter by now!'). Arguments staggered on with Leslie Julian Jones's agent: 'Threatened him with Skid. It worked like a charm. Must threaten people with Skid more often.' Bergel was taken to hear some of the Russian revue material: 'The room rocked with his disapproval of (a) the work under discussion, (b) everything I've ever written, (c) especially the Stroganoff books. Unlucky!'

The closeness of their relationship is amusingly confirmed by another entry.

CB The Bergel, who said he would 'phone this morning, has made no sign all day. Doubtless he will come to life tomorrow. I would give our joint fortune (say, 4d) to sulk and not be available. But I bet I go and get compunction trouble – can't bear to cloud even a second of their leave. So I absolutely bet I'm tactful, and pretend that I didn't stay in all morning. Men! Even nice ones!

NS In compensation she discovered, rare wartime treat, a new restaurant.

CB Dined tonight at a Czechoslovak restaurant. An ample *table d'hôte* that also contrives to be the best dinner in London at 3s 6d, but you've got to eat it in the Edgware Road. The Czech government has taken over the ground floor of the block of flats where I live and Ferdie Four flourishes. Our reception halls are always full of well-fed men and plump women billowing out of their honeycomb of offices. Now I know exactly why it is. I'm rather expecting to billow myself after a week or so of Czech eating.

NS On 7 August Bergel came to heel. 'Twenty minutes before curtain rise, the Bergel arrived to be taken to the Ambassador's show. Claims to have 'phoned five times yesterday. I couldn't be less convinced. Borrowed £2 from him and invited him to take me to Simpsons.'

Caryl's highly suspicious nature soon put her on the track of more perfidy in the plans for stage *Dizzy*. '*August 9th* – Shown some sets that Jack de Leon, who had told me that it was altogether too premature to ask Karl to show designs, had ordered from someone else.'

'Someone else' was Richard Berkeley Sutcliffe, a distinguished designer in the decorative Oliver Messel tradition. He became one of Caryl's closest friends, designed many of her book jackets and several of our theatre musicals, as well as the 'weather house' clock outside

Fortnum and Mason. It was characteristic of her that, however suspicious she was of this new designer, confronted by the work she kept an open mind.

CB Blast it, they were good! Also the designer is in the Army and is managing to get them done in his spare time, which I found touching . . ." [Along with Oliver Messel, Berkeley Sutcliffe was appropriately in the Camouflage unit.] Moreover, he has read *A Bullet in the Ballet* in the Underground and gone on past his station. But I feel very angry that I have been 'managed' in this way.

Warded off Elsie Randolph and Jack Buchanan. For the time being.

August 10th – Broke the news . . . by phone, to Karl about de Leon's perfidy. He couldn't have been nicer.

August 12th – Today we did the opening for the *Rousska* show.

> '*In Russia where the rivers flow*
> *Beside the trains, and just as slow.*'

I have started reading Russian fairy tales in search of material for seven-minute operas – two minutes too long, by my reckoning. Touched to find that where we would say 'the great wide world', they say, 'the great white world'.

NS The bombing had stepped up again and Caryl addressed her journal sternly on the selfishness of the people of Oxford and Cambridge. 'They have had some small anti-personnel bombs dropped in Cambridge and they are still talking about their Blitz in an exhibitionist and sickening kind of way.' She contended that the terror which made some people outside London think only of themselves, made almost any Londoner do more and more for others. 'One day the horror will end. Meantime I've borrowed ten shillings from the hall porter.'

Lunching at the Czech restaurant during the only time Simon could steal from the ARP, they worked happily on a drinking song for the Russian show. 'There we sat, humming and ti-tumming to each other, forgetting the clatter all around. A fierce-looking Polish officer, a general at least, sat opposite us and beamed when we got to a mention of vodka and kvass.'

CB *August 15th* – Today I received £1 12s 8d to be divided between

Skid and self, being the royalties over three weeks on our two numbers in the *New Ambassador's Revue*. There's only one thing to be said about the energy, interest, hurt pride, hopefulness, sweat and blood that went into my half of £1 12s. 8d: *Palooka!*

NS More backsliding by Leslie Julian Jones – 'he wants to do a second edition of *Rise Above It* before he completes stage *Dizzy*' – caused a delay that threatened Bea Lillie's availability – if she were indeed to do it. However, Caryl drowned her sorrows with Mrs Jones.

CB Tight as a tick on champagne before lunch, so off I streaked with Virginia Jones, utter sisters, to buy fur coats. I chose a lovely blue-fox bolero for Skid to give me on the first night of *Don't, Dizzy*, and just in case there should be no first night of *Don't, Dizzy*, what with Blitzen and managements and one thing and another, such as the effect of the champagne wearing off, I brought the coat right back with me. Skid calls it a 'conditional present'; 'and not the usual condition either,' he remarked dourly.
August 18th – Final notice for telephone today. Couldn't be more depressed. The only thing I care to record is a food announcement by Our Wonderful BBC: *onions*. These vegetables have been rare lately.
August 20th – Skid enlivened today's work session, a *Stop the Banns* number for stage *Dizzy*, by an account of a Skidelsky wedding. His eldest brother, Archie (Arkadi?), was getting married. The ceremony was to take place at the Brook Street Synagogue. The entire Skidelsky family including Uncle Bounya (whom, I am reliably informed, looked just the way his name suggests) started out from the Savoy and coasted round and round in taxis looking for a street that looked like what Archie thought Brook Street looked like. He had forgotten the name; nobody else had ever known it. At last they found it. Out got Mamoushka, Tante Gitya, Archie, Seca (who is S. J. Simon, known as Skid), Mischka, Bobka (for whom, on an evil day, I found a job as games and drawing master at the prep school of the husband of a girl who has since ceased to regard me as her best friend). Also there were the bride and the bride's father. It was a long time since the bride's father had found himself in a synagogue. What with the marriage of his only child and memories of his own wedding, he was prepared to be deeply affected. So with the choir singing their heads off and Tante Gitya meanly sobbing on

Mamoushka's shoulder, the bride's father was soon needing his own handkerchief. A *Shamuth* came creaking up the aisle. He tapped the bride's father on the heaving shoulder: 'Don't forget to tip the choir,' he breathed o'er this very Jewish Eden.

August 23rd – I'd like to take a sleeping draught tonight, but I think there'll be a Blitz, for I heard a 'plane purring low over the sky just now and I figure it was one of our fighters streaking out after Jerry. So I'll lie awake, waiting to be called out, and get to sleep just before the siren sounds, as absolutely usual.

NS Rumours of a September invasion were rife: 'For the last two days cars have been stopped and drivers asked what they would do if there were an invasion.' Leningrad was threatened: 'I would feel worse if it were still called St Petersburg.' News from Bloomsbury packed a more immediate punch.

CB *August 26th* – Can the stars have lost their grip? This afternoon Trusty Lusty came through with the news that the printers made a mistake in their calculations and that *No Bed For Bacon* is only seventy-four out of the stipulated seventy-five thousand words. You can't publish at 8s 6d if you're under seventy-five thousand. So we're all in favour of cheating our public.

I feel very tired tonight, I can't think why, and just about as old as the world . . .

NS They solved the length problem by 'chucking in the Armada', but there was another shock at the Ambassador's. 'Our producer has ripped out Our Number while Our Backs were turned. Our Author, however, bethought herself of a long-distance 'phone and now has Our Situation well in hand.'

Caryl had time, after a dinner at Beguinot ('scene of my first Soho binge with a maiden aunty and a cousin') to reflect on the Blitz and a mysterious sense approaching relief when a much loved, much feared for building was suddenly destroyed.

CB For I had fed my eyes on the buttery terraces of Regent's Park and the lovely Georgian squares, Park Crescent (where Skid lives) never to be complete again, the smooth round spire of All Saints, Langham Place, and Cumberland Place – half-destroyed – and all the quiet streets and squares – how almost unbearably lovely they were in July and August of 1940 when we knew that we were very near to losing them. We looked at London then with forever eyes. Each time was a last time, then. It was – almost – a relief when the last time happened.

August 28th – Driving home through the park I looked at London with remembering eyes. I wondered sadly if my own order was passing, had passed already. And then I remembered that the thing about being a Jew is that one's order doesn't get swept away – though clearly it gets knocked about a bit in the process of surviving down the centuries, which is a comfort . . .

. . . When I got back, Skid arrived tight, which was *horrid*; but very, very Russian.

. . . A dubious locality. From an open window the sound of a gramophone. Two demolition workers look up from out of their cloud of dust. ''ear that music playing in that tart's room?'

'Music while you work, I shouldn't wonder.'

NS Caryl began to talk to Peter Hebden, the lead salesman at Michael Joseph, about launching *No Bed For Bacon*. 'He says it is the apple of the autumn list. This would be more exciting were it not for the fact that M.J., poor wretch, hopes to get to heaven by virtue of the humility he brings to advertising the latest Brahms-Simon.'

CB *August 30th* – Week ends on its starry form with a letter from the bank. Despairingly borrowed 7s 6d from the hall porter. Why can't I learn to be properly poor?

. . . Blitz with Skid at today's work session. The British Empire featured largely. So did my awful selfishness. It started rather sweetly, though, over a sentence we both finished in different ways. I liked his way best; he was sold on mine. So we both lost our tempers . . .

September 1st – We had yellows last night at Ferdie Four. So what? Symptomatic of September . . .

The Bergel's brother, Hugh (Mark 2, a less definite, slightly slicker model), once had a job with a very fine firm of engineers. They made bits for large-sized bridges, and very exquisite artificial limbs. Indeed, they made legs for Bader of the RAF. But long before his day they made a leg for Sarah Bernhardt. It is in their museum to this day. It was a very fine leg, and Sarah was delighted. Till they sent her the bill. Then she was livid. 'Think of the *réclame*,' she insisted.

'So the manufacturers wrote to the old lady,' said the Bergel, with relish, 'and said if she didn't pay she would have to send it back. So the old lady sent it . . .'

Agate would trade in his ration of *potage* for that little item, I'll bet my ballet shoes . . .

. . . To see our producer (Cyril Ritchard) between shows at the Saville. Herbert Farjeon was there for the same purpose. This created an embarrassing bottle-neck. It seems that our 'Left-behind Balletomane' was five years too late. Attempted to point out that five years ago there was no call for home-sickness for a Russian ballet in America. Foiled by sheer charm impact. Leslie Henson, hearing I was in the theatre, sent for me to tell me that he had read *Dizzy* aloud to the wretched company while they were on tour. Rushed madly out before my head got turned.

NS   This is the last reference to the *New Ambassador's Revue*. It must have closed soon afterwards, for theatrical records show that a new show was occupying the stage by the end of the month.

Invasion scares proliferated and a renewal of the bombing was threatened. 'Skid told me of a while-you-wait shoe-menders. "I've been here an hour and twenty minutes," he had grumbled. The assistant pointed to the while-you-wait board. "Well, you're waiting, aren't you?"'

Jack Bergel seemed to Caryl to get more leave than the average man. 'He came to eat out of tins this evening, in one of his rare and valuable sweet moods. After we had played *Petroushka* and *Brigg Fair*, we talked a bit about Lady Macbeth . . . The Bergel is a special and unusual person. His quality as a companion comes from perceptiveness, irascibility, low humour, amazing energy, a cloud-of-glory egg-shell left over from his mother's knee and Balliol, quickness, grasp, horse-sense and the capacity for wonder.'

They dined; they went to the ballet; they played records. Caryl went to Queens to watch him skate. They sat on sunny park benches and swapped stories. 'The Bergel told me that a hitchhiker in a desolate bit of country thumbed a limousine that happened to be luxuriating along. It wasn't until he settled into the saloon that he realized that he was facing Queen Mary and the Duchess of Kent. Disconcerting.'

Caryl, always keen on a royal anecdote, had hers to offer in return.

Ernest Thesiger, the actor, was the source. Queen Mary was visiting a children's hospital. She paused by the bed of an 'utter angel child'. The utter angel child had a doll. She was banging it against the wall like anything.

'What are you doing, little girl?' asked Queen Mary, interested.

The utter angel child beamed. 'Banging 'er bloody guts out, Miss.'

They shared wartime rumours and letters from friends. 'Finding himself stationed in, I think, the Outer Hebrides, A Strong Man in a Pre-war Tank Corps wrote: "*Darling, There is nothing to do here, so I have read a book. It is by O. Wilde (Salome). It is very hot.*"'

And Bergel provided a constant critical commentary on her work. 'It is for his ruthless, dead true attitude towards my work that the Bergel is so valuable and so touchstone-like. But how exposed and flinching I feel while it is happening. And how I hate him for twenty-four hours after.'

He left after lunch on 7 September. 'I was a bit behind my face.' The next day Caryl dined in Bayswater.

CB On the way back I walked up one of the quiet familiar squares. It was so lovely, so still and so complete. The sky was clear and light and the trees were deep green with silent torrents of leaves. And the houses were good Georgian brick, rich and formal. Two windows were glowing out in glorious orange squares, for the lamps had been lit early and they seemed to float in the evening air. And it was familiar and dear and quiet. And I was the only person walking in it. I remember driving through this square with a friend before the war and how he pointed to a house with a red-striped awning. 'I'm going to a dance there tonight, we shall stroll in the gardens, I expect.'

London tears your heart out of your body in the autumn. I would rather be a good Londoner than a good writer – or even a good ferry pilot, like the Bergel.

September 10th – Today, watching for news of Jean Abady (a friend having an operation) has been endless. 'The trouble with you,' said Skid in the middle of Dunkirk, 'is that you take other people's troubles so much to heart.'

One night in the September Blitz last year, they dropped a stick while I was at supper with Skid. It wasn't a particularly delicious supper, though it would seem so now by contrast. It was an egg, which was about all I ever felt inclined to eat in the state of fatigue

I was in that autumn (every other night on duty all night, and parts of other nights, and most days) but I had prepared that egg and I was eating it with my guest. The thunderbolts were shattering and very near. And the great building I lived in rocked a bit. 'My poor Caryl,' he said, 'such a nervous little woman,' for I had gone on eating my egg. Not enjoying it. Just eating it. I've often been too angry to be thoroughly frightened.

The design for the wrapper of *No Bed For Bacon* came by the early post. Have written Trusty Lusty to point out that I have a prejudice for having my name spelt correctly on my own wrappers . . .

September 11th – Skid being a dog-race-goer in a big way (he has been known to say to me, 'It's the only thing I've got in my life,' his face white with self-pity; and how my heart ached for him – until I clicked back to the times he used this argument, with just this white look, about bridge, pin-tables, and without the slightest embarrassment, his girl-friend), we went together to the race meeting at Stamford Bridge.

This time I saw a young man in the RAF, half a wing up, win £100 on a bet. 'Two fifties will do,' he said, in a voice he did his best to make level, his face flushed and his eyes showing his excitement. This seemed to me so unbearably pathetic it quite ruined my day. Reported to Skid. He said, 'You're crazy! Now, if he'd *lost* £100, I could understand it!' (Skid had just lost ten and was feeling grim.)

Skid once went through a very taking phase when his betting activities appeared to depend upon his turning his back while the dogs were racing, to watch the last-minute figures on some sort of board at the back of the stand. He was, I think, collecting data for an infallible system – a system which, to judge by results, made it certain that he would lose. Right now, he wanders whitely about, making last-minute dabs and backing every dog in the race. He also carries a stock of winning tickets from last week's meeting that he can't be bothered to queue up to cash in.

A rare dog-race-goer myself, three meetings remain vivid in my mind.

One was at Bournemouth, a clear September evening. Chamberlain had flown to Munich and the whole world was waiting for him to emerge from The Presence. They lit a great brazier in our enclosure. And right then we were all thinking that perhaps there wasn't going to be a war. It was only when we were told the terms of the peace that we knew there must be one. I can

point to that bitter little poem in *Punch* to prove this. And one still
later that *Punch* wouldn't publish:

'*We'd like to keep the Isle of Wight,*
We think perhaps we may . . .'

The second dog-race meeting that I remember vividly was held in
the sunshine of a rackety and slightly home-made track on the bricky
borders of London. That track had charm. It was so palooka. It also
held a meeting during the peak point in one of the post-Munich
crises – don't ask me which, they were all so agonizing. A newsboy
came along calling a scare-line. Even Skid noticed him and bought a
paper. A woman with a red face and a nodding feather turned to
me. 'There mustn't be a war,' she said, explosively. 'There can't be.
And there mustn't be!' That's all she knew.

The third dog-race meeting lies snugly in my memory for quite
a different kind of reason. I met a Russian at the White City who knew
me vaguely and so kissed my hand. The 3s 6d ring nearly
over-balanced itself in its efforts to see more of this fascinating
encounter . . .

Today's meeting was notable only for the fact that I backed a dog
called Temple Light, on account of H. Temple Abady, as a direct
result of which I left the course losing 3d.

Trusty Lusty writes, 'I am thankful to find I haven't forgotten to
announce *No Bed For Bacon* in our autumn list.' Thoughtful of him!
September 12th – The thing I most like remembering about today is
Jack de Leon's expression when we told him that we had once had a
sketch turned down by the Windmill because it was too dirty for
them . . . we were a bit surprised about this, too.
September 13th – Listened to one of the Dvorak Centenary Concerts
– but without much love. To tell the truth, the Czech government,
who have taken the whole of the ground floor of this block of flats,
have beckoned away my daily Mrs Lollipop by paying her twice
as much as I can afford. I just can't compete with government funds.
I take this behaviour on the part of our gallant allies hard . . . Pinching
other people's Mrs Lollipops may be an old Czech custom, but it's
jolly tactless of them to continue it here.

John Byron, on leave from the RAF, took me out to late breakfast
at the Corner House. Rolls and honey. He looks bronzed and
rested, and is having a lovely leave. He told me a charming story.

[100]

Tanya Moseiwitch was listening to her father on the wireless playing the 'Emperor' Concerto. With her, listening intently too, was her landlady's little son. During the break between the first and second movements, Tanya felt that A Few Words were definitely called for: 'I expect he's wiping his brow now with a big white silk handkerchief,' she observed.

'Like Hutch,' said the landlady's son.

September 16th – Loyal Little Woman

The Bergel's name bubbled into conversation. Celia (Ramsey) looked severe. 'I once told Jack Bergel he was the most offensive man I have ever met,' she said with an air of defiance.

'And he wasn't even trying,' I observed coldly . . .

NS The Czech restaurant, or rather the Czech government in exile, was out of favour with Caryl that week. However, she still ate their food.

> Old lady dining there turned to her table:
> 'Do you speak English, my dear?'
> CB (sadly): Rather better than I write it.

The Jewish New Year on 22 September yielded a bonus. 'I have discovered a dive – wild readers will not drag its name from me – where caviare toast is to be obtained at a shilling a round. Red caviare it is true, but very delectable for wartime.'

On one occasion, Caryl returned to Furzecroft to find Jack Bergel on leave again. She had been in a rage:

CB I have been rude to Michael Joseph. I have called him blind, crass and probably incontinent. I have added an irate postscript and dared him to skip it. Was this undignified? I wrote the four furious pages standing up to make the letter stronger, while the bathwater brimmed over and flooded the bathroom floor. To me, bent double, mopping up, the Bergel on sudden leave. He seized up the situation inside of two seconds – and I was crying with rage. 'How dare Michael Joseph suggest I have a *sense of proportion*?'

NS The reason for the rage is never explained, but there had been another dispute about the picture of Queen Elizabeth on the amended dust wrapper for *No Bed For Bacon*; 'Elizabeth of England, still in pink but this time back to front. Better.' Bergel took her to dinner and to

Disney's *The Reluctant Dragon* (a meal and a movie would almost invariably change Caryl's mood, temporarily at least) and produced for her amusement a familiar waiter who, asked why he was looking glum, sighed heavily. 'Well, sir,' he said, 'the food's so bad and I've run out of lies.'

Bergel had another revelation. 'One way and another,' he babbled, 'it's been a grand day. Why, do you know that Fay Compton and Mrs Dudley Ward have both been made a grandmother by one and the same action!' And Caryl quotes another exchange:

> CB 'Can't think why I put up with you, Jack.'
> JB (cheerfully) 'Catch 'em not so young, and treat 'em rough!'

CB *September 25th* – A day. The proofs of *No Bed For Bacon* to hand. 'There will not be much for you to do,' writes Trusty Lusty, on the note that came with them, optimistically . . . It's always a moment when proofs come in. Sentences we never specially thought about leap out and make us laugh. Sentences we sweated blood over ride the page with ease. Sentences we thought so good die on their commas. And, most satisfactory of all, there's still a chance to put things right. We have a new printer, for our old one was blitzed at Plymouth with all our set-ups, *Bullet*, *Elephant*, *Dizzy*. If they had to be blitzed, I'm glad it was in Drake's town.

Skid looked up from his proof-copy. 'Remarkably correct,' he said, impressed.

'How far have you got?'

'Two pages.'

NS Proofing was Caryl's job. Simon was back at his wartime task:

CB *September 26th* – Skid's ARP post has a nice little problem of its own. Yesterday, his Senior Warden, who had been scanning the list carefully, called him over. 'Take a look at this.'

Skid focused: Finklestein, Rabinovitch, Rappaport, Kissinsky, Appleblossom.

'Well?' asked Skid.

'All due to register on Tuesday.'

'What of it?'

'It happens,' said senior, with awful dignity, 'to be Yom Kippur.'

NS   Suitably ecumenical, the next day she went by the twice-bombed St James's, Piccadilly. 'I never expect to see it wrecked. It is a fresh sorrow every time. Whenever I pass I feel I am trespassing upon some privacy and must turn away my head. It is like looking at a sleeper whose face is unguarded and exposed to impertinent, exploring eyes.'

She turned, as so often to Pepys (April 1671): 'Mr Young was talking about the building of the City again, and he told me that those few churches that are to be new built are plainly not chosen with regard to the convenience of the City, they stand a great many in a cluster about Cornhill . . . thus are all things in the world!'

'The other fire,' she wrote, 'gives our present woes an historic respectability.'

She was late to bed. 'Reading Bacon by candlelight at three o'clock in the morning, it has been nice to come upon this passage: *Walled Townes, Stored Arsenalls and Armouries, Goodly races of Horses, Chariots of Warre, Elephants, Ordnance, Artillery and the like: all this is but a Sheep in Lion's Skin, Except the Bread and Disposition of the people be Stout and War-like.* No good the District Warden's sending an Elephant along, I just happen to feel peaceful, right now . . .'

CB   *September 28th* – Skid and I spent some time grumbling about the state stage *Dizzy* has got itself in. No opening till next spring, and all the stars we want going into other shows. 'Never mind,' I said, 'we'll soon have enough experience to write our own shows by ourselves.'

Skid's face lit up. 'Enter a lunatic,' he murmured raptly.

He had a very taking little story of a pre-war wedding. A friend of the bridegroom arrived at the reception very windblown, very flushed and very late. He had recently become the owner of a secondhand car – his first – and had driven himself to town very enthusiastically and with much arm-wagging, brake-grinding, and many heated explanations. The time came for speeches. The little man rose, glowing, to his feet: 'Speaking as a motorist,' he began.

I wore my new furs to the ballet. Nina Tarakanova stroked them lovingly: 'But they are beautiful, Caryl. Tell me,' she leaned forward confidentially, 'you borrowed them, no?'

October 1st – Simon and self are to be on a Brains Trust in a large, tough shelter tonight. Only Casabianca Flan could get me to go through this terrible ordeal . . . The questions they looked hopefully to us to answer ranged from What is Electricity? ('What they've

[103]

just cut off in Miss Brahms's flat,' said S. J. Simon, playing for a laugh) via Is The Tomato a Fruit or a Vegetable?, to How Far From the Sun are We? and How Do We Know?

October 2nd – Anna Duse and I showed The Man With The Money the *Rousska* designs. The first half of this homely Russian show is finished.

NS She took an afternoon off to go to the ballet, *Les Sylphides* being once more on the programme. Her report combines her severe attitude to the spirit of the Wells Company under de Valois and her appreciative but less than starry-eyed view of the emerging Fonteyn.

CB How they dragoon their sylphs at the Wells. Everything about the gossamer spirits of the glade is martial, from the roll of the drums as the *pas-de-deux* ballerina takes her *arabesque* to the trumpets in the finale. The Company has lost touch with the intangible. The *corps de ballet* go through their paces with the demeanour of ATS volunteers and the faces of King's Chapel choirboys. Someone must have told the Company that the work is a classic. It ought to be given a rest for a year and then produced as though it were a new work.

Margot Fonteyn alone comes near to the feeling of the spirit of the moonlight, the light night-winds, the moving branches of the trees. This dancer has a childlike simplicity – as well as the graces of line and facility – and shows a grateful compliance to her choreographer. When she is dancing she seems always to be a child, alone on the stage, grave or gay, who has slipped away from her playmates and is dancing alone, with ecstasy.

Perhaps this is not the best place in the world to add that she has no *dévelopé*, the ugliest *fouetté* that I have ever seen, and that never has ballerina worked on more disappointing *pointes*. In spite of these defects her great quality persists, and her lovely line is a delight and an enchantment.

NS A few evenings later Fonteyn was dancing the Sleeping Princess 'with an easy brilliance that made me forgive her entire lack of *pointes*. The little *variation* the seasoned ballet-goer knows as Nemchinova's was most superbly danced.'

Influenza, ARP duty and stories prepared long ahead for Christmas magazine issues kept her prostrate or busy through November; and another welcome letter from Christopher Fry in his non-combatant corps cheered her:

> I can as easily write letters now as a rich man can enter the kingdom of heaven; when I'm not on the parade ground I'm doing the garden of the officers' mess, and when I'm not doing the garden I am guarding Bootle docks; and when I'm not doing any of these things I'm preparing to do them, or recovering from doing them, or else my brain is wading about in a commotion of canteen-radio, piano-playing and general hubble-bubble.
>
> Or else a corporal is telling me the story of his life (without reservations).
>
> Or else I'm asleep.
>
> In between these things, so that frustration, boredom and despair shall not send me Nijinskying out of time altogether, I sandwich rehearsals for two scenes out of my play about Moses!
>
> [I feel like] so much green scum, so much duckweed, apart from the occasional lucid moment, at which I may alter one word of a speech in Moses. But the rest of the time, while history is piping hot the world over, and action and suffering are like a twin epidemic, and if ever a man should be geared up it is now, I am locked in a nursery in khaki, being taught fantastically silly games, being told nonsensical fairy stories, compelled to be less of a man under the heading Conscription of Man Power, made use of to be useless, forced to be helpless on the pretext that everyone must help.

A pre-war friend, now an instructor of elementary arithmetic in the RAOC, took Caryl out.

B *October 8th* – It has been decided today that I am to have a month's holiday from working with Skid. My idea of heaven is, on the whole, quite a simple affair – it's just not having to see Skid *every* day.

Mike told me over oyster lunch (4s 6d a dozen) that he was walking up Regent Street last night when a shady lady said good-evening to him.

'*Pas ce soir, chérie,*' said the virtuous Mike.

'*Dommage! car je suis en forme,*' returned the shady lady unexpectedly.

NS During the Brahms-Simon working lull they got together to sign a contract with de Leon for stage *Dizzy* and to celebrate the event with Leslie Julian Jones. They also tangled with the BBC again: Max Kester, a radio variety producer, suggested six half-hour revues, inviting them to devise an entertainment containing 'laughter and loveliness and tears' – an instruction they had difficulty accepting with straight faces. It provided an excuse for the re-united collaborators to share oysters, discuss it and call it *Dear Me, Mr Donat*. 'Work should always be done over oysters and champagne at mid-day . . .' Kester spent a deal of time insisting that they could not use the phrase 'body-urge' on the wireless; but told a very BBC story about the evacuation of his department to rural North Wales.

CB One sunny morning he was walking up the High Street humming a bit and wearing his usual bright check coat and flannel bags, when he heard two women discussing him:
    'He's from the BBC.'
    'How can you tell?'
    'Where else could he be from?'
October 22nd – Skid got back from the first lecture of an advanced anti-gas course in a depressed condition.
    'What was it like?'
    'Grim. Full of threats of what he's going to talk about in other lectures.'

NS Later the same week, Caryl read a book written by two English prisoners of war about Christmas in the Cotswolds, an area which had always been a solace to her and was soon to be so again.

CB I have always been marvellously happy in the Cotswolds. Its ways are the ways of happiness and its paths are the paths of peace. No matter where I go in the Cotswolds, I know I have been there before. The Bergel flies over them most days. But I shall not go back and walk in them again until after the war, those sturdy villages built in ancient honey-coloured stone, the small rich sweeping fields, the gentle rivers spanned by small humped bridges, the thick compact coppices, the smell of leaf and log on the frosty air. The straight tempting roads. The self-respecting farms. Chipping Camden built of basking stone that seems to hold all the sunshine in the world, where once I heard an old man play a tune on bells.

Bibury, where we watched ducks on a pond. Bourton-on-the-Water
– little bridges span the stream, there; and that was where we
scooped up snow in our bare hands for the feeling of glowing warmth
when the numbness stopped. The Slaughters with their five times
gated road. And, dearest of all, Burford, built on a hill. The Cotswolds.
Nothing can make them alter or falter. They will be there waiting
for us all after the war . . .

MS In late October she dined at the Moulin d'Or in Soho. 'Ma, who, with
her two sons, George and Ernest, runs the Mill at the age of seventy-
five, waxed confidential. We gathered that her vegetable marrows
refused to pollinate. "Homo," she told us with infinite scorn . . .' A
week later Caryl dined there with Bergel 'in one of his rare, sweet
moods, docile and simple. When he talks about flying he looks happy
and young . . .'

CB *October 27th* – The review copies of *No Bed For Bacon* go out today.
Feeling awful about this.

I've acquired Edith Sitwell's collection of poems for children,
Look the Sun. How magnificently right for late childhood is her own
'Aubade'.

Jane, Jane,
Tall as a crane
The morning light creaks down again.

. . . I came, too, upon two Cotswold jingles among these poems for
everybody's nursery. The first is by Lord Berners:

I went to Noake
But nobody spoke;
I went to Thame
It was just the same;
Burford and Brill
Were silent and still.
But I went to Beckley
And they spoke directly.

I specially love '*Burford and Brill were silent and still*'. The other
Cotswold poem has no author's name, but I strongly suspect the
same pen:

At Brill on the Hill
The wind blows shrill
The cook no meat can dress;
At Stow-in-the Wold
The wind blows cold;
I know no more than this.

But I know more than this; I know that outside Stow-in-the-Wold there is a hill from which you can see five counties. And that it lies on the left driving from London. And that it winds down past a lane that leads to the Stantons, built long, long ago in Cotswold stone for palookas like Harold and me to go and remember. And I know that at the bottom of tilted Burford there is an orchard. I have seen it bearing apple-blossom, and under snow. You walk through it to get your Sunday papers. *Burford and Brill are silent and still*, and waiting for us to go back to them, after the war.

October 30th – Skid and I behaved like a couple of lunatics today. We raided our publisher demanding an early copy of *No Bed For Bacon* due next week. We smuggled it out for fear of Trusty Lusty turning Crusty. We rushed madly to de Bry's where we read it aloud to one another over toast and caviare, gloating over the cover, giggling at the refeened maize-coloured binding with our names in purple on the back, and we bellowed at our own jokes – and even at one another's!

October 31st – Guy Ramsay phoned today. He has read a review copy of *No Bed For Bacon* and claims to like it. Queer! But infinitely comforting, for this is the first word from the outside world. He says he has been walking about all day in our Elizabethan world. While the book is nothing like so good as we should have made it, I begin to hope that we haven't let down the hopeful people eager for us to make them laugh.

November 6th – The first review of *No Bed For Bacon* has appeared, five days before publication, in the *Daily Sketch*. Civil!

November 7th – Amazing whoopee! Out with the Bergel to celebrate the publication of *No Bed For Bacon* (before the Sunday press cramps my style) and to mark his promotion to larger, louder and more lethal planes.

November 9th – *No Bed For Bacon* came out today! Skid and self greeted by Mr Wilson of Bumpus's with a whoop that brought book-loving heads up from quiet browsing with a click. Mr Wilson introduced us to H. M. Tomlinson . . .

November 11th – Armistice Day. Thoughts not for these pages. A letter from M.J. [Michael Joseph]: 'This is Bacon's birthday – may he furnish all your dreams of luxury. Not Skid's – we don't want him turning up at the office with a string of expensive greyhounds . . .' Our special book assistant at Selfridges spoke warmly of *No Bed For Bacon*. Celebration lunch of oysters with Skid.

November 12th – My new Mrs Lollipop* arrived to do for me today, plump and twinkling, announcing that she too is a humorist (can't help feeling that two of us in this minuscule flat may prove to be a bit too much!): 'I often say to my husband, "You've married a very funny woman."' The humorist departed with a horrid threat: 'I'll bring you down the reports I wrote for the British Legion – you'll enjoy them!'

November 13th – *No Bed For Bacon* is reprinting, before the end of its first week . . . Elizabeth in pink looks awfully good in the middle of Selfridges' Oxford Street windows.

November 14th – The loss of the *Ark Royal* has been announced in the one o'clock news.

November 15th – The humorist arrived today to find me lying with lack-lustre eye, loathing the world. 'That's right,' she said, ''ave a good time while you can. It isn't so nice when you're married . . .'

A sober and good notice for *No Bed For Bacon* in the *Manchester Guardian*. I would rather be praised in a sober manner by the M.G. than by any other paper in sight. And the book has been called by a Birmingham paper 'a merry vindication of Shakespeare' – after all the great tomes that have been written to prove that Bacon wrote the plays and then considerately left masses of clues in them so that we should know it. So much simpler, I suppose, than signing his name.

November 16th – Oysters with Skid to celebrate our second imprint.

The humorist informs me that she has been called Little Sunshine in eight hospitals. Hell!

November 18th – The Bergel was killed on Saturday, November 5th, ferrying a bomber to the RAF.

s The journal is silent for seven days.

---

* Caryl's word for all her housekeepers.

In his book, *Fly and Deliver: A Ferry Pilot's Log Book*, Hugh Bergel, Jack's younger brother, analyses the reasons for the latter's crash and the nerve-racking circumstances in which he reckons it occurred. He concludes: 'In order to spare a close friend of Jack's [Caryl] the shock of seeing his death reported in the newspapers, I wrote saying, "Surely he was one of the lucky ones, to die with barely a moment's foreknowledge, at the top of his form, doing a job well." Let that stand as my epitaph for my much missed only brother.'

Hugh Bergel went on to explain that he had minimized the pain that Jack must have suffered in the crash. In 1982 Caryl reviewed the book for *Punch*, her last book-review for that magazine, in the year of her death. Hugh Bergel confirms that the two had talked of marriage, 'after the war'. Jack Bergel was thirty-nine when he died. Caryl would have been three weeks short of her fortieth birthday. *Fly and Deliver* was the first inkling she had of the true circumstances of Bergel's death. She did not refer to it.

She resumed her diary from Quinton in the Cotswolds, where she was staying with Charles Landon, who worked for the BBC and had for a brief spell, long before, been engaged to her. She always insisted that it was a 'convenient' engagement to a suitable Jewish boy to keep her parents quiet.

CB   *November 25th* – I am staying in a rural isthmus almost entirely surrounded by the BBC.
    December 2nd – Nice notices for *No Bed For Bacon* arrived, including one from Clifford Bax who declares stoutly that we are not 'fundamentally unsound' as we have blithely admitted on our title page. Fundamentally, he insists, we are sound, and it is only superficially that we are absurd. Couldn't like this more.

NS   On the 4th Caryl was interviewed again for a BBC job. This time she 'passed the general knowledge test!'; but her impression was that the encounter did not go well; 'And I'm not completely sure about taking the job when and if it is offered.'

CB   *December 5th* – I heard a charming story from one of the BBC sub-editors. It seems a certain section is housed in a mansion to which there are some great, wrought-iron, gilded gates. Jean Chevreau, the harpist, was due to play in a programme for this section, so she arrived together with her harp and started walking up the drive. The gate-keeper 'phoned through to what he took to be the upper lodge – actually it was the private line of a departmental chief – and reported: 'Madame Chevreau has just gorn through the golden gates along with 'er 'arp.'

'Who do you think you're talking to,' asked the departmental chief, exasperated, 'St Peter?'

December 7th – An attack on Pearl Harbor has been announced in the nine o'clock news. So America is to fight the Japs. And I had the remarkable experience of waiting, in this ancient cottage that had seen in a great many wars and a great many peaces, to toast in my birthday, and to learn if we were at war with Japan at one and the same chime. We were.

12th December – A long walk among the orchids. In the distance I could see the blue line of the Cotswolds that I love so dearly, and pick out Broadway tower and the clump of trees that make the cut that the Bergel told me he beat up in his plane. I scolded him for his foolhardiness, but he said that wasn't the way you got killed. It was when you were just doing ordinary things.

JS On the 16th she left for London. 'I have often looked over to green Bredon from the Cotswolds. This afternoon I stood on the slopes of Bredon looking over to the Cotswolds – my blue remembered hills.'

B *December 17th* – To a rehearsal of the second edition of *Rise Above It* with Skid. All very listless, save for the pianist who was very determined. She wanted to get away by 5.

December 20th – To lunch at the Moulin d'Or. Dorothy Sayers lunching across the room, talking religion with great determination. With Skid to the second edition of *Rise Above It*, a first night. Thoughts not for these pages.

The management reiterated their determination to get *Dizzy* going immediately after Christmas.

S By now the collaborators had decided on their next book. Its precise inspiration is not documented but it was to begin in the reign of Queen Anne and to end the day after the fire blitz on the City of London. It was to be set principally in a house in Berkeley Square and called, of course, *No Nightingales*. Caryl went to the London Library in search of books. The librarian returned, panting, with two armfuls.

'These will do,' said Caryl.

[111]

'I see,' said the indulgent librarian. 'Just a preliminary romp through.'

On 22 December she travelled back to the Cotswolds. On Christmas Eve, 'midnight mass in the ancient church . . . it is rumoured that we are to have an egg for breakfast, but I, for one, refuse to count on it . . .'

CB *December 25th* – An egg for breakfast! Boxes of matches in ruby tin-foil for *everyone* on the Christmas tree. Christmas cake with soft sugar icing. And at night a party. Who said we've got a war on?

But in the afternoon I was told secretly of the fall of Hong Kong. And at midnight they confirmed it on the radio.

NS On Boxing Day there was marmalade for breakfast – another wartime rarity worth recording – before stepping out into 'this fine frosty, gilded day. Sun on my nose and ice at my toes. The world one vast, bald horizon. The Cotswolds vanished. Bredon, too.'

CB *December 31st* – A cold misty day to end the year. At eleven o'clock I retired to watch the New Year in with thoughts of my special people – amateur sailors, soldiers, airmen, wardens – all palookas in peril.

1941 brought London a lull in the Blitz. It saw the fall of Greece and the fall of Crete, it was punctuated by the final stages of Wavell's advance on the Eastern Desert, the retreat to Tobruk, and the sally forth again to Benghazi . . . Russia came into the war . . . America came into the war. But in London we call it the lull . . .

My parents are still in unoccupied France. Skid became a full time ARP Warden. But I shall remember 1941 as the year in which the Bergel was killed ferrying a bomber to the RAF.

He did so love his 'planes.

I can still say that this is the only age to live in. If I could be sure that it is the best age to die in I would be reconciled to what has happened and all that is to come.

NS By 2 January 1942 she was back in London.

CB . . . On to see Jack de Leon at the Comedy Theatre to discuss stage *Dizzy*. Arrived to find a photo call going on for *Rise Above It*.

Up in the Manager's office, Honest Jack produced a mass of disapproving notes: 'The material is too dirty,' he said. 'Too much sex,' he pointed out virtuously. Even the walls raised their eyebrows.

Gladly I tore out an earlier page from my notebook. It recorded an earlier pronouncement on our material. It read:

'*Longer,*
Stronger,
Meatier,
Dirtier.'

S Over dinner at Scotts, a friend suggested that she should do factory work: 'My advice to you,' he said, 'is, put on overalls. Take the varnish off your nails and go, if they send for you, with a light heart. We realize that you'll be raw and won't know much, and we'll go very easy with you.' She did not heed the call.

B *January 8th* – . . . To lunch with Skid at Canutos. Oysters. Together we composed the blurb of our Penguin edition of *A Bullet in the Ballet*: 'Lunatics of genius. Gifted idiots. Cracked-brain collaborators. Impudent wits. These and similar aspersions have been cast at the heads of Caryl Brahms and S. J. Simon by an admiring press. It is sad to note that this is maintained even when the authors pride themselves that they have been poignant,' is the way we began it . . .

January 10th – The rest of the week has slipped away in frenzied arguments about stage *Dizzy*, a great deal of dipping into Queen Anne and the Georges for the new book, masses of typing and planning for the stage show (*Rousska*) with Anna and Tim Abady. Somewhere at the back of it all there has been a war going on. I have been notified that the BBC is sending for me in its own sweet time, and that will mean a full-time war job and the end to Caryl the careerist. I'd be sad to be finishing the Brahms-Simon collaboration were it not that I feel pretty sure the BBC will sack me the minute they get a load of my spelling*. . .

January 13th – Firth Shepherd is to see our *Rousska* show in two weeks' time. This means that our output must quicken . . .

Skid arrived today, having triumphantly lost all our yesterday's work. 'I have a superb memory,' he gloated. 'Now, *how* did the beginning go?'

---

* The BBC summons never came.

January 19th – A letter from my father in unoccupied France. He asks me not to wire him any more.

January 20th – *Rousska* session with Tim Abady. Firth Shepherd is to hear our material on Thursday of next week. It would be funny if our little Russian show were to beat *Dizzy* to the stage.

January 21st – To the Trading With The Enemy Board about a letter to my parents in unoccupied France. Like all English people who were not able to get away when France fell, they are treated with suspicion by both sides, though my father remained there only on account of my mother's health. During the Blitz I had a pathetic letter from him saying how he wished he were here in London helping to fight the fires. He was seventy-one on the 6th of this month.

NS Her friendship with Richard Berkeley Sutcliffe, the young designer whom she had met so warily in the previous year when Jack de Leon foisted his designs for *Don't, Mr Disraeli* on her, had ripened.

CB *January 22nd* – To lunch at Rules with Richard Berkeley Sutcliffe who is designing the décor for *Don't Dizzy*. We sat on the crimson plush beneath the varnished eyes of great actors looking down on us from the past, and purred over Richard's designs. The first time the Bergel took me out, and the last time, he took me to Rules. Other times too. And I have lunched there with almost every ballerina I know.

January 26th – To see my bank manager. So far as we could both make out I have just £2 to spend until 16 April. This is a bit of a bother . . .

January 27th – Unexpectedly this morning . . . a cheque from Merrill Rogers in New York City. I might even pay the rent . . .

The Management for stage *Dizzy* are strongly urging three top-liners from the Halls on us. In a fit of rage I suggested throwing in a troupe of performing seals. 'Animals are so unreliable, Caryl . . .'

NS The Brahms-Simon attack on the theatre was beginning to peter out in despair. Although their Russian show went to Firth Shepherd, it did not find a home. They postponed writing *No Nightingales* in favour of a modern backstage novel, *A Revue Has Been Arranged*. 'I shall not have to read for this book. All I have to do is to survive living it. And there

is a chance that we can get it done before I go to the BBC – if I go.'
She did not go to the BBC, and before long they had abandoned the
modern novel and returned to *No Nightingales*.

There was one more false start on *Dizzy*. Leslie Julian Jones rehearsed some of the songs for a try-out in a small theatre in Henley.
On the world stage Malaya had gone and Singapore was going. Brahms
and Simon sat in 'that empty icy little theatre watching them work our
numbers – a sobering experience. At least it sobered me. Skid was
slightly more boastful than usual, if anything.'

The nervous authors decided to stay away on the first try-out night
– 'The cast want to feel their way into their words before Skid and I
see them.' As soon as that entry had hit the page, a 'phone call advised
the diarist that the opening had been postponed. Caryl's sentences,
often long and involved, were invariably shorter when she was annoyed.
Capital letters crept in. 'A last minute argument between the Management and Mr Jones. The Play Must Not Go On . . . Blast!'

At about this time the diary stops – except for a brief flurry of activity
in July 1944. Neither the Russian show nor the BBC series was
produced. The skeleton version of *Don't, Mr Disraeli* was performed a
few times at Henley (Caryl later claimed that in one moment of
desperation she herself choreographed a can-can), but the try-out did
not lead to a West End production. Had I known this back history, I
would have been more surprised when the association with Leslie
Julian Jones was picked up again for *No Bed For Bacon* in the 1950s.
Meanwhile, the impresarios George and Alfred Black took a series of
options on the stage rights to *Don't, Mr Disraeli*, and eventually George
Black went into hospital for an operation. At last he had a chance to
read the property he had acquired. As soon as he was better he called
Brahms and Simon to his office, asked them if they were mad, and
withdrew from the project.

I have chosen to end this chapter on one more entry which hints at
the variety of experiences and emotions so evocative of those years. A
pre-war friend, Niki (his surname is not recorded in the journal), had
been a naval officer on the *Hood* before the war. Caryl recalled the fact
when she recorded the sinking of the *Hood* in May. Later he had been
at Dunkirk, and then joined a Polish destroyer, the only English officer
('The Poles will think that English sailors are uncommonly comical,
kindly and stout-hearted fellows'). Later she wrote:

B Niki has had a miraculous escape. He was just about to board the

Isle of Wight ferry steamer on his way to rejoin his Polish destroyer when he met a friend and decided to go by the next ferry instead. The first boat hit a mine. There were no survivors.

You may say that it was Providence – or that ferry just didn't have Niki's name on it . . .

I have been reading a novel about Dunkirk – vastly over-written. Yet from the torrent of words emerges some terrible detail. I would have said that the only way to record great times is to write simply of them. But the dissected, spot-lit, wriggling congress of words in this novel did more to drive home the ghastliness of the tragic seascape than my own spare phrases – of the heroism of a whole army in a desperate position, each man behaving as well as he could as a matter of course.

Niki said that when he was there the sea was a sheet of flame, and that there was no time that you could not have read a paper by the light of the burning town – always supposing you had time to read a paper. So the troops must have stood there, tired and patient and hot and hungry and thirsty and hurt, before their eyes a sea of fire, behind them a town that was a blazing furnace. It must have seemed to them that it never would come to be their turn to be hauled into the boats that were ferrying to the ships, or even to arrive at last at the top of the lines, standing waistdeep in the flame-coloured water. What a moment it must have been when their toes first touched the sea after days of waiting – the beginning of just a chance to come home.

NS As so often she ended her day going home alone to her flat in Furzecroft off the Edgware Road.

CB Walked most of the way home for love of London. It floated quite perceptibly in a silver-lead haze.

Post-war

NS When Caryl started to keep her diary again for a short time in mid-1944, she listed the novels she and Simon had so far written together, 'to get a perspective on us'.

CB *A Bullet in the Ballet*: Rich in characterization and unexpected situation. The first of the funny detection books, it seems to have founded a school. (Film rights with Ealing Studios. Penguin Book 1942.)
Casino For Sale (the sequel): Stinko. But still much funnier than anything other people seem to produce. (Film rights with Ealing Studios.)
The Elephant Is White: Comedy of characterization – the first of the crazy Russian books. (Film rights with Gaumont British.)

IS I have already quoted her considered opinion of *Envoy on Excursion*. ('Stinko; film rights couldn't be more available'.)

B *Don't, Mr Disraeli!*: Vintage book. An abundance of invention and a line of faintly surrealistic flick-scenes. (Play and part film rights tied up with Eric Wollheim but look like coming untied right now. *Evening Standard* Book of the Month.)

S Her pride in *No Bed* had grown since its successful publication.

B *No Bed For Bacon*: A very fine book about Shakespeare at work in his theatre with Elizabethan England working, playing and strutting through the pages. (Film rights ours – substantial offer would be considered.)

S By now she and Simon had abandoned their contemporary back-stage novel and completed *No Nightingales*, published in February 1944. It told the story of Number Seven, Berkeley Square, built before the Nightingales invaded the place and acquired in 1708 by two retired soldiers, General Burlap and Colonel Kelsoe. Benevolently haunted after their death by the two Old Boys, it passes through various hands – a merchant grown rich in the South Sea Bubble, a refugee from the French Revolution, a King's mistress, a suffragette, and other nicely chosen tenants. It ends too soon for the era of Stroganoff, but Diaghilev makes a brief prophetic appearance at the London première of *Petroushka*. His trusted Grigoriev intervenes to quieten his nerves: 'Courage, Sergei, Benois 'imself will be 'ere soon.'

The large black head shook its one white lock.
'If 'e come,' said Diaghilev doubtfully . . .

The book ends with a zeppelin raid which destroys the house in 1916. On the morning after, the old soldiers sit atop the rubble as Queen Mary visits the bomb site, freeing them from the need to haunt.

'What a pity,' she said. 'It was such a nice house. I do hope nobody was in it.'
She returned to her car.
And two old soldiers, standing rigidly to attention, watched her out of sight before they faded slowly away.

The diligence of the authors' research was acknowledged in a note of gratitude to the staff of the London Library. 'The learned librarians are in no way responsible for the manner in which this material has been used.'

Caryl's verdict, some months after publication, was: 'Faintly attractive. (Film rights with British National.)'

Later the same year they brought out *Titania Has A Mother*. A wartime note explains that the book contains 82,000 words crammed (because of the paper shortage) within 195 pages. 'This novel,' it proclaims proudly, 'would ordinarily make a book of about 320 pages.' The authors were asked to describe their book. 'We found it easier to write this book than to describe it. Briefly, we have blown a bubble and hurled into it every nursery rhyme in sight. We have devised a ballet and wandered out of the theatre in the intervals. We have gone behind the scenes in a cloud-cuckoo fairyland to tell the story of Titania and

Oberon and Cinderella's husband; and we hope that the shades of Mother Goose, Charles Perrault, the Brothers Grimm, Hans Christian Andersen and Pushkin will not mind.'

To her diary Caryl confided sentiments mingling fear and pride. 'Due this autumn. A bubble into which we have thrown every fairytale and nursery rhyme in sight. A shimmer of a book.'

By July 1944, when the diary was picked up again, the pattern of the war was changing and London was adjusting to a new threat – the flying bomb.

CB *July 6th, 1944* – Churchill has announced in Parliament that 2,754 buzz-bombs have been launched at us in three weeks. The death toll is 2,752 with 8,000 injured, i.e. one kill per bomb launched (with a higher proportion to those that arrive) or just a shade higher because some of the serious casualties will inevitably die. The highest figures in the worst months of the Blitz were:

September 1940:   6,954 killed;   10,615 injured.
October 1940:   6,354 killed;   8,695 injured.

I am glad the Primo has spoken at last, for we all prefer to know just what we are facing; and Churchill has put us all into history once again with a phrase:

'London will never be conquered and will never fail in her renown. Triumphing over every ordeal, her light will long shine among men.'

It's weeks since I heard from Harold (Kahn) in Italy and they're sending my charming Richard (Berkeley Sutcliffe) to India – the other end of the world – for at least a year. He's been such a life-belt. When things were grim I used to go to Farnham or Norwich to be with him, and we'd laugh our heads off. I feel so bereft and at best *yellow* about these pilotless aircraft they lob at us all day long and all night long, suddenly, out of a quiet sky. They sound like a motorbike at 350 miles an hour, roaring up from nowhere and subsiding into silence – with luck – and there's no kind of warning, but from two to thirty seconds later a sickening bump and an evil cr-r-unch – stomach-turning – and, if it's a count of two, the awful acrid taste of dust; but at least it means it was making for me and not for Richard or Harold or any of my friends. It gets under the skin as no ordinary bomb did. We're on call all the time and we live, eat, sleep to the sound of sirens. You can sleep through anything if you're weary enough.

NS To another friend she wrote:

CB Now we are used to the fly-bombs we don't mind them so much – though they were very hard to bear in the beginning, and we expected to be scared out of our wits three times a night and twice a day, roughly speaking, and feel a bit uneasy if there is what the papers describe as 'a lull' – which means a few hours without a silence with an earthquake at the end.

In the middle of today's scripting my accountant 'phoned to tell me that yet another of my father's properties has had blast. This makes the fourth lot – one rubbled in the old Blitz and three slightly blasted in this. And all in outlying and widely separated districts.

NS On another day she recalled the mournful story of a publisher who had taken to spending his nights in the Strand Palace, leaving his comfortable bed in his hotel bedroom to sleep more safely, or so he felt, in the hotel lounge. That night, in his absence, thieves broke into his room and stole his best suit.

'London has been given back to the Londoners,' she wrote, 'and to our crew-cut allies, the American troops.' She likened the noise of the bombs 'churning through the air' to 'teams of high-powered motor-bikes tearing through a million miles of calico'.

CB A power-bomb landed in Piccadilly last Friday. It destroyed beauty in the form of a Wren church and had the impertinence to rock Fortnum and Mason's. We were waging a story conference in Wardour Street over the film script of our novel *No Nightingales* at the time. Glass flew out of the windows opposite and the blast made my cheeks go in and out like a concertina. I remember the taste of the dust and Skid, particularly bland and undisturbed, coming up for air and blinking benignly through his crooked specs. I would not know if his knees were knocking like mine – I certainly needed the brandy he gave me with lunch. Before, there'd been a little light relief when the film tycoon, emerging from under the Bechstein grand, said: 'I wouldn't mind for myself, but it gets the girls in the outer office scared.'

[120]

We were in a sterner mood after Hitler broadcast an offer to stop hurling his blasted buzz-bombs at us if we would stop dropping bombs on German war-plant.

NS The strain of the flying-bombs persisted. On one occasion after a sleepless night, Caryl recalls crawling into a sunny Hyde Park and sharing a Buchanan tartan rug with the actress (now agent) Myrette Morven, a neighbour. 'We cradled our heads in our arms and fell, exhausted, to sleep, to awake to find that we were being nuzzled by a flock of sheep.' On another night, 'I awoke to the sound of the All Clear, having been plunged in a sleep so deep that I hadn't heard the Alert. I sat in bed shivering because I thought the siren must be one of those new rockets they threatened to send.' In the same week she heard from Robert Gittings, the poet, biographer and broadcaster, that he had been typing his new play during the alert that night. 'It's a good way to take your mind off things,' he said, 'and if you happen to be writing in blank verse you can stop at the end of lines and listen.'

Her own next experience was less literary:

B I was chased home by flying bombs tonight. To be exact the siren sounded shortly after I had left a Soho restaurant where I had been dining. Since I am allergic to the Underground, since the last bus had gone, since London taxi drivers prefer American soldiers, I set out to walk it.

I pounded along Oxford Street so fast that I nearly brought on an attack of asthma. Past an American officer giving another American officer a pick-a-back. (Will our gallant allies ever behave like an Army? And echo answers, 'I doubt it.') On and on towards Marble Arch . . . past the Cumberland, up Seymour Place, and round into George Street, and it wasn't until I got within a couple of arrow flights from my block, Furzecroft, that I saw a sinister whizz-bang making a nasty, low, purposeful bee-line for me. I had a thousand years in which to see the silver gleam of its wings, the golden light in its tail and the ribbons of searchlight threading the clouds behind it.

Managing not to run was one of the most difficult things I have ever made myself do. Yet when the explosion shook the block and the swing doors blew in, I realized what a long way off the bomb actually fell.

NS Three nights later: 'Forced to break into my own flat, having left key in other bag, for the third time this year. And it wasn't funny the first time.'

Wartime life continued to revolve around Ferdie Four, and the warden's duties had extended to include Shelter Patrol.

CB Down to the war caves where sleep the workers of this city. In one of the larger shelters on our sector a 'regular' had lost his wallet. He'd gone to the canteen, and while he was away, 'a strange man in a brown homburg' (the shelter bay was quite unanimous about his head-gear) had been seen rummaging in his bunk. And not one of the shelterers made any attempt to stop the stranger or even to ask him what he was doing. And not one of them called the Shelter Warden. This is typical of their irritatingly helpless attitude.

Another shelterer, a poor little sweaty, white-faced, rabbit man, had lost his false teeth down the gents, where the trap had, for some reason, been removed. 'And they were a new set, too,' complained his wife. The little man was so good about his misfortune. 'I know I never ought to wear 'em there with my corf, but you don't always think, and before I knew, my corf came on and they was gorn.'

Later we came to a very quiet cave full of seemly old people, most of them already asleep. 'This is a very good little shelter,' said the Post Warden, who habitually accepts the universe as her nursery. 'They never give me any trouble at all down here.' It was the Almshouse shelter.

The night before, our Shelter Warden had come upon two ancient hags having a rough and tumble in one of our larger shelters. 'Two old ladies,' he told me, not without awe, 'seventy-five and seventy-two, and they were going at one another – would you believe it? I says, "Calm down and tell me what it's all about." So they both start crying and I had my hands full – and do you know what it was all about? Two old girls, seventy-two and seventy-five?' said the scandalized Warden Sprossen (a mere sixty something). 'One of them said the other one snored!'

As for myself, I have long since decided that hell will certainly turn out to be one vast eternal air-raid shelter with me there to keep the peace.

NS However, ARP work still had to be reconciled with the writing pro-gramme.

CB I find it a bit trying to work in the warden's rest-room – endeavouring to remember not to raise my voice and yet making myself heard above the clatter of Skid's typewriter. The wardens couldn't be kinder and they bring tea and they stay away – what more could authors ask? And it's our only way to get our scripting done, now that on-call leave has been stopped for full-time wardens and Skid cannot leave the post when he is on day duty. We shall manage some way, of course. Thank heavens we get some free days next week.

NS Simon was created Salvage Officer, 'which gave him a splendid excuse for looking as though he had been sorting through the dustbins'. Caryl was offered a job as press officer to Mona Inglesby, the British ballerina who was forming her own company which was to run for several years – the International Ballet. Although Caryl felt that she had good qualities, she did not see her as a *prima ballerina*, starring in her own company. On the other hand, her family was able to help financially.

CB Mamoushka Inglesby wants me to write a book about Mona. Papoushka Inglesby, a man of good sense in spite of being a seller of armaments, wants me to do NO book about Mona. Me, I do not want to do a book about Mona. The three-pronged war was prolonged and bitter. Outside we are waging another kind of war, but Mamoushka Inglesby appeared to have little time to notice that. In the end I lost my patience: 'If you're so keen on publicity, why not bring out an issue of postage stamps?' I asked, with all the cutting edge I could command. I left Mamoushka Inglesby giving stamps her serious consideration.

NS Nor did she approve Mrs Inglesby's trait of refusing other dancers the proper costumes when they danced her daughter's roles, insisting that they wore their *corps de ballet* clothes in spite of their promotion.

Soon afterwards, a member of Miss Inglesby's *corps de ballet* was surprised by the ballerina when reading a Penguin edition of *A Bullet in the Ballet* on a train call.

'What are you doing reading that dreadful book?' she demanded, and without further ado pitched it out through the window.

By now the predicament of Caryl's parents in the South of France had eased.

CB They announced the next evening in the nine o'clock news that there was to be an exchange of British civilians in Germany and the occupied territories. I wondered if my parents would be able to return from the South of France. It depended, I imagined, on my mother's health, and I hoped that they would be allowed to wire me from Lisbon. I waited, just as I waited through the fall of France, for a wire to tell me they were on their way home.

NS The ray of hope prompted Caryl to be philosophical about the prospects of life after the war.

CB I dined with Guy Ramsay. His wife was going to the country and Guy was about to become a 'buzz-bomb widower'. We talked about the perils of a premature peace and agreed that it seemed expedient that one nation should suffer for the peace of the world. 'If,' I said, 'the Russians get into Germany before we do I shall pull down the blinds of my conscience and say, "The stories of brutality are greatly exaggerated!"'
    'That's what makes me hate the Germans,' said Guy. 'I hate them for *making* me hate them.'
    In my heart of hearts I know we're going to find it awfully hard to hate them the minute they stop hurling their bits of nonsense at us. Yet, paradoxically, I know I can never not hate them, save for their artists – the singers, conductors, performers, soloists. How ambivalent can one get?

NS She conquered her hatred after the war, but not an overwhelming feeling of reluctance to travel in Germany, an experience she risked on only one occasion. Music and musicians encouraged her most to forget, as they had been her greatest comfort during the Blitz.

CB I've a feeling that when we think back to these war days from out of their heritage of secure and peaceful years, it will be the wartime concerts, the gatherings of such different sorts of people in all kinds of uniforms, service and civilian, that will seem to be a symbol of the times. People with faces softened by music, in uniforms ready for war. I am always conscious of being glad to be one of the softened people listening there, as well!

NS On 13 July 1944 she was still waiting for news from France.

CB A bit edgy all day, wondering if every footstep in the corridor would be that telegram from my parents. Every step is the telegram boy until it isn't. [*In a subsequent note she adds:*] Later it was announced that the exchange was delayed – my parents were never to return to this country – and there was no need to expect that every step in the corridor was bringing a telegram.

NS Caryl's parents died soon after the war. Her father, who had stayed in France to nurse his invalid wife, died before her. Caryl travelled down to his funeral, and wrote from Nice to her friend Mrs Toye (*née* Doris Sonne, who had partnered John Byron as a dancer and earlier had danced with de Basil). Mrs Toye writes: 'Amongst facts and the usual banter, there was this: "He was my friend. If there is anything firm or constant in my nature under all the chi-chi, it is directly due to his influence," and in a postscript: "No words to tell you of my father's courage when the Germans put him in a concentration camp. And of my grief and sense of loss."'

Pearl Abrahams died more than a year later. I understand that Caryl's relations with her mother were not cordial in the last years, and that they were never reconciled. Max Landau and his wife Helen visited her in Villefranche after her husband's death and confirm the rift, though Max writes: 'She hinted she had something stowed away for Caryl. Perhaps a Turkish carpet. The Behars [relatives] were carpet people.' Any discussions that I had with Caryl about the quarrel, if such it was, were abruptly closed, and suggested that two powerful women wished for different objectives from life, and from each other, and that as both grew older, both grew more stubborn. Certainly Caryl could not bring herself to visit the villa in Villefranche after her mother's death. She sold the property and its contents hurriedly, distressed by her memories of it, and of her parents; and in doing so she contributed greatly to the financial difficulties with which she continued to battle for the rest of her life.

Another vignette puts that insecurity sharply into focus:

CB Skid and I had met, one winter's afternoon, to work at my flat. We were in our customary financial condition – skint. But as usual we laughed immoderately at our own jokes, then shook our heads over the images and adjectives that a second ago had surprised us into laughter, and pronounced them 'out', and out they went. We worked on cup after cup of tea and Woodbines.

[125]

Towards dusk, ring went the front-door bell. 'The electric light man, called to mend a fuse,' I said. I showed him the meter cupboard, indicated the step ladder, took him tea and biscuits, and went back to work. In due course, he departed, looking, I thought, a little dazed. Dusk set in.

'Switch on the light, sweetie,' mumbled Skid from the typewriter, a cigarette in the corner of his mouth fountaining over himself – it was normal.

After a bit I said to Skid, 'Switch on the light.' He blinked. He stood up, stretched and yawned. We completed our sentence. Thought of another; laughed in delight; rejected it. By now the sunset was climbing the wall. An awful thought struck me. I jiggled the light switch.

'Skid,' I said, 'that man who came to mend the lights – I don't think he was here to do that at all! I think he came to cut them off!'

'And you gave him tea *and* a biscuit,' Skid said in disgust. 'You palooka!'

NS There were other irritations. Her 'wartime nadir' was reached with the withdrawal by the Post Office of the Special Messenger Service, an emergency invention staffed by 'mostly decrepit old men in coming-to-pieces clothes and scarecrow shoes. Special Messengers were invented for me!'

CB Only twice during this war have I caught myself unexpectedly in tears. The first time was when the army got back from Dunkirk, when I was told that the Grenadiers had marched and counter-marched in the square to remind our men of discipline and to raise their hearts.

The second was when, walking in Hyde Park, I came upon a bed of wonderfully coloured tulips. I had forgotten in the drab cold wartime world that such colours could still be found.

NS Bright moments ('Batsford have got hold of enough paper to print a second edition of my book, *Robert Helpmann, Choreographer*', but the news went almost unnoticed by its loving author in the general excitement over Hitler's Bomb) still jostled with work problems – 'I tried to do a work session with Skid who has been seconded to a different post – net result, two alerts and four lines written. We have been just managing with full days for working every other week, but Skid needs a large part of those days for sleeping now that wardens are kept on watch by flying bombs all through the night. We never really get going until we have chewed the cud for half an hour when we first meet, and what with frequent cups of tea and gossip, even more laughter, and with collaborators' tiffs . . .'

She was still in John Byron's flat at Furzecroft at this time – 'all ferro-concrete and still housing the Czech government.' One of its principal defects was inadequate soundproofing. 'Every time my neighbour's wife threatened to leave him, I could hear just how glad he'd be if only she would.' On another occasion she overheard the same woman chiding from the bedroom while her husband sluiced himself in the bath to the strains of 'Onward Christian Soldiers'. 'Irreligious as I may be – am – at least I obey that commandment that tells us we may not covet our neighbour's wife. I did not even covet my neighbour's husband.'

John Byron's leaves were occasions for intense activity. 'Into a week we crammed *Hamlet*, two films, two pantomimes, supper with John Gielgud, several prowls in bookshops, and many talks about his future.'

More publicly, the first Brahms-Simon venture into the cinema was about to reach the screen. The collaborators were as excited about the movies as they had been about their abortive forays into the theatre; but they were apprehensive. *Give Us The Moon* was an attempt by the director-screenwriter Val Guest to make a funny film out of the delicate humour of *The Elephant is White*. The principal comedians entrusted with this task were Margaret Lockwood and Vic Oliver. Jean Simmons made her screen début.

B *July 19th* – . . . Many forebodings about *Give Us The Moon*. Reduced to reminding myself that it will not be the first film to flop . . . To the ballet to take my mind off the wretched film. Jerry Sevastianov there. Asked him if Hurok's new choreographer was as good as rumour has it?

S Sevastianov was an impresario with a long connection with the de Basil company. His tale of woe cheered her up no end. Apparently Hurok, in desperate need of a new, audience-pulling, choreographer for his New York season, had chosen one at random and told the press, 'He is genius!' The choreographer, however, read his publicity and believed it. Now he was demanding a huge rise from Hurok. It was a situation that would have fitted neatly into the new Stroganoff saga which they were beginning to mull over, *Six Curtains For Stroganova*.

The next day, 20 July, was the occasion of the press show for *Give Us The Moon*, which gave Caryl little opportunity to relish Hurok's problems. The screening coincided with the Generals' plot to assassinate Hitler and with a particularly heavy buzz-bomb raid.

CB   *Give Us The Moon* press show today, to a salvo of four bombs –
distant. I choose to consider this a salute of honour. People
laughed in ripples at 10.30 in the morning. It goes to the New
Gallery in Regent Street on the 30th of this month. I am compensated
for the emptiness of town and the sparseness of audiences by the
honour of having an escapist film on a London screen to help people
to laugh among the flying bombs.

Through all the emotions of the morning – anxiety, pleasure as
crack after crack got its laugh, horror at some of the crasser
touches, and the awful suspicion that my hat was a mistake – I was
conscious of how marvellously lucky Skid and I have been to have
stayed alive last night, and that we were able to see our film, however
bad we knew it to be, and feel the theatre warm with laughter – a film
which would never have been made if a Shepherd's Bush film
executive had not come upon his twelve-year-old daughter laughing
over the paperback!

NS   The opening at the New Gallery was on the 30 July 1944. A couple of
days before it, the reviews started to trickle in and find their place in
the journal.

CB   *The Mail* calls it 'the film of a very funny novel which was never
funny'.

The Sketch just gives the title and adds tersely, 'Give us anything
but this.'

The Evening News observes: 'If this is an attempt at American
crazy comedy, it certainly is crazy.'

The Express puts it last and labels it 'fair'.

The Star . . . 'a version of a very amusing book about non-workers
which inundated it with boredom.'

On Sunday Dilys Powell got cracking all right: '*Give Us The Moon*
. . . Sarah Churchill has charm, Vic Oliver has comedy. For the rest,

give me the exit!' Agreed. But there's just one thing. Sarah Churchill wasn't in the film!

We went to the New Gallery, not particularly abashed by our peculiar press (one critic said, 'to be quite candid I haven't the vaguest idea whether you will smile faintly or yell with mirth'), to test with our own ears the reaction of a Sunday afternoon audience. Sparse, but warm and friendly. Nobody roared very often, but everybody rippled continually – even when a particularly low-flying doodle came over.

At the end Simon and I stood watching the audience trickle out.

'They look a bit stunned,' I suggested.

'Only half-stunned,' said Simon hotly.

At last we got (in the *Telegraph*) the sort of notice that I expected the film to get. '*Give Us The Moon* is an enjoyable cracker about a band of pseudo-Russians, definitely pre-Stalin, and their efforts to avoid work in post-war, organized England. Margaret Lockwood and Vic Oliver were very funny indeed . . .' And even then the reviewer had to go and put the film at the wrong cinema!

Two days later I was reading Quiller-Couch at a late session at the post C-for-Charlie One. I came across the following in a lecture on Dorothy Wordsworth: 'But – to put one side of a case as soberly as possible – all biography and all autobiography suffer from this; that no man can tell the truth about another's soul and no man dares to tell it of his own.'

Thus prodded, I steeled myself to admit that I went once more to see my own film. On the threshold I came upon S. J. Simon!

S   While *Give Us The Moon* was languishing at the New Gallery, Brahms and Simon were at work on another screenplay, a version of their novel, *No Nightingales*. The film was called *Two Ghosts in Berkeley Square*, produced by Lou Jackson for British National. The collaborators were not pleased with the final version – especially the rewriting, which, Caryl always claimed, Robert Morley volunteered to do while playing one of the old boys in order to augment his acting fee. Felix Aylmer played the other.

B   I went with Skid to a story-conference on the script of our film. Brahms and Simon call these one-sided arguments a 'schmooze' – we protest and they just go on saying 'you gotta'. Our producer is a man like a well-pleased, yet rather wistful, O. Rumour has it (but

[129]

you know what rumour is) that he started by being a prize-fighter,
then an uncle died and left him a flea-pit cinema in the days of
the dear old galloping piano. While he was trying to sell it he made
so much money that he bought another. Now he is the managing
director of a film-distributing company with its own film studios. I
recognize this as success. He brings an earlier technique to bear
upon his present problems which is most engaging. He told us, for
instance, about a temperamental stage star about to start working
in a picture for him.

'I called her in. "Now, look," I said, "you've established yourself
as the greatest actress of the age. The . . . the . . ."'

'Sarah Bernhardt,' I was about to prompt him, but he'd got it.

'"The Theda Bara of 1944. Well, all right. You've established
that. Now you've got to learn *to be quiet*. You've got to get dignity,
see?"' She could have had much worse advice.

'Well,' he said to us, 'and what do you think of the bad press you
got for *Give Us The Moon?*'

'We had one good notice,' said Simon defiantly.

'Two,' I backed him up.

'It's a very fine film,' we said together, and roared with laughter.
The producer blinked.

It's the only way. This producer was much given to asking us
what we thought. He asked us what we thought when another
buzz-bomb came flying rather low over Wardour Street. 'Well, what
can I do about it?' asked Skid plaintively as the thing went off in the
distance.

NS   On the evening of 5 August 1944, a bank holiday Saturday, Caryl went
to the New Theatre 'to the last night of the ballet'. The Sadler's Wells
Company had concluded four years of frequent seasons there, broken
by short provincial tours. The New Theatre was to be handed over to
the Old Vic for its spectacular post-war productions and the ballet was
to move to the Princes (now Shaftesbury) Theatre, en route for a
refurbished and re-opened Covent Garden.

CB   They gave *Coppelia* for their last night at the New. I am very fond
of this old and ample ballet for pigeon ballerinas – its sturdy humours,
its dancing cadenzas and the batty old workshop of the batty old
doll-maker. Margot Fonteyn dances the first two acts enchantingly
and superbly. But in the *divertissement* act she lacks the authority of

the *ballerina assoluta*. Robert Helpmann continues to give what, when he does not let it play him, is probably the richest bit of clowning of the age.

NS She summoned the season up as 'one of promise rather than achievement and so more interesting to the attentive observer.' Beryl Grey was 'accepting her height and the large hands and feet that go with it.' They were no longer allowed to come between 'this gifted young dancer and the roles she takes.' Moira Shearer had been seen in *Spectre de La Rose*, 'a role which she can – only just – not manage . . . she would be a sensation in Monte Carlo; but in London we take her pretty much for granted.' Pamela May 'danced *Lac des Cygnes* in its entirety. She has great courage and is intelligent and decorative. But that lake of hers lies somewhere between South Kensington and Streatham.' Andrée Howard choreographed the one new production, 'a rather lowering affair in which a spider eats a butterfly . . . adolescence haunts her choreography as a dancer's mother haunts the dress circle.'

The last diary entry was for 6 August: 'The war goes wonderfully well.' Caryl's completed memoirs made no reference to its end in Europe but they contain one recollection of the news of the bombing of Hiroshima. She heard the report at Oxford, to which she was a frequent visitor at this period.

CB I was on the roof with the Playhouse ASM on the morning the story of Hiroshima broke. Such a sunny morning. I remember thinking the atom bomb would save thousands of lives in the long view by bringing the war to an end, but when I spoke of this, the ASM said the use of it had filled him with shame, which made me feel crass and insensitive.

NS Post-war Britain saw the publication of *Six Curtains for Stroganova* (1945) and *Trottie True* (1946). It was the last novel Brahms and Simon were to complete together – researched largely from the memoirs of the stage-door keeper at the Gaiety Theatre and from Caryl's collection of Edwardian picture-postcards. She lent a ready ear to ageing purveyors of Edwardian gossip.

CB I have been told a charming story about the Edwardian beauty who starred in *The Merry Widow*. Many, many years later, in a marble terraced garden in the Californian moonlight, the figure of a very old lady valsed up and down some marble steps to the strains of the Lehar 'Staircase' waltz coming through the open windows of the country hotel. Two onlookers stood gasping at the vision, who smiled at them delightfully.

'I just wanted to make sure I could still do it,' explained Lily Elsie.

I would like to think this story is true.

NS In *Trottie True* Caryl told another story of Lily Elsie, this time at the height of her youth, beauty and fame. She had gone to the salon of a couturier, probably Worth or Paquin, who admired the beautiful sable coat she was wearing. 'A present from the Duke,' she said, and stroked the cuff lovingly. 'You see,' she explained, 'he did not want me to be cold.'

But the project which most excited the collaborators – and occupied their time – was a scheme to bring *A Bullet in the Ballet* to the stage. Val Gielgud had produced it as a radio play and the Penguin edition had helped to establish it as a comic classic; but the idea of a spectacular theatrical production was irresistible.

CB Shortly after the second war-to-end-war was won – believe it or not, by us – we were approached by a funny little rotund pigeon of a man whose name was Dr Braunsweg, Jule Braunsweg ('My younger brother, he is Baron: me, I am Doctor'), with a view to getting *Bullet* on the stage. He was, I think, Polish, and the English language had a hard time of it with him. We were taken to a snack at the Trocadero, where we met his partner, another Pole whose name I no longer remember. Dr Braunsweg's saturnine colleague, however, is clamped to my memory with imperishable bonds because each time little round Jule's podgy pink hand reached out for a smoked salmon sandwich the saturnine one slapped it down. Together they were presenting a most peculiar entertainment called *The Wednesday After The War*. Legend has it that they were running out of funds for it when Jule bumped into a fortune-teller of his acquaintance.

'Today I have beeg backer come to call,' he is said to have confided. 'So you come also to my office. I introduce. You tell him fortune. You say he make beeg money *Wednesday After War*. Him, he put two and two together and it make Ten Thousand – you understand?'

Apparently it worked.

[132]

S Braunsweg had connections with the de Basil ballet. He was later an impresario, an architect of the Festival Ballet, and a permanent sparring partner for Caryl in the foyers of opera houses and concert halls. I remember vividly her contempt when he boasted proudly of the new costumes he had bought from the Ballets Russes de Monte Carlo for *Petroushka*. 'You could have sent them to the laundry,' she sniffed. He turned on his lighting man: 'I *tell* you there is too much light on stage!' he shouted. Once he asked Caryl to write his 'official biography'. She made one stipulation: 'The truth, the whole truth and nothing but the truth, Jule,' a requirement which proved a very quick deal-breaker.

In 1946 he was wooing Brahms and Simon fervently.

B Little Round Jule, eternally an optimist, met us at the Ivy the following week to discuss the *Bullet* project further. He told us in a flood of fractured English that he would bring the distinguished choreographer Massine over from America to re-create *Petroushka* and portions of various other ballets for our play. We were sitting in the ante-room, waiting for a table. 'Some day,' Little Round Jule told us, 'they no longer force me to wait for table. Some day I, VIP.'

Skid and I were, quite rightly, somewhat sceptical about his ability to finance stage *Bullet*. He arranged to prove it to us the following week, and so he did. He turned up with a suitcase full of five pound notes. The dazzled Skid blinked. 'Lend me a fiver,' he said, and put out his hand, but Little Round Jule snapped-to the lid.

Some years later, his 'secretary confidential' fell out with him and became a lot less confidential. She telephoned me.

'You remember that caseful of five pound notes Dr Braunsweg showed you? – They were borrowed,' she said. 'He had to take them back next day. And,' she capped it, 'the suitcase, too.'

Time passed. Cables whizzed to and fro across the Atlantic. Sure enough, small, compact, neat and impish, Massine arrived in England. His large, brown eyes set in a face like an animated walnut. Irina Baronova flew over from America, too. No longer the sylph of yesteryear; indeed, to my distress, somewhat portly – a wet-nurse from the entrée in *Petroushka*, rather than, as of yore, one of Nature's beautiful wax dolls. Little Round Jule engaged Marcel Varnel, a French film director with an egg-shaped face and a hurt

look in his eyes such as one sees in the eyes of a royal child who
has started to realize that he is not as other boys. Hein Heckroth was
Little Round Jule's choice of designer – never mine.

NS Caryl always described *The Red Shoes*, which Heckroth also designed,
as 'a work of unbelievable vulgarity'. She had already enlisted the taste
and good offices of Val Gielgud as some sort of professional chaperone
– she was always addicted to bringing in colleagues to back up her
argument, at least until they diverged from her point of view. On this
occasion the trio arrived at Dr Braunsweg's flat before he got there.
His maid let them in. Gielgud, in particular, viewed the disorderly
sitting-room with disapproval. The chief feature was a very long brown
cushion on which sat a large, empty, omelette pan.
   'What's that for?' he asked.
   Caryl had an inspiration. 'He stuns them first?' she suggested.
   Doom dogged the production.

CB Stroganov, our lovable Russian impresario, played by Charles
Goldner, a Central European actor whose broad black eyebrows,
thatch of inky black hair, and saturnine features made him a dead
ringer for Dracula, Struwelpeter, and any father turning his
daughter and babe out of his house into the snowstorm with the
inhospitable instruction: 'Nevah darkenn my dooors agenn!' Beside
him, your common or garden Sir Jasper seemed like a wild rose
growing in an English hedgerow. Ivy St Helier played opposite
the satanic Goldner: she was our formidable Arenskaya, teacher of
the Stroganov Company. These two adversaries were born to
snatch each other's lines and to fight to the death for a possible
laugh. Fortunately, Ivy will be better remembered for her eloquent
cabaret artiste in Noel Coward's *Bitter Sweet*, singing *If Love Were
All*. We were to find that she would refuse to speak some line on
the grounds that 'blood was such an ugly word', whereupon Goldner
would dwell on it with relish in a deep basso profundo and reap
a loud laugh. The words, I think, were, 'bullets, ballets, blood!'
Some nights later, having heard the laugh he got, Ivy would grab them
back without warning.

NS The Company had a cold, slow, foodless progress on the Sunday train
call to Edinburgh for the out-of-town opening. However, they arrived
at the King's Theatre in time for their dress rehearsal. There, the

extent of Braunsweg's double-dealing could no longer be concealed. At the fittings, it had proved impossible for performers to move in the costumes. Braunsweg had cancelled the fittings lest the news got through to Massine, and now none of the costumes fitted.

But Braunsweg's manoeuvres had not stopped at the costumes. His principal backer James (Jay) Pomeroy was investing his own money in *Bullet*, a gamble which he had not confessed to his *prima donna* Daria ('Dasha') Bayan whom he was presenting at the Cambridge Theatre in a season of opera. 'Do not tell Dasha,' he warned the world, 'or she keel me if I lose money on *Ballet* which I should lose on her!' As dancer followed dancer on stage, unable to rehearse in costumes in which they could not move, Pomeroy's frenzy grew.

'Vere is Braunsweg?' he roared. 'I will wring him by neck!'

Braunsweg was in a box, hiding under a seat.

Simon was 'so fascinated by the spectacle that he lit a cigarette and leaned back the more to relish it.' Caryl tried to soothe the backer, who resisted her sympathy and announced his intention of taking the Company back to London. Brahms and Simon demanded to be allowed to take the costumes around the tailors' shops of Edinburgh. Somehow the entertainment staggered into dress rehearsals.

CB By this time Massine was not speaking to his Director or his Management except through 'Miss Brahm', on the grounds that I was 'creator'. However, he was also wily enough to see a chance of grabbing the stage for his ballets without the irritating interruption of our dialogue, had seized the opportunity and was raptly rehearsing *Petroushka* with his semi-clothed dancers. After all, costumes that did not fit or had not yet arrived and were acquiring last-minute stitches in traffic jams, were the mere *plat du jour* of any Company worthy of the name of Ballets Russes. Now it so happened that only one of our acting cast had to appear in the ballet, not actually to dance but to shuffle round the stage as the old Puppet-Master, dragging the straw-stuffed puppet of Petroushka after him by one long limp limb while the spirit of Petroushka shrilly mocks him from the top of his fairground booth. The chill of the winter's evening in St Petersburg has set in. The fair is all but over. All this the Puppet-Master must convey. It had to happen, too, that no understudy had been rehearsed in the Puppet-Master's couple of entrées with the ballet. It will no doubt be a foregone conclusion to any reader of these pages that the Puppet-Master would be the one member of the double cast who would fall down a stage-trap at rehearsal, break an arm and three ribs, concuss, and generally do his damnedest to ensure that the Edinburgh opening would be a non-event.

Palely, jerkily, we did open two nights later, with a novice Puppet-Master shoved around by any dancer in whose way he happened to be. Poor terrified Thespian, he must have been black and blue when, the nightmare over, he shuffled forward to take the curtain-call. Miraculously, someone had passed on a much-travelled, rather dusty, laurel wreath, which dropped from his shaking hand.

Not that his had been the only problem the Company had to rise above on that Scottish opening night. The sets were mounted on a trolley which took up most of the space. Each time the ballet took the stage, the trolley had to be trundled into the wings to be re-set. It rumbled like the wrath of God. One night it rumbled the wrong way and swung down towards the orchestra pit with its stunned human cargo, who bailed out in time.

NS After Edinburgh they played Leeds. Adam Quill, the detective who brings some puzzled sanity into the narrative, was played by Barry Morse, later to make a name for himself in the American television series, *The Fugitive*.

CB For reasons, known only to himself, Morse insisted on playing one scene in the auditorium with a 'charwoman', before racing through to enter on stage from the wings. One night, by some innocent human error, the pass door which leads to the stage in every theatre, was locked. Sergeant Banner, his slow but worthy assistant, was on stage alone, awaiting Quill, who was at that moment galloping round an interminable outside block to get into the theatre by the stage door. The stage waited.

'Mr Quill,' called Banner on stage.

'Mr Quill,' shouted Banner.

'Mr Quill,' bawled Banner.

'No answer,' he told the audience truthfully.

'Oh well,' he resigned himself. He picked up his newspaper, a prop, and settled down to read aloud to the audience from it, until such time as whatever was detaining Quill would release him from its clutches.

In the stage box Skid and I hugged each other, half-way between ecstasy of 'We told him so' – we hated the way Morse insisted on playing that scene – and the agony of the hundred years we seemed to be living through while (unforgivable offence) our hero kept the stage waiting.

s It was not the only open-door problem the production faced. 'Our designer had painted coy little scriggles where practicable door-handles should have been. So, back at Edinburgh, the cast when making exits had to step down in full view of the audience and insinuate themselves between the footlights and the errant trolley to pass into the wings.'

B It was at Blackpool that it became apparent that *A Bullet in the Ballet* was not to see the bright lights of Seven Dials. How could it? By then we had uncovered another of Little Round Jule's dastardly plots. For our play, Massine rehearsed and staged three ballets – a Chopin and moonlight mix which came as close to Fokine's *Les Sylphides* as it safely could; *La Vie Parisienne*, his popular Offenbach opus, and *Petroushka*.

s For all these works Braunsweg now had the elements of orchestration, scenery and costumes. If he extracted them from the débris of the detective plot, he had a programme of ballets which he could use as the nucleus for a touring company. If he could retain Baronova and Massine, he could perhaps build a repertory from this beginning at his backer's expense. He had already begun to see himself as Stroganoff.

Brahms and Simon felt that the piece had been staged at their expense. 'Clever? But cruel. We were allowed only eighteen minutes of dialogue in our last act to stage our dénouement and tie up the red herrings in our plot.'

B It was at Blackpool that Dasha Bayan discovered that the impresario she loved, or at least who loved her, was losing his money on us, not on her. It was at Blackpool one morning, out of season, that Skid and I trudged round the deserted fun-fair in a bitter easterly wind. We had long decided, in our innocence, that bitterness had no part in humorists' philosophy; and there we were, the only paying customers in the Golden Mile, getting rid of the Marah – the bitter herb of the Seder Night service – within our souls. Grimly we went round the arena of gaiety, sampling the hollow mirth of the Chinese Laundry, going on the Ghost Trains – the only passengers –

failing at the Hoop-la, watching the empty roundabouts and swings, all the fun of the fair that was suddenly so unfunny.

At the end of the pilgrimage I said to Skid, 'Never mind, we can still write our books. We'll do a story about this fun-fair and rid ourselves of the sour taste of defeat.' So, *To Hell With Hedda*, the only Brahms-Simon book of short stories we were to write, was born.

NS   They sold the film rights in the title story for 'a pittance'. The film was never made. Some time later Caryl was patrolling the back of the stalls circle at Covent Garden and loitered by an aisle to catch a moment of the ballet. An assiduous eavesdropper, she saw a plump girl nudge her companion and say, 'Who's that in the box?'

Caryl ducked to see. It was Irina Baronova, and she told the girl so.

'Oh,' the girl replied, 'I saw her in *A Bullet in the Ballet* in Blackpool.'

Caryl felt guilty, and offered the girl the price of her Blackpool ticket back. She refused to take it. 'Oh, no!' she said, '*you* didn't see Mae West in *Diamond Lil* in Blackpool!'

To the end of her life Caryl had to steel herself to say 'Blackpool' and always started in distress if someone used the word unexpectedly.

Another of de Basil's dancers, Nina Tarakanova, became a close friend during this period. She had married and settled in London, and she enters the diary with yet another abortive stage project.

CB   To lunch with Nina Tarakanova who wants us to do a sketch for her in the new Anglo-Russian show. Found her at work on the huge stage of the Stoll Theatre – it seemed as vast as the stage of Drury Lane, and the scatter of ballet girls and the slim lithe figure of the choreographer shouting instructions to the rhythms of a Strauss waltz, did little to lessen the shadowy distance across the great stage in the cavernous dark house. The last time I was in front at the Stoll Theatre was to see a circus – a wartime travelling circus – dancing ponies, but mostly little dogs.

NS   Nina Tarakanova had telephoned as a flying-bomb buzzed overhead, interrupting her flow. 'There is one right above my head,' she had cried, 'I must immediately to my cupboard.' As 'the most charming and merriest of the Russian soubrette ballerinas', Tarakanova was a favourite source of Caryl's ballet stories, whether 'cooking a joint for me with almost as much emotion as when she prepared for a gala night at the ballet'; or recalling Berlin before the war when, presented to Goebbels and his wife, she was so impressed by the tall blond soldier in the line-up that she entirely failed to notice 'the ugly little man himself' and left his outstretched hand unshaken.

Caryl's two favourite Tarakanova stories concerned, first, a young Russian dancer who, finding himself alone in New York, decided to call on his first wife. He surprised her in her peignoir arranging her hair. *'Ciel! Mon mari!'* she exclaimed to the ceiling before settling down to a good chat. Ten minutes later, they heard the sound of a key in the apartment door. *'Ciel! Mon ami!'* she cried in confusion, and looked wildly for a hiding-place for her husband.

The second anecdote involved a ballerina of 'theretofore unassailable virtue'. Her Russian friends felt it was high time she was deflowered – good for her art. An elaborate plot was hatched to leave her in her apartment with the ladykiller of the company. Next day the man appeared on time for class, but in an ugly mood. Questioned – 'for the ballet knows no reticence' – he was heard to observe that the lady was *peu intéressante*. When the ballerina arrived she remarked with a sniff, 'For my part, leave me as I was yesterday!'

The loss of virginity in the ballet seems always to have held interest for its closed world. During the war, when Caryl was at Oxford, she went to a Russian Easter service with her great friend, Nora Nicholson, who was playing at the Oxford Rep.

CB It lagged behind our customary Easter-tide by something like twelve days. I accompanied Nora, most stylish of actresses, most modest of ladies, most loyal of friends. One was expected to stand throughout a service which lasted half a lifetime. The Russian priest, to my surprise, spoke perfect English – and so he should, for behind his long white hair and holy hands this living ikon had been English tutor to the Tsarevitch. What amused me greatly, once I was over the awe engendered by the occasion, was the black-clad female busybody shoving the congregation around, presiding over the holy wine and little loaves, muttering the while like a humming bee.

'Look,' I whispered to Norushka, as the busy old girl gave an extra hard shove at a ministering blonde, 'just like a dancer's Mamoushka.'

'Yes,' Norushka said, 'indeed, she is one – Madame Eglevsky, she has a rather fat son, André, who is a dancer, and she lives in Oxford and builds corsets for a living.'

[139]

'Shsh!' said the humming bee, giving us a glare; and quite right too.

Anyone can spin like a dervish. André Eglevsky was noted for his eight slow spins, *sur place*.

NS Caryl then goes on to say that 'in addition to deploying the slow eight-fold spin, André was said to have been Madame X's first lover'. I have checked this with Madame X, and since she denies it there is no point in mentioning her name. She denied it quite happily and certainly without embarrassment, and spoke warmly of Eglevsky and his wife. However, Caryl continued:

CB It is part of ballet folklore that Madame had gone to class the morning after, and with a hitch of her tights had sniffed: 'Is that all it is?' Sniff. Hitch.

NS Another loss of virginity, not in the ballet, remained one of Caryl's favourite stories: 'A cousin of mine, returning from her honeymoon ('My darling's name is Weinkronk'), remarked to me: 'Sex is very much overrated; both Harry and I are agreed about that.'

By the 1950s, although Caryl was still writing about ballet occasionally, she began to spend more of her time writing for radio, television and the stage, and her criticism concentrated more on the theatre. However, in 1951 she brought out her *A Seat at the Ballet*. She had shared the excitement at the re-opening of the Royal Opera House after the war and formed a close friendship with David Webster who ran it, and Michael Wood who presided over the press room. It was at that time that she acquired her regular seats – A76 and A77 on an aisle in the stalls circle, from which she could slip out and up to the back of the grand tier if she wanted an overall view of a work from any particular point.

CB But if it was easy to slip away from those seats, it was easier still to stay and, alas! like justice in English law, to be seen to have been there, or not, as the case might be. One day I received a letter from an angry fan of a conscientious, uncharming charmer from the Antipodes. Why, demanded the writer querulously, was I never in my seat for Rowena Jackson's *Sleeping Beauty*? Nemesis, thy name is A76 and 77.

S She always had a particularly soft spot for the less disciplined repertoire of the emerging Festival Ballet.

B I was at the birth of the Festival Ballet from the moment when it was nothing but a babble in its impresario – Braunsweg's – famous broken English in some other company's foyer. Led by Alicia Markova and Anton Dolin, it was born in the Grande Salle of what was formerly the Duke of Sutherland's town house and later the Arts Educational Theatre School. Massine had called a rehearsal of *Le Beau Danube* but was late, having been held up by the filming of *The Tales of Hoffmann* – in which he was appearing. Dolin, Director of the Festival Ballet, filled in the time with a brisk rehearsal of *Chopiniana*. At last Massine, all straight brows and neat utterance, placing his syllables as meticulously as he placed his feet in the dance, arrived to take over and the familiar music of Strauss filled the room with the strict tempo of the dancer's carefully counted abandon.

S She could hardly believe that the fledgling company would 'get it together' in time.

B Although I am accustomed to the ballet metamorphoses, from its seemingly inextricable tangles, false starts, catastrophic scene changes, disarranged orchestral rhythms, to the apparent smoothness of a professional performance, this was a surprise. (And here I would stress the word 'apparent' above – for only another dancer knows how much effort, fever and the resignation of despair goes into all that floating from the heart of one chord to the heart of the next; how much strain lies behind the line, the lightness, the radiant smiles and the authority of the dancer in the dance.)

I was quite unprepared for the standard of the first performance I was to see when the Festival Ballet Company opened at Southsea. I had gone down in the company of a heavy cold. I felt a little lost in the strange foyer filled from steps to staircase with holiday-making ballet-goers, and not an enemy to call my own among the lot of them. Markova was off – convalescing in the stage-box; the guest ballerina, neat, elegant and charming, was Krassovska; and from the bones of rehearsal chaos bloomed the recaptured laughter that once blew down the air of Strauss's Vienna. Suddenly, in the most certain way, it no longer mattered that I was feeling wretched and had nearly sneezed my head off, for I knew I had come home to the ballet.

A certain extra nervousness characterized the impresario that night – he knew that I was due to report on his Ballet's début for the BBC's 'Woman's Hour' on my return, and radio was a potent crowd-puller before it was swamped by television.

I made my report through my head cold but, if intelligible at all, with much the same enthusiasm that I have recorded here. When the Festival Ballet opened at the Stoll, I met Braunsweg, who was all smiles. Clearly he had got the general message.

'Caryl,' he kissed my hand, 'I was so moved. I say to myself, "What can I give her to show appreciation?"'

Was a bribe lurking?

'I think a pearl necklace?'

It certainly sounded like it.

'Or perhaps a diamond bracelet?'

This was a new experience. How to refuse it?

'Then I say to myself, "No, this I will not do; I will thank her from bottom of my heart!"'

NS   In the memoirs which she left, Caryl's memories of the ballet range at random over the eight decades during which she witnessed it.

CB   The limelight of memory swings over a montage of recollections. Tamara Toumanova, as I once saw her, in an arena of all places, dancing the second act of *Giselle* in a way I never could forget; or Markova, as so often a beautiful butterfly at last breath, but a steel-accoutred butterfly, whose artistry was dedicated to authority and emotion; or Violetta Elvin in the white act of *Lac des Cygnes*; Fonteyn, a beautifully cut diamond gleaming at a woman's throat; Moira Shearer in the early years of her career, when she frequently did so much better than could have been foreseen and her work was alive with triumphant surprise – a quality that entirely won me; Nina Tarakanova, gayest of ballerinas; Danilova at her wittiest and most dazzling.

Dearest, certainly longest, in my memory, is Markova. Dear Alicia. She has always been sweet to me. I could never forget the day, one sunny Saturday, when Markova confidently supposed that she would be dancing the Doll in *Petroushka* as rehearsed, and all Monte Carlo knew she would not; Alexandra Danilova, a noted

[142]

Pearl Abrahams and her sister Sarah on a Riviera promenade

Caryl on the Thames: the family lived near Kingston for a while in the late 1920s

Louis *Carabbale*
3, RUE PAGANINI - NICE

'Pampered gypsies' in the south of France – Caryl (foreground) at a party in Nice

Caryl with her mother and 'convenient fiancé' Charles Landon

The Blitz: Skid (left) and Caryl (centre) in the Wardens' Post
where the 'F-for-Ferdie Four' stories were born

A publicity picture of the 1940s

Caryl with her *Footnotes to the Ballet*

Caryl in the late 1940s: always a passion for hats

Opposite: Lunatics of genius – Caryl and Skid

Charles Landon: a trusted friend until his death

Jack Bergel: 'my very dear young man'

Richard Berkeley Sutcliffe: 'my charming Richard'

Herbert Sidon: 'the Hapsburg one'

exponent, had flown in that morning. Alicia went early to her dressing-room in the crimson and gold Casino to don the Doll's costume, but Shura Danilova had travelled her own.

I, with the responsibility of five London publications, had been summoned to speak to Blum, the impresario, early that morning, and under the seal of confidentiality – a vile word – had been made aware of the situation. Of the two loyalties, that to my friend Alicia and that to my five papers, I had to commit myself to my profession.

Danilova, inspired soubrette ballerina at this time, reaped great acclaim that night, and things have always been just a little taut between the two *assoluti* ever since.

I checked this story with Dame Alicia, who did not in fact dance the Doll in that Monte Carlo season – indeed, she did not dance the role until some years later in America, with Massine and the Ballets Russes under Fokine's supervision. She did say, 'Could it have been another ballet?', but was inclined to doubt that since she and Danilova have always been and are still 'such good friends'. She has no memory of Caryl's story of Danilova in New York which follows almost immediately, but as I was there I can confirm it. However, Caryl's relish for the tradition of competition among ballerinas may well have increased the sharpness of the tale without stopping off to acknowledge the affection in which the two great dancers hold each other.

Markova was created a Dame, following Fonteyn into that distinguished company. I am told that in an elevator in New York she was heard to say to some over-casual citizen who had hailed her as 'Alicia', 'I do not care what you call me, but the Queen likes me to be called "Dame Alicia".'

When I was in New York, staying with Ned at the Algonquin, Alicia asked us for a drink. Stretching her goodwill, she asked Shura. Darling Shura arrived already bristling: Darling Alicia, dangerously bland. Shura lost no time waging the war in the enemy's camp: 'Me,' she announced to the ceiling, 'me, who am *not* Dame, I wrote book about me.'

'That should be . . .' said Markova, seeking the right word through the window, 'interesting. I've had so many books written about me,' she told the room at large, 'you know, I've quite lost count.' And she smiled equably.

NS Caryl's next reminiscence of Markova can be traced (thanks to Katherine Sorley Walker's book, *De Basil's Ballets Russes*) to the summer season of 1938.

CB Alicia is a woman of courage who never hesitates to call upon it. She had to call upon it again when the Ballet Blum cabrioled, entrechated and arabesqued itself into London – where it became to all intents and contents, Sol Hurok's Ballet. With the Hurok take-over in full Franco-American-Rouski operation, the Ballet Blum opened at the Theatre Royal, Drury Lane. That Colonel de Basil opened in the same season at the Royal Opera House, Covent Garden, served to sharpen the rivalry. I found myself a human pendulum between the two belligerents as did all the ballet magazine critics. I think I was on *Punch* at the time.

Markova was dancing Giselle to Serge Lifar's Prince. In the middle of one of the white act's ethereal variations, the ribbon of the ballerina's ballet shoe came undone – a vocational risk – and I sat in my box and trembled for her, as meticulously she picked her steps through that trail of pink ribbon. When I went round to see her she gave me the offending pink satin slipper.

Where is it now? Gone with the *pas de chat volante*?

NS The slipper was, in fact, in one of Caryl's wardrobes, where I found it after her death, meticulously moth-balled underneath her grand-mother's elaborately embroidered Edwardian gowns which she willed to her cousin Zoë Dominic, who has the shoe as well.

There are a couple more points which need clearing up here. Dame Alicia remembers the incident vividly. The ballet was *Lac des Cygnes*, not *Giselle*, and her partner was not Lifar but Panieff. She also adds another string to Caryl's bow. When Hurok arrived in London, he brought with him two high-powered American publicists, Ruth and Gerry Goode – only to find that an English public relations front-person had to be employed also. Alicia suggested Caryl, who served in some PR capacity. Quite how she reconciled this with her role of critic for *Punch*, I am not sure, but the attempt was typical of her eagerness to get into the thick of things. As she was a notorious maker of waves, I would have thought that the ingratiating cloak of a PR person would have fitted her oddly; but at the same time I cannot see her missing the chance. Later in these pages she describes her role in Hurok's early days in London as 'telling him who in the capital was who'.

3 I cannot vouch for the next Markova triumph over catastrophe, although I see the scene so clearly that I feel I must have been there. Feuds broke out in the hot-house ambience of the Ballets Russes with the persistence and plenitude of daffodils in spring. One such feud, it seems, flourished between Markova and Lifar, both former Diaghilevians; and looking back I think its roots were in the furious soul of Lifar – furious because, dancing at her home base, Markova, slender as a lily bud, took more curtain calls than he – always a subject that engendered heat in the ballet – and Lifar had put on weight and although his manner when not actually executing the classical steps was unimpeachable, his dancing was more akin to prancing. As the enthralling rumour had it at the time, he decided to make the ballerina pay the price of her popularity. He is said to have sneaked into her dressing-room and stuck a needle in her knickers, laid out ready for the first act of *Giselle* – the Peasant act. If this is true, his revenge was indeed fiendish, for the poor girl never knew when next the needle would prick.

Fortunately, Markova, like her long-time partner Anton Dolin, is a survivor. They have both needed to be. Besides, Dolin's method of dealing with his ballerina, like his Albrecht, was more subtle than Lifar's.

'One day,' Alicia told me, 'Pat and I were dancing in an out-of-the-way town in Australia. It was a flying visit and we were giving our *Casse-noisette Variations*. Pat had finished his solo entrée and I was starting mine. Pat had often sworn that if I did a certain applause-pulling movement of my arms at the end of my solo variations he would leave me with egg on my face. I finished my variation and was about to sail into the supported *pas-de-deux*. No Pat. I improvised. Still no Pat. I was not aware of having pulled applause, and whatever was I to do?

'Suddenly, not a step too soon, Pat landed beside me in a great leap. As soon as I could, I whispered, "When did I do it, Pattie?" Turn . . . turn . . . turn.

'"You didn't," hissed Dolin. *Brisée . . . brisée . . . brisée.* "I'd got to the end of my own music and forgot to come back."'

3 Dame Alicia has a couple of comments about this passage. She did have trouble with Lifar in the production of *Giselle*. Excited by the prospect, she found that the version Lifar was producing was substantially his Paris Opéra production. The role of Giselle had been heavily

cut and what remained was often upstaged by the reactions of Lifar's Albrecht. After a while she pointed out that her Giselle was well known to the London public and the London critics, and might they not wonder why she was only giving half the role? Lifar said: 'You do not realize. In Paris, I am God.' To which Dame Alicia was surprised to hear herself saying, 'Yes, and in London *I* am God.'

Later, in New York, she remembers the volatile Lifar challenging Massine to a duel in Central Park. Massine squelched the idea quite simply by telling Lifar, 'Go away and take a couple of aspirins.'

The needle incident happened much later, in Los Angeles. She does not choose to remember the name of her Albrecht on that occasion – it was not Lifar – and in any case she has no definite knowledge that it was her cavalier who planted the needle.

Of the *Casse-noisette* story, Dame Alicia confirms the gist of Caryl's narrative, underlining that it was a minor – almost an affectionate – tiff on both their parts: but since she never danced with Dolin in Australia, she would prefer the correct location – the incident happened on a Canadian tour, in Montreal.

Caryl's frequent clashes with Dame Ninette de Valois were remembered with gusto.

CB On one occasion Ninette and I, screaming at one another in the Crush Bar, were so intent on our battle that we failed to realize that the Interval had occurred and that we had a fascinated audience of onlookers. What was the bone of contention this time? Well, it could have been that I was advocating the importing of a Russian male dancer.

'It would break my boys' hearts,' says Dame Ninette stoutly.

'And for every broken heart you'd have a boy dancer who could really dance,' says La Brahms.

Or it might have been my insistence that critics be invited to see dress rehearsals – to see them, but not to write about them. I argued that if I, with all my experience, could not assess a ballet at sight, my colleagues, less adept at it than I, had not a chance of a laurel wreath in hell.

Colonel de Basil, in contrast, kissed my hand and begged me to get Dame Ninette de Valois cornered so that he himself could take over the Royal Ballet and run it; a plot in which he so strongly resembled the Brahms-Simon Stroganov that I marvel we did not pinch it.

'I always think of de Basil,' she wrote, 'as a bland expression behind a pair of non-intimidating spectacles guarding a world wide memory for faces. Like any administrator who would keep his company together through the saturnalia of intrigue, financial and artistic, that permanently surrounds the Russian Ballet, the Colonel had to develop the tenacity of an octopus with a pronounced facility for never letting his left tentacle know what his seven right tentacles are doing; but still, a man with a talent for giving genius its head.'

Sol Hurok, alternately de Basil's colleague and his enemy (sometimes both at the same time), also fuelled Caryl's passion for eccentric impresarios.

He started in some Central European ghetto selling papers, and ended in America impressing every ballet company in the world. In the days I am doing my best to summon up, he was grim rather than grand.

In Hurok's early days in London, Caryl was 'of some assistance to him, telling him who in the capital was who'. Her attempts at smoothing his way were not always appreciated. The painter, Edward Seago, once enlisted her help on behalf of John Masefield, the Poet Laureate: together they were compiling a ballet book with Seago's sketches and Masefield's commentary. Masefield, in full flight of fan worship, was ambitious to meet Lifar to tell him how beautiful his ballet *Icarus* was. Seago had taken him backstage, only to find that Lifar had not bothered to wait for them. Caryl was summoned to Seago's studio to see if she could fix something. A painting of a horse and rider stood on Seago's easel. As Caryl left, an open-air looking man arrived. He stared at the picture for a long time before saying, 'I know the horse, but I've no idea who the man is!'

Caryl hurried away to enlist Hurok's help. She explained that the Poet Laureate was upset. 'Poyits,' said Hurok, unimpressed, 'we have two a dime in Noo Yoyick.' She pointed out that this was the King's poet. Hurok relented. 'Tell him to come Friday when we give *Seventh Symphony*. Tell him he don't be late!'

'You will be there to receive him, won't you?' tried the unaccustomed go-between.

'Receive a poyit? Me? You receive him.'

Poor Masefield had to make do with a brief meeting with Massine and an audience with Markova which, judging by Caryl's opinion of Lifar, she probably considered an improvement.

One recollection of Fokine lingered in her memory. 'The Master Choreographer was onstage at a dress rehearsal at the Royal Opera House at Covent Garden – could it have been for *Coq d'Or*? Be that as it may, Fokine was not happy with the lighting. He strode to the footlights, "M'sieu La-haut," he called to Joe, the electrician, "M'sieu, put me the lights in the footsies."'

Although her visits to the ballet grew infrequent after the 1950s, Caryl continued to write about the ballet into the '60s and very occasionally in the '70s, her criticism as sharp and her occasional enthusiasms as fervent as ever. In 1950, considering *Les Sylphides*, she examined the theory that the male dancer is, as some claim, 'the spirit of Chopin, summoned by the strains of his music to linger among the spirits of the trees'; and she dealt with one of her favourite targets in one of her favourite footnotes: 'Certainly this would account for the agonized expression to be seen on the face of the *Danseur Noble* at Sadler's Wells Theatre. He could well be Chopin listening to the orchestration.'

Earlier, in 1948, she had seen Carmen Amaya and her Spanish gypsy dancers at the Princes Theatre. She was, perhaps, chancing her pen with: 'She gets her audience so steamed up that I almost expected the theatre to go up in Ole smoke'; but is more assured with: 'We are told that her supporting company are all relatives, and I daresay they do better than yours or mine would in similar circumstances.'

Her account of Eglevsky's *Colloquy Sentimental* at Covent Garden in August 1948 conjures up all the ultra-modern ballets her fictional choreographer, Nevajno, might have devised. 'This is a ballet about a backcloth. It was designed by the surrealist painter, Salvador Dali. On it are a number of bearded Brahmins on bicycles with boulders on their heads. There is also a grand piano. This lets in water through a fissure in the lid. Before this fascinating scene, Rosella Hightower and Eglevsky do a distraught *pas-de-deux* interrupted by a boulder on a man on a bicycle and a dressmaker's dummy in white satin drapes on a turtle in a tank.'

She admired John Gilpin's dancing but, confronted by him as the Young Napoleon at Nice in one of the Festival Ballet's less successful new works, wrote: 'The sight of poor Mr Gilpin trying heroically to rise above his wig brought those tears to my eyes which well up only when I see a bear in captivity.'

[148]

A lifelong friendship with Sir Anton Dolin and a profound admiration for his skill as an artist, and especially as a cavalier, did not obscure her vision when she went to Beriosov's production of *La Esmeralda*: '. . . Anton Dolin strove valiantly to persuade us he was rightly cast as Frollo, the lecherous monk.' She never quite excused Dolin for his mischievous promotion in the 1930s of a rumour that she was a lesbian – far from her instincts – but 'wicked' was the affectionate adjective she applied to him most frequently.

She was always ready to expand on one of her regular dislikes, the work of Serge Lifar. She was convinced that the choreographer once spotted her from a taxi wondow as she was walking down l'Avenue de l'Opéra towards the Paris Opéra, which he directed. She was on her way to collect tickets for which she had arranged. He, she was sure, urged his taxi on so that by the time she reached the box office it had been informed that there were 'no tickets for Caryl Brahms'. She may well have been right, in view of notices which usually implied her stupefaction, 'that the French ballet could go on trotting out their bogeys by Lifar – astonished that this excellent band of dancers seemed deaf to the death-rattle of a long outmoded determination to be *moderne* at all costs.'

Of another French dancer, Violette Verdy, she was inordinately fond; but I could never quite decide the precise balance between romance and accuracy in her story of calling to interview Nelly Guillem, as Violette was then called, when she was in London with Roland Petit's Ballets des Champs Elysées and finding instead a pathetic, wide-eyed waif backstage, who said sadly, 'I suppose you are looking for Nelly – nobody wants to interview me.'

Always kindly to an unknown, Caryl asked her name. 'Leslie Caron,' said the unknown.

As a postscript to her disagreements with Ninette de Valois, I notice that in her meticulously kept cutting-books Caryl has pasted in a *Daily Express* account of the Sadler's Wells Ballet's first triumph in New York. Under a picture of the de Valois, Caryl has vigorously underlined the words: '. . . her (de Valois's) biggest disappointment? That British ballet critics who should have known better were so slow to recognize a good thing.'

She greeted the arrival of Nureyev with enthusiasm, but her last 'discovery' was made when she went to the Coliseum with Nicholas Dromgoole. As they waited for Barishnikov to make his entrance, she spotted a *corps de ballet* dancer who took his stage somewhat diffidently.

She nudged her host vigorously. 'Now that boy will be good,' she said with certainty. She had 'discovered' Barishnikov.

CB Ballet-going is an exercise ad nauseum, and your ballet critic is impelled to return to the scene of the crime as strongly and far more often than a murderer. Eventually I tired of swans and I began to see more grace, more eloquence and more animation in watching Marian Mould or Harvey Smith or David Broome coaxing their long-limbed show-jumping horses over the obstacles on television, or eventually in person at the all-England show jumping course at Hickstead.

NS After their disappointment over *Give Us The Moon*, Brahms and Simon tackled an original screenplay for Two Cities films, *One Night With You*. It was always called 'The Italian Tenor in the Square' by Caryl. Directed by Terence Young, it was a vehicle for Nino Martini who, as *Picture Show and Film Pictorial* told its readers, 'you may remember lent his really glorious tenor voice to the Hollywood successes *Here's To Romance*, *The Gay Desperado* and *Music for Madame*.' The opening scenes, which satirized a movie producer and his writers beating their empty heads for an idea, amused the critics in 1948; but the plot which they devised – a tenor who has lost his cash sings for his supper in one Italian Square after another, accompanied by Patricia Roc, also penniless – pleased them no more than it did Brahms and Simon. Stanley Holloway, as a tramp, collected the good notices, but, according to the *Brighton Argus*, 'a young actress called Irene Worth makes her first film appearance, and appears to possess a sharp personality and sense of humour which ought to bring her before us again.'

Meanwhile, they had sold the film rights in one of their short stories from *To Hell With Hedda, Shorty & Goliath*.

CB Our outfit for the film was enchanting. There was a little Central European refugee named Juddicke writing with us, who turned white with passion if we tried to cut any of our 'chokes'. He was an amiable, rueful, histrionic egg who acted out our sentences all over the flat. The film was never made, but I might usefully have referred to my diary some thirty years later when there was another attempt to film it. The producer called me and I had completely forgotten the earlier transaction. I met him with Ned and he outlined his plans, the very reasonable price he was offering, and the enthusiasm of the distributor to whom he had already spoken. Elated, we went away to celebrate the sale. A couple of days later, the anti-climax; the distributor's script department had made a search – they discovered that they already owned my property!

Caryl was an inveterate diner-out and at this period she was able to indulge her passion daily.

I have always liked eating out. I like every day to be a birthday so that, following the nursery tradition, I am allowed to choose my own dinner. My restaurants are my clubs. They are the places to which I go when I want to relax but not to be alone, and they have ranged from the Ivy and the Ritz and the Savoy Grill to my special, steamy little haunts. I am lucky to have counted Monsieur Abel at the Ivy, Monsieur Mario at the Caprice and George and Ernest (as indivisible as Swan and Edgar) of the old Moulin d'Or as my friends. More recently, the Casserole in the King's Road during the heady days of TW3 was a haunt, and Toscanini's, next door; of a later vintage, Lacy's, Beotys, Joe Allen's, and the impressive, though expensive, Inigo Jones, the wonderful Wheeler's Oyster Bar at Whitstable, an unpretentious lock-up presided over by Delia Fitt, succeeding her equally apple-cheeked mother in oyster-opening, lemon-slicing and brown-bread-buttering. Then there was that anonymous cabmen's pull-up – anonymous because I don't think we ever knew its name – where Skid and I used to work when the tea ration got really low towards the end of the month.

The Ivy was to the theatre world what Tattersalls' is to the racing man. It was so restfully, so discreetly decorated, that though I used at one period to eat there several times a week, I find it hard to remember just how it looked. Unobtrusive walls. Unobtrusive upholstery. Monsieur Abel was an impeccable host and perhaps I can best describe him by saying that on one occasion when I entertained a bishop I took him to the Ivy, where Monsieur Abel, being bland and benign, looked so much more like my idea of what a bishop should look like than the bishop himself. When I was sweating over every sentence, every word of a ballet notice, Abel would bring me a brandy, and when the Blitz was at its height the Jenkins brothers plied their taxis from the Ivy, ensuring that Gingold and Lillie got safely home from their war work and, that precious cargo safely delivered, I was piloted back to Furzecroft.

[151]

Then M. Mario opened the Caprice, the walls lined with ruched claret silk, the tables running the length of the room, the atmosphere different from the Ivy. The stars of the Ivy had been stars for so long that only their public remembered it; but to get a table at the Caprice made a new star feel she must have arrived. What a relief to find its reincarnation in the '80s a triumphant success for its young *maîtres d'hôtel*.

The Akropolis in Percy Street was the creation of Mr Ktouri, a Cypriot – how many Christmas dinners did he send me with his greetings? How many times has he sent me over good chicken soup when I have had my winter flu? His children really were, in the words of the Bible, like olive plants round his table, and he seemed to have as many smiling, bowing sons as a baker has loaves. The Akropolis – always a pilaf for me, chicken or lobster, with raisins and mushrooms in it and each grain of rice a separate entity – was full of colleagues and editors and publishers – very much the feeling of today's L'Escargot, presided over by the beaming Elena Salvoni and her Aldo, my particular friend.

There was one other restaurant which had a special place in my wartime heart. Each day during the Blitz it was more or less obligatory to walk from Furzecroft, George Street, W1 to Pitta's restaurant in Old Compton Street, Soho, if only because it eased in the conversational, 'See you at Pitta's then, and if that's been bombed, at the Restaurant des Artistes.'

'And if that's down?'

'At the Akropolis. But if Furzecroft gets blitzed there'll be nothing I can do about it!'

Grim jokes make grim possibilities easier to bear, and so less frightening. The walk to Pitta's, too, meant that if an alert was sounded on the siren one did not have to wait for the passengers on a bus to disembark.

Arrived *chez* Pitta, the first thing that met your eyes would be the *caisse* and sitting in it, Madame Pitta, a black-clad island entirely surrounded by high piles of bills on skewers which were Pitta's method of credit accountancy. Every now and then one would pay off a few, after which the credit would continue to climb ceilingwards.

The next thing to greet you would be Andy's smiling, round, tawny-skinned countenance. Andy was the establishment's waiter and uncrowned king, under whose sway came every client, and whose

hoarse whisper would decree whether one could be regaled with
a steak* or a real egg, or condemned to pasta which filled you up
for the moment but soon wore off and left your stomach
clamouring twenty minutes later.

I was Andy's favourite customer. Andy's word was his bond.
Once, when I had quarrelled with a friend whom I called the
Hapsburg One – he of the fractured English – I told Andy he was
to have nothing but macaroni for three weeks: 'Three weeks,
Andy, and not one day sooner.'

'Certainly, Miss Caryl, just exactly what you say.'

Mr Pitta was the sputtering frying-pan and the delicious smell of
fried onions coming from the kitchen at the back, otherwise invisible
as an astral body.

The clientèle at Pitta's was totally theatrical, composed as it was
of very young actors whose names appear twice in a programme, in
tiny parts; chorus girls rehearsing dance routines for weeks for
shows that will close in a fortnight; old actors stiff in their joints but
behaving like dukes or butlers according to professional bent;
comedians fresh from making Skegness laugh on a Number 3 tour
and hoping to be invited to join another while boasting that nothing
would induce them to accept, in case they weren't; Frank Muir; ladies
who earned their spaghetti by hanging upside-down on trapezes;
nephews due to be fed in grander but arguably less colourful
restaurants in the hope that a word would be put in for them to the
great Grade himself. Violetta Elvin, Russia's answer to Fonteyn
(but not Fonteyn herself – she would be lunching Chez George and
Ernest at Moulin d'Or, with Constant Lambert), and a chirruping of
the *corps de ballet* who supported her. Bob Beatty; the bottom of the
bills at music halls; Francis Bacon; singers living on Masonic
dinners and home-on-leave Sunday league concerts;† a simmering
of dress designers; scene shifters; would-be agents; Diana Menuhin
née Gould; and anyone else on the midwifery side of that magic
word, Theatre.

There were more deals a day mooted at Pitta's in Old Compton
Street than at the Savoy Grill, the Café Royal, Rules, the Ivy,
L'Ecu de France, Scotts, and Claridges all put together; and even
if the sum total of all those Pitta deals amounted to less than a

---

* Rare, in both senses of the word.
  † Their skewered bills, blown at the edges, very nearly ceiling-high, recognized as
lost causes.

single salary agreed over a Crêpes Suzette in the Garden Room at the Ritz, the jubilation would be greater, for at Pitta's a deal stood for Opportunity at Last, and no one asked you for a cover charge.

One girl looked like Theda Bara, but she knew her Pitta's price list by heart: 'I think I will have' – pause for pretended thought – 'spaghetti.'

'So will I,' says the girl who looked like Norma Shearer, far too quickly.

'Escalope de Veau?' suggests Andy paternally.

Nazimova steels herself against temptation and shakes her curls till they rattle: 'Spaghetti,' she insists.

'Spaghetti,' says Norma Shearer.

'Spaghetti,' say Vivian Leigh and Edith Evans together.

'You will *all* have escalope because you are clever people and I have full confidence in you. *With* spaghetti,' Andy emphasizes. 'Actors,' he philosophizes, 'must eat!'

The door opens. In comes Donald Wolfit – as near as makes no difference: 'Gotta job,' he announces, 'understudying Donald Wolfit. How much do I owe here?'

Andy flat-foots his way to the *caisse* and returns with an astronomical amount.

'Oh,' says Donald Wolfit, his sun behind a cloud. He digs into his pocket. 'Here's seven and six towards it.'

Andy trundles off with it to the *caisse*. 'We will not argue,' says Mrs Pitta, 'we are ruined every day of the week.'

'Actors must eat,' says the resigned Andy.

'As I tell the Puppa,' she agrees, 'actors must eat.'

NS Caryl has referred to 'the Hapsburg One – he of the fractured English'. Fractured it was, and still is. Unlike all the impresarios who came to believe that they were Stroganoff, Herbert Sidon flourished his own highly idiosyncratic Central European eccentricity to Caryl's delight, especially his 'enchanting derangement of the English language'. As Caryl characterized him, 'Herbert von Steinbrecker, anglicized Sidon, was a couturier of *haute école*. Also, from time to time a stage designer, director, translator and impresario. At times the *haute* in *haute couture* slipped a little; times dictated by the ebb and tide of high finance.'

CB It was on one of these occasions that I met – for the only time – a conjuror and his lady. The Hapsburg One had accepted a commission to design a set of silver costumes with emerald-green pompoms and stiff tarlatan ruffs. 'Also I must collect a cheque from this conjuror at Wood Green. Come with me, my darling, for moral support.'

It was a prospect I could not resist. So donning a reasonably anonymous grey suit and vicar's wife hat, I set forth, every inch Miss Brown the couturier's assistant, my fragile identity considerably strengthened behind a veritable mountain of cardboard boxes. What I did not know was that once the silver-threaded canvas-like tat with the bright green pompoms and bortsch-coloured pierrette ruffles were unveiled, the high cardboard boxes could be reduced to flat cardboard pancakes if one dealt them a smart blow on the lid.

'This man,' Sidon told me in the taxi, 'this conjuror, he smiles all the time but pay he does not. Always he has just given the last cheque in the book, or he cannot find pen to write, or ink is run out – excuses, excuses, excuses! Never I go alone to him again!'

I took his point.

'But with the two of us . . .?' I suggested.

'With the two of us,' he concurred.

There were six costumes, so diminutive they must have been for dwarfs, as well as a resplendent concoction – sequins gone mad – for the Conjuror's Lady when he sawed her in half. I assumed a confidence I by no means felt. But before long the confidence took over.

'Unpack the costumes, Miss Brown.'

'*De suite*, M'sieu Sidon,' I said.

We had worked out a routine for me in the taxi. As each of the no doubt effective costumes for midgets emerged, I shook out the creases, handed them to the dressmaker, stood back, clasped my hands in simulated rapture and breathed an admiring 'Ah!', every inch the Couturier's Assistant. But the Conjuror's Lady sent for her husband. True to form, the Conjuror produced a thin chequebook and a pen. He shook it. Nothing happened. He shook it again.

'No ink,' he pronounced, beaming. 'My dear?'

But his abetting spouse had no ink, either.

'Oh well, next time,' she cooed, and flung open the dressing-room door. Sarah Siddons could have done no better.

This was where the Couturier's Assistant – me – found the limelight. I produced my own pen.

[155]

'*M'sieu*,' I said, '*à votre service!*'

The Conjuror shrugged. The Conjuror's Lady shrugged. The signed cheque changed hands.

The Couturier pounced and jerked his head to the cardboard box mountain. 'Those now can go back to the taxi,' he directed.

I was dismissed. I stacked as many of the boxes as I could carry and wobbled towards the door under it. I could feel a furious glare piercing my spine.

'Not like that,' said Sidon. 'So.'

He bashed the boxes one by one, and the cardboard walls telescoped into carriable pancakes. I made for the door, and as I dwindled down the corridor the Conjuror and his Lady called out: 'Good-bye Miss Caryl Brahms, thank you *so* much!'

Some you win, some you lose.

NS In between their falling-outs over the next twenty-seven years, Caryl continued to collect examples of the Hapsburg One's 'derangements'. Most spectacular, perhaps, 'You see, my darling, I have only three teeth in my bottom.' Violence sometimes crept into his life and deranged the language vividly: 'He gif me the gifle' and 'He give me the plonket' were both meant to suggest that blows had been struck.

The couturier in Sidon was further outraged at Pope John Paul's habit of kissing the earth of strange lands when the Papal plane touches down. 'In this lovely garment of white Italian silk,' he inveighed, 'which cost a fortune, what does he do? He throw himself in the mud.' Unpacified, he continued, 'I desiccate this John Paul person! And I do this thing as a Catholic!'

'Herbert,' Caryl said accusingly, 'how long since you've been to church?'

Guilty silence.

In the late '40s they travelled abroad together.

CB I was a slow developer, as I have pointed out. Once I went to stay with the Hapsburg One, with his Mamma in Amsterdam. One night he took me to a cathedral-like church entirely surrounded by lighted windows, some of them with pretty ladies – distance lends enchantment – sitting at them; some empty, but all of them lit by red lampshades. Clearly, thought I, they were the *grande vogue* in Amsterdam cathedral circles.

'Look,' I said to my cavalier, 'all the ladies of the Cathedral Close have red lampshades!'

'My darling,' said the Hapsburg One, 'it is the district of the Light Red.'

How naïve can one be?

s I am indebted to Herbert Sidon for some notes on this period. As confirmation of Caryl's accurate appreciation of his 'enchanting derangements', I have not tampered with his prose, though I have omitted his account of some incidents already described. He writes:

At *One More Mile* [a revue] in the spring of 1945 at Unity Theatre, a show directed by myself under the name Herbert de Wilde, I met Caryl Brahms after the show. In the show performed David Kossoff and the later wife of Ted Willis, the director of the theatre. Caryl found my stage name not suitable and christened me with the name Sidon. She lived in the basement of Furzecroft in George Street. The flat had been lent to her for the duration of the war by John Byron. As it was only a basement one-room flat, of 20 sq. metres, it was a miracle how she ever got into her bed as the entire room was piled high with books, records and paper. But it was luxury compared by S. J. Simon. Skid lived (later) with his wife on a mattress in a small room, there he did his writing so the bed was covered with the typewriter and books and papers, a piece of string attached to the ceiling held his clothes – but I think a corduroy trouser and some sort of jacket was really all he ever wore. Caryl had a lot to complain of Skid's way of Bohemian life, mostly that he never closed the lavatory door when doing his business.

Our daily luncheon was taken at Pitta's café in Old Compton Street, together with ballet boys and girls – mostly with Gordon Hamilton who lived in my flat and sometimes a beautiful, long-haired blonde little girl, Diana Dors, as well as Diana Gould, the present Mrs Yehudi Menuhin.

Andy, the owner [sic] of this café had a pile of unpaid bills next to his till. This was very helpful for all concerned – indeed for Caryl too. 'Can you change me small cheque?' was her way of getting through the day. She had an instinct deep insight into my friends and told me about a friend (John Elliot) – 'he will have six children' – he had – about my secretary, Mary Williamson – 'this is the future Duchess' – she married a son of the Duke of Richmond.

At the first night of *Talking of Tightropes** came all the stars of the London stage – Hermione Gingold and Beatrice Lillie had to be turned away – with many others. The show to put on cost me only £400 – for me a fortune those days. And she refused to give me the future rights of the script. Not that it mattered, it was a flop, only lasted ten days and mostly Caryl and I were the only people in the audience, but we laughed so much every performance – the cast had a good idea always to tease us, with smashing-up old antiques that I had bought at the nearby market.

Christmas 1945 we spent in my flat and we agreed no present should cost two shillings sixpence (Two and Six) but we found plenty for this amount in those days.

I made a red coat with golden sequin embroidery in leaf design for her. She wore this coat every night at Covent Garden until Richard Buckle wrote that a well-known designer can easily be recognized by the coat of his companion. Then she decided that she needed another outfit. From there on Caryl was brave enough to wear the sort of clothes a designer dreams unfortunately of.

When Massine and Baronova arrived for *A Bullet in the Ballet*, we fetched them from the airport. Baronova went to stay with Yul Brynner at Noel Langley's. At the clothes fittings Yul used to lay on the floor with his lovely hair like an aureola. When asked by me 'Why?', he said that he was more interested in what was under a woman's dress.

NS When Herbert Sidon travelled in Europe with Caryl, he was able to observe her tendency to communicate with Roman traffic policemen by singing Puccini at them. In Germany she got by on bits of Wagner. In Austria they called on Sidon's grandfather at Igls near Innsbruck – the Archduke Eugen Hapsburg-Lothringen, whom he describes as 'my illegitimate grandfather'. (His mother, born in 1888, married a Von Steinbrecher and came to England in 1936.) He writes:

One afternoon in the Archduke's house my Aunt was in the garden. Eugen was in his study. There came a knock at the front door. An American lady informed Caryl and myself that she had brought a lady called Marie in her car to Zels. So I went into the Archduke's

---

* A Brahms-Simon radio play about circus life which Herbert Sidon adapted and presented at the New Lindsay theatre in 1946.

[158]

study and fetched him. Caryl told him there is an American lady called Marie at the door. 'Oh! The Queen of Bavaria,' replied the Archduke.

Herbert Sidon has another anecdote about Caryl's pen-name. He referred one day to the fact that her original name was the same as that of Doris Abrahams, the wife of a prominent businessman. Caryl had no intention of reverting to her old name and character, or talking about it. 'Don't talk to me about a woman I have discarded,' she snapped.

In 1948 Brahms and Simon had just started work on *You Were There*, a nostalgic documentary look at the century with a slender thread of story woven through it. The title page carries a subtitle, 'Eat, drink and be merry for yesterday you died'; and inside is the warning, 'This is less a novel than an out-of-date Newsreel'. The collaborators were a couple of chapters in when Caryl heard the news of Simon's death. He was only forty-six. The *News Chronicle* carried a diary piece on 29 July 1948:

> It was not until midday yesterday that Caryl Brahms heard of the sudden death of her collaborator of twenty years, S. J. Simon. She had been away for the weekend and returned expecting 'Skid', as he was known to his friends, to be on hand to work on their twelfth novel, *You Were There*. Theirs was an almost word-in, word-out collaboration, and when the books were published they could not remember which passages each of them had written . . . 'Most of our work,' said Caryl Brahms yesterday, 'was laughing and eliminating.'

The *Star*'s bridge expert, Edward Kempson, remembered Simon as one of 'the most absent-minded people I have ever met . . . once he had two haircuts in one morning, having completely forgotten the first.'

Terence Reese, who wrote in the *Observer*, had been with him earlier on the Monday night when he died. 'He had done a television show (about bridge) with me. He had a new tie for the occasion, buttercup yellow. "Thought it was Technicolor," he said.' Reese goes on to evaluate S. J. Simon, and his bridge.

> Writing about bridge on this page, he was as amusing to those who do not play as he was instructive to those who do. To his friends he

[159]

was a constant joy and a most lovable personality . . . His biggest success was the classic *Why You Lose at Bridge*. He had two more books at the press, one on bidding and one about the inimitable Mrs Guggenheim and her colleagues. As a player he won countless tournaments, and this year was a member of the British team which won the European championship at Copenhagen . . . As a theorist he had a big influence on the development of bidding and was contemplating a monograph on his latest quirk, the bidding of three-card suits . . . His appearance was memorable. A mop of black hair overlapped a broad forehead, jutting brows, owlish spectacles, and a humorous mouth always ready to break into a chuckle, generally (and why not?) at one of his own jokes. A line by Skid was as clearly his own as a line from Damon Runyon or *Alice in Wonderland*. The literary marks were the clipped speech, the omission of article and pronoun, the disregard of syntax. The humour always touched the human comedy but never with malice . . .

The loss of such a close collaborator from a sudden attack would have been distressing in any event, but it was exacerbated by the obituary in *The Times* which twice referred to 'his wife, Caryl Brahms'. A few years before he had married another bridge player, Carmel Withers. Though *The Times* corrected their mistake the next day, the distress, to both women, had been caused. Mrs Simon died just over a year later. Caryl finished *You Were There* and prefaced it with the touching note: *'Dear Skid, I have finished the book. But of course it will be obvious to all who read it that their host was from home. Caryl'*. Her agent at the time, Joyce Weiner, paid eloquent testimony to the determination with which she kept working at, and completed, the novel.

Caryl faced the prospect of writing fiction alone for the first time. Afterwards she remembered vividly the challenging advice of Noel Coward and Ivor Novello: both told her peremptorily to apply herself to work at once; and to the imaginative gesture of Hermione Gingold, who had not been a particularly close friend but immediately sent for her and asked for a revue number. In a letter to a friend, she examined her predicament:

CB The world is fairly overwhelming. Financially it is so difficult that I wonder I'm not in ulcers. Still, at least Skid's estate is very nearly solvent now, so soon maybe I shall be able to make a start on my mountain of income tax. It's the problem of day to day living while I work at finishing the novel which we started together – grim task – which is falling so heavily on me. The two films which should have materialized under contract this autumn but somehow did not, the extra time it took to finish the ballet book. The printers' hours which delay publication, and all the strain not to let these things show in one's public demeanour. I have managed it, in spite of more illness and effort than you can conceive, and it is not helped by weeks of grief and sickness.

Started my first solo novel and it's going better than I dared hope.

NS That book yielded another disappointment. Brahms and Simon had written ten novels and a volume of short stories for the publishing house of Michael Joseph. Caryl had finished the last book herself. As she told the story, she then asked Joseph to commission her own novel, *Away Went Polly*. She was told that it was too great a risk for them to publish the book she wished to write alone ... without Simon she was an unknown quantity. She was shattered. This is the incident she refers to in Chapter Four ... '*Later, after Skid's death, Trusty was nearly to end my span as a writer altogether – but that is a story for another, sadder day.*' We have now reached it and it is only fair to report that Sir Robert, as he now is, has no memory of the incident ... He writes:

> They and their books added enormously to the gaiety and success of the scene. But the humiliating aspect which I have to confess is that I have no recollection at all of coming to the end of any day with Caryl or of not wanting to commission *Away Went Polly*. Alas, I have no records here and everyone except myself who played any part in the scene is dead ... in my own long-remaindered book, *Bound to be Read*, I refer affectionately to Caryl and the early books, but that seems to be all.
>
> My memory in any sort of detail has become appalling, but I will certainly write to Michael Joseph and find out if they have any records ... If Peter Hebden were alive he would probably be helpful, as I invariably found Caryl and Simon a rather alarming pair to deal with. They called me Trusty Lusty and regarded me as rather dim as they wandered around my office reeling off bright remarks, few of which I could hear or understand. I am a little wondering if, in fact, the break came after 1956? I rather hope it did, for I would hate to think that I was regarded by Caryl as something of a villain ...

In a further letter, Sir Robert says, 'If the Michael Joseph records had not been destroyed, an explanation might have been found. I would not have turned down Caryl's project without consultation with some "reader" or "literary adviser" as such were then called, since I never regarded myself as a Brahms/Simon expert.'

The late Joyce Weiner, however, confirmed Caryl's recollection. *Away Went Polly* was published by Heinemann in 1953, a year before I met Caryl. It was well reviewed.

7

Brahms and Sherrin

The gap that Simon's death left must have been incalculable, but Caryl felt that she would never find another collaborator who matched him, and did not look for one. (She did briefly attempt a stage adaptation of *Away Went Polly* with Christopher Hassall, whom she admired and whose gentle company she enjoyed, but the play was never produced. Her own radio adaptation was recorded in the late 1950s, with Yvonne Mitchell. Her favourite memory of the working partnership was an agonizing night during which she thought she had lost three pages of Hassall's hard-fought first draft. She had A, B, C, and G, but could find D, E, and F nowhere. She hunted to no avail and was in a suitable state of exhaustion, embarrassment and penitence when her collaborator arrived for work. She confessed. He studied the pages.

'That's all right,' he said, unruffled, 'it's all there – A – B – C – G!')

It was necessary for her to reshape and reconsider her life. But her resilience was formidable. She told me that this was the one period during which she considered ending her life, but always rejected it as an abdication of responsibility and an intolerable betrayal of her friends.

She was still living in Furzecroft, the flat she had borrowed from John Byron 'for the duration of the war'. When the war ended, Byron went to Bristol to play leading roles with the Bristol Old Vic. In 1949 he felt that it was time to move back to London, but the news surprisingly dismayed Caryl. With a recognizable single-mindedness, she had come to look upon the flat as her own and showed a marked reluctance to move out. She and Byron had been close friends for years, and he is eloquent of her kindness and her imaginative friendship to him. However, in almost farcical circumstances he was summoned to his own flat and confronted by a very formal Caryl, accompanied by her old friend Charles Landon who assumed the role of arbitrator. After a solemn discussion they all decided that Byron should repossess, and Caryl set about finding a new apartment. She moved in 1950 to

No 3 Cambridge Gate, a Victorian block in the Outer Circle of Regent's Park, where she lived for the rest of her life.

While continuing her child verse and the ballet criticism, she stepped up her journalism, particularly for *Picture Post*.

CB There was at the time a splendid illustrated weekly news magazine called *Picture Post*. Soon after the war I composed for the editor, Tom Hopkinson, a long list of subjects I hoped, fledgling optimist that I was, he would be panting to publish. The list was cold cod in the next day's grey morning light and as much to cheer myself up about it as for any other reason, I found myself tapping out: *The Business Side Of Being A Bishop*. Back came the commission to write the wretched thing.

Panic.

And where to find a bishop?

There weren't any at the synagogue.

I consulted my amiable friend Michael Wood, PRO to the Royal Ballet and Opera at Covent Garden at the time. 'Michael, how on earth am I to get my hands on a bishop?'

'Remember that chap you took backstage to introduce to Svetlana Beriosova for me?'

I did. The chap had been in charge of the crew of the Cambridge boat; the ensuing conversation had been sticky on both sides, and had soon taken on the form of a monologue by me. But Michael Wood had had royalty and the concomitant Court Circular on his plate that night, and one would and will always do anything for Michael, so I had battled on under Svetlana's calm but apparently tongue-tying beauty.

'Well,' Michael said, 'his name is Tremlett – Tony Tremlett – used to call him Trubshaw in the army, and he's the domestic chaplain to the Bishop of Trinidad. He's your man. Ask him.'

Off went a letter to Tony Tremlett, later the Lord Bishop of Dover, who lost no time in telephoning. 'You're in luck,' he said, 'I spent a couple of nights down at Wells in Somerset last week, so Bath and Wells is practically in the bag. Know him?'

'No.'

'You'll like him. Talkative kind.'

But will he like me? I thought. The odds were against.

'My paper wants to give £50 to any charity he cares to nominate,' I told Tremlett.

'For heaven's sake, don't waste it on Wells – we could do with it in Trinidad.'

'Right,' I said, 'I'll suggest it to him.' The bargain was struck.

Next I turned to my friend Tony Gishford, formally a co-PRO with Michael Wood. Tony would know exactly how to address a member of the royal family or a dignitary of the church.

'How does one address a bishop?'

'My dear Caryl, you say, "Nonsense, my dear Bishop!"'

Somehow I did not see myself saying 'Nonsense!' to a bishop of the Church of England, one of whose offices was to stand at the left hand of the Queen at her coronation.

For Caryl, meeting and becoming friends with Bishop Bradfield added focus to her interest in Christian attitudes and practices. She never, I think, wished to be anything but a Jew; but she was fascinated by the ritual and the mystery of an unfamiliar religion, and when she rediscovered her second cousins, Anthony and Peter Levi, a few years later when both were Jesuits, the extra complexities of their calling intrigued and concerned her. For the moment, however, she was characteristically worried about the social side. Having learned the correct address she began to hunt out the right wardrobe, and above all a suitable hat. She had written to Wells and received a prompt and welcoming reply: she was invited to attend a Meet at the Palace, and to stay on for the Hunt Ball.

Panic.

I searched desperately among my little black dresses, *de rigueur* in town, for some really old tweeds suitable for country wear. But nothing would do, for we had not long been released from the dictatorship of wartime coupons. In my despair I telephoned Madame Rose Vernier, Bonnet-maker to Princess Marina, several Duchesses, and me, and fortunately my good friend.

'Bring me everything suitable you've got, and I'll see how I can help,' said Vernier.

Timorously I presented myself *chez* Vernier. On sighting me she shrieked: 'No, no, no and no,' tearing me to pieces. 'Shoes wrong! Skirt wrong! Sweater wrong! Scarf wrong! And hat,' she tore it off my head and flung it into the waste-paper basket, 'IM-possible!'

I had been rather proud of that hat.

'Now let us see . . .' She rummaged. 'We shall begin from the hat downwards like we were trying on our corsets. Ah!' She produced an appalling brown felt hat and routined it. 'Now pull it down *hard*,' she ordered.

She stood back and surveyed her more-or-less stripped-to-the-buff client.

'Will do – for a beginning,' she decided. 'Now show me your gloves – you have none? – but this does not *exist*! Out of the question! Convolvula, fetch the pair that Lady Troutbeck left behind.'

Convolvula jumped to it.

'Scarf,' pondered Rose Vernier. 'Brigitta, my cook, has the very thing. I gave it to her last influenza. When you have finished admiring your nails, Fiona, you shall run to my flat and borrow back.'

Thus, we went through the accoutrements of a country lady, plundering largely from her stock and her staff who dared not object.

Finally, kitted out, I made my somewhat self-conscious way back along George Street, cravenly crossing the road whenever I saw a pair of raised eyebrows I knew.

NS (Here Caryl allowed herself a diversion on the subject of Vernier's hats. The one she had worn to Aldeburgh, 'an inverted miniature beehive with a single corn-stook across the front', blown frantically by a gust of gale-force wind across the Festival front. 'Oh, Caryl,' said a fellow music-lover, 'we do so look forward to your hats each year.' For receiving an Ivor Novello Award, much later, 'a deep cream soufflé in chiffon'. Another 'twentieth-century, lightly-whipped-together confection' to accompany our entry for, of all un-chic things, the Eurovision Song Contest; 'a dream of black mink with oriental decoration'. She was to have worn another to the unveiling of the Roosevelt statue in Grosvenor Square, but for a 7.30 a.m. call from Vernier. 'Caryl, you must not wear today the hat I have copied for you. Princess Marina will be wearing the model at the ceremony.')

Vernier from head to foot, Caryl went west.

CB There is nothing like a slow train for unsealing the lips of usually silent passengers. The slow train to Wells was no exception.

('Faith – well it's a very simple matter really, my dear Caryl. Every time we go to the booking-office and pay the price of a railway ticket we are making an act of Faith – faith that the little piece of cardboard

[166]

will take us to our destination.') My 'little piece of cardboard' afforded me the information that Bath and Wells was well-liked in the diocese, and energetic. ('See more of 'un than the last one.')

Arrived, then, at Wells, off I went to the local newspaper offices.

'You'll like him,' they encouraged me. 'He'll say, "Come in. Take a chair. Cigarette? Well, let us take an unaccustomed glass of sherry!"'

And that was how a sudden brisk gust of wind caught the brim of my hat and nearly deposited it in the moat – the swans would have been disappointed – on this, my first visit to Wells.

And sure enough, the Bishop's first words to me were: 'Come in. Take a chair. Cigarette? Well, let us take an unaccustomed glass of sherry.' (Who could have foreseen the time would come when the Bishop would say: 'Now for the washing-up, Caryl – you wash and I will dry.')

I had arrived at the Palace of Wells to find the drawbridge up. Lacking the courage to pull the bell to admit my very old, mud-splattered car, I sat there contemplating the moated swans. Presently help arrived in the sprightly form of some minor cleric, and I was in. Up the drive I drove, past the walls of a claret-coloured brick ruined abbey, by no means 'half as old as Time' but a folly committed by some Victorian bishop, to be shown into the Canterbury Room. When his Archbishopship last graced it, I was not told nor dared to ask, but it was suitably vast and sparse and shining, and colder than any spare bedroom I have ever lodged in. My suitcase, borrowed from Vernier, looked like a very small, self-respecting craft braving a very large ocean of varnished floor-boarding smelling like an upper-crust schoolroom. A pleasant and clean smell. A daughter of Israel alone in the Canterbury Room!

Now, if there was one thing that terrified me more than any rearing and nostril-dilated neighing quadruped, or even Vernier, it was the terror of all terrors of being late for meals in my exalted new surroundings. And so next morning I arrived in the breakfast-room before even my hostess emerged, feeling as self-conscious as the first prize-winner to mount the presentation platform. The Bishop was still in his domestic chapel. ('When I christen a baby the parents often give me a pound or so as a gesture of gratitude and I always use it to decorate my domestic chapel – I hope to leave it a little handsomer than I found it.')

Mrs Bradfield was a statuesque lady of great outer severity and

even greater inner kindness. She seized the opportunity that the
tardiness of her two daughters gave us for uninhibited chat about
them. We could have been old friends. She might have known
me for years. 'If ever you can help my younger daughter, please do,'
she said.

I felt it to be unlikely, for our worlds were far apart, but I said,
'Of course,' and I hope I have.

Before leaving for Wells that first and most exercising time I had
sent Tony Tremlett the list of questions I proposed to put to the
Bishop, for fear that out of ignorance I might unwittingly offend.
Tony had told me I could go ahead.

Did he get his suits from a clerical outfitter as did, I was given to
understand, the Bishop of Chelmsford?

'Good gracious, no. Certainly not.' I gathered that Bath and Wells
had them built by his tailor.

Question by question I edged up to the sixty-four-thousand dollar
– or rather, the fifty pound – one. 'My paper would like to give £50
to any charity you care to nominate. I dare say you would wish them
to give it to Tony Tremlett for some Trinidadian charity?'

'Certainly not,' snapped the Bishop, 'I shall get something for my
domestic chapel.'

It was all very well for him; he was not required to face Tremlett
with the bad news. No doubt Tremlett was livid. But if so he did
not let it stand in the way of our becoming good friends.

Nor did I take offence when he referred to my 'old-fashioned
religion', though I did point out mutinously that if it had been
good enough for my Sephardic grandparents, it was good enough
for me; and that if I am slack on the dietary laws it is my own
fault, and anyway they were laws for a hot country made at a time
when Himself had not yet created the fridge. Amused, and on a
later occasion, I told the Bishop about my 'old-fashioned religion'.
Thereafter, he often asked, 'How is your old-fashioned religion getting
on, Caryl?'

'Well,' I said, 'it's no use trying to convert me. There's no
news-value when yet another Jewess becomes converted to
Christianity. But if a Jewess were to convert a Bishop . . . think of
the headlines!'

The morning of the Meet, which was the *raison d'être* of my visit,
dawned bitterly cold at the Palace of Wells, with a spicing of ice on
the easterly wind, and was definitely fraught.

There I stood, feeling at my most highly unsuitable, for all Vernier's care, dreading to make an ass of myself among the horses, and all of them champing and rearing and hoofing the air in my heated imagination – indeed my imagination was the only warm thing about me. Then there was the Bishop's wife, dear lady, tense as only elderly ladies of considerable *embonpoint* can be, a purple kind of pink in the face from pent-up nerves. For the relict of a former and possibly richer Bishop of Bath and Wells – doubtless a second Mrs Proudie, and experienced in Meets at the Palace – had signified her intention of attending, and that seemed to catch everyone but the Bishop by the short hairs. The relict, I was to find, was Queen Candid Criticism in person, and coming so soon after the end of World War II, with everyone's domestics in short supply, even the two daughters of the house were buzzing around like experienced bees.

Soon the Pink-Coated Tally-ho's were assembled on the Green, champing at the bit to be in pursuit. Meanwhile, the daughters of the house were cheerily about bearing stirrup cups, a couple of female Ganymedes, ignoring the restive steeds, leaving me with the largest, heaviest tray of sandwiches I have ever toted before or since, and urged on by the Bishop – 'There's a man over there on that restless horse who's got his hands full and doesn't seem to have had any comestibles – go over and minister to him, Caryl' – or words to that effect.

Panic!

But a daughter of Israel could not allow herself to chicken out with the Church of England's eyes on her. Forward I went among the flying hooves of the neighing quadrupeds.

It was on my way back to the buttery that I met the relict's butler-chauffeur, a sterling sort who took in my predicament at a glance. 'If I were you, Ma'am, I'd leave the sandwiches to the young ladies – they look very strong young ladies. And if I may take the liberty of making a suggestion, I'd slip into the house and watch from a window.'

To the Hunt Ball I wore a black velvet picture-gown and I had brought with me a Victorian necklace of stage emeralds, the size of pigeon's eggs – a parure that had made quite a stir when I wore it at the Royal Opera House. Alyson Bradfield, the younger of the two daughters of the house, came up to the ice-cold Canterbury Room to supervise my last touches. She eyed the pinchbeck emeralds with a strong look of Vernier at her most disapproving in her habitually laughing blue eyes, but all she said was: 'I don't think that necklace is altogether suitable.'

She had it off before you could say Moody and Sankey, and clipped me into her own necklace of seed pearls, and all went merrily as a peal of bells, save that I am not your seed-pearl type.

Later, I shared another sporting occasion with the Bishop; or nearly. It was his habit to go to Lords' cricket ground and leave a message with my answering service: 'Tell Miss Brahms I shall be calling in after the match for a little light supper.' I remember that the first time I met him he told me that somewhere along the way of a hard-fought day in the diocese 'a Bishop gets fed as the sparrows are fed'. The crumbs from my table, though biblical, would not have done. So I would whip round the local shops and prevail upon them to credit me with a bottle of Madeira, luscious smoked salmon, cold chicken moist as a virgin's eye (which I cook Spanish fashion), fruit and several cheeses, black coffee and brandy, which we would consume later on my balcony. In short, and vulgar with it, I did my nut.

'It's surprising how good these simple meals are, Caryl,' his Lordship would say.

NS Their friendship continued until the Bishop's death. She had a missionary zeal for encouraging into the theatre people who might not ordinarily find themselves there. Her last visit with Bishop Bradfield lived up to expectations.

CB I took him to see *Love's Labour's Lost*. I had planned the outing with more care than is my wont. My aim was to make the Bishop more aware of theatre as an art form, so our evening was shaped to have supper at the Ivy, planted firmly in almost totally theatrical soil, in West Street off St Martin's Lane. Simple enough, one would think – but was it? For one thing, there would be the dreaded – by me – grace before meals. Would we be expected to stand around our prominent table under the astonished gaze of Monsieur Abel, who, as I have remarked, looked so much more like a bishop, I thought, than our veritable Bishop? Luck was on my side, however, for the Bishop had a couple of words for it and the moment passed. Over dinner he remarked: 'Do you know, Caryl, I had no idea that Shakespeare was such good money's worth.'

[170]

Dorothy Ward, the great principal boy, was another friend whom Caryl met through her journalism in the early '50s. Dorothy lived across the grass from her in Regent's Park and walked purposefully around the perimeter taking her daily exercise. Meeting in the forecourt of Caryl's block of flats in Cambridge Gate, they presented a fascinating picture of dignity and impudence.

One of the women I have admired down the years is Dorothy Ward – Principal Boy *par excellence*. In the days of which I write she must have been sixty if she was a day, a beautiful and fulfilled woman.

'You see this dressing table set – the King of the Belgians, dear – solid silver.'

She was blonde – still – gorgeous – still: 'My hairdresser says I haven't a white hair in my head.'

Above all, she was trusting and friendly. My lucky star must have been in the ascendant, for *Picture Post* invited me to write a profile-in-depth of Dorothy during the putting together of a pantomime. I saw to it that this entailed my being closer to her than her shadow for two glorious weeks. Dorothy Ward was married to the late Shaun Glenville, the battered Pantomime Dame. 'I like to wake up in the morning at nine,' she told me once, 'have my breakfast brought up on a tray – just a boiled egg and two pieces of toast – and see how my shares are doing in the *Financial Times*, dear.' She was no mean businesswoman.

Her son, Peter Glenville, is a gifted director of stage plays who now lives in the States, but in the days of which I am writing he was a close friend of Oliver Messel, the great designer of décor who influenced his era of stage design and did the cerulean blue and gold, delicately traced dust-cover for my book, *A Seat at the Ballet*.

'People are always asking me when Peter is going to get married, but as he says: "Where am I going to find a girl who can discuss a script, Mummie?"'

Dorothy put the point to me: 'I knew that while Peter was living in Oliver's house, no one would take his own work seriously. They would just label him "Oliver Messel's friend". So I bought him a house of his own. And do you know, dear, from that day on Peter became someone in his own right!'

The Pantomime Dame deserves a digression of his/her own.

[171]

Have you ever watched the pitying expression on the face of an American as you have tried to explain the duality of this peculiarly British seasonal travesty? Dorothy put it in a sentence for me one weary night after I had spent that fortnight dogging her every footstep. The pantomime was *Jack and the Beanstalk*. Dorothy played Jack, a kind of thigh-slapping Rosalind straight out of the Forest of Arden; and Shaun Glenville, her husband, was playing the Dame. Jack, sent to sell Jessie the cow at market for his widowed mother, had instead swopped her for a bag of beans, which the old lady, in a burst of anger at the boy's shiftlessness, had thrown out of the kitchen window, not knowing that the beans were such stuff as magic was made on and that they would grow at the end of Act I as high as the sky, and Jack would mount them with the resounding cry: 'Now God for Harry, England and St George!' and bring the house down.

Dorothy and Shaun were rehearsing Jack's return to the cottage with the bag of beans while the stage carpenters were hammering away at lofty beanstalks substantial enough to bear the weight of her ascent to the land of milk and money and her descent at the beginning of Act II to the Village Green, rich beyond the dreams of avarice. Loud was the sound of hammering by night. Dorothy strode to the centre of the stage, an offended Sarah Siddons.

'Gentlemen, gentlemen,' she expostulated, 'how do you expect me to play this intimate little scene with my husband who is my Mother, if you make so much noise?'

She liked what she called 'a good acting rôle, something I can get my teeth into'. Jack was all right; so I suspect was Dick (Whittington). Aladdin was too urchin, too gamin for her striding style; Prince Charming perhaps not lively enough. The role she despised was Colin in *Mother Goose*, 'no character . . . nothing to play'.

I have noticed a strict scrutiny and a rivalry among Principal Boys. Dorothy again: 'Imagine it, dear, she gave her Robinson Crusoe at Liverpool last year, and do you know she sang into a microphone in the shipwreck scene? What the children must have thought of a' – with infinite scorn – '*microphone* coming up through the waves, I shudder to think.'

The scrutiny was extended to externals. 'Take Newcastle,' Dorothy said. 'I had to travel two skips of costumes. Duggie Byng was playing the Dame, and you know what a dresser he is, Caryl! I went straight to Oliver Messel and he designed the little parma violet crêpe de Chine tunic I wear when I come down the beanstalk.'

'But Mummie,' Peter objected when Oliver told him, 'you *couldn't* have a change of costume there.'

'Oh yes, I could – the fairies brought it to me in the interval and it will have my initials embroidered on the breast pocket, I told him – D.W.'

'There's one thing I'd love to do, Caryl,' she told me on another occasion; 'I'd love to go with you to see Margot Fonteyn dancing at Covent Garden.'

I chose one of the season's press nights when Fonteyn was dancing *The Sleeping Princess* for the first time in that season. As we stood together in the Crush Bar of the Royal Opera House – Dorothy, a snow-white vision in a long fox coat, all her pearls and diamonds on display, bracelets from wrist to elbow over long white kid gloves; me in journalist's non-committal black – she said: 'Oh Caryl, don't we set one another off well. Me so blonde and you so dark! I should have borrowed Nora Littler's tarrara – tiara,' she corrected herself swiftly, 'if only I had thought of it.'

Given that those were the days when one went *en grande toilette* to a Covent Garden first night, it would still have needed to be a very Royal Gala for one to remain reasonably inconspicuous in a tarrara.

(One such high occasion is, as it were, glued to my memory, for Michael Wood's wife Edmée, a tall, large-boned woman, wore a tiara and a long white gown with black brogue shoes. How it happened baffled the imagination. Was it absence of mind, or lack of time? Or just that the diamonds were real and she felt that there would be such a crush that no one could step back and catch a glimpse of her comfortable, sensible, but in the circumstances risible, footwear?)

The two weeks sped by. I continued to play page to Dorothy's Queen Wenceslas. We must have resembled an elegant Gibbs-built launch (her) and a very determined mud-caked tug (me). Together we went to do a 'Workers' Playtime' – how they loved Dorothy's party piece, '*Everything is peaches down in Georgiah*'. How *I* loved watching Dorothy and Shaun putting the panto together:

'This is the scene where you do the milking business.'

'No, that's on the Village Green.'

'Well, I *am* on the Village Green.'

'Now I sing the first verse and you sing the second.'

'No, I sing the first verse and *you* sing the second!'

[173]

'That's not the way we did it at the King's Theatre in Edinburgh.'

'*This* is not the King's in Edinburgh – it's the Chiswick Empire, practically the West End, and Tom Arnold's given us his new scenery . . . well, all but.'

Driving home from the night of the technical rehearsal, which went on till four in the morning and involved the cast who were lucky if they got away by five a.m., Shaun said to Dorothy: 'Miss Brahms must be very bored and tired.'

'Caryl bored?' Dorothy gave the matter her considered attention. 'Oh no, she was talking to the Lady Lion-Tamer!'

NS   When I came down from Oxford in 1954 I was committed to sitting for my Bar examinations, if only to give me more time to make up my mind about a career. However, I cherished an ambition to adapt *No Bed For Bacon* as a stage musical. My intentions had been two-pronged until a Cambridge group got in first with my other choice, Max Beerbohm's *Zuleika Dobson*.

From the flat in which I had a room on Chelsea Embankment I wrote to Caryl. Her name and address were in the London telephone directory and it seemed a sensible step to take. I asked if I might 'send her some lyrics'. They were, as yet, unwritten. Before nine the next morning my landlord, the late Kenneth Fortescue, was yelling up the stairs: 'Telephone! It's Caryl Brahms.' Caryl, who later said that my named sounded 'Tin-Pan Alley', insisted that we knew one another. I denied this. She then discovered that Oxford was common ground – so had she met me there? She had not: I denied that too. She was insistent. Finally I capitulated; it seemed the easy way out.

CB   When Ned came down from Oxford he wrote to ask me if he could 'send me some lyrics' for a musical version of *No Bed For Bacon*. Panicking at the prospect of losing his verses or of having to find brown paper or string in which to return them, I telephoned him to let him down gently. He sounded so nice that I agreed to give him a glass of sherry. I had not wanted to work with another collaborator after Skid's death – apart from one attempt to adapt *Away Went Polly* as a play for the stage with Christopher Hassall. However, I could see at once that Ned would challenge no comparisons with Skid, and we decided to try.

NS   I cannot separate my first impressions of Caryl from the view I had of her over the next few years. Physically she had that aspect which appeared not to change for two decades, until the noticeable enfeeblement of the last four or five years: friends like Richard Berkeley Sutcliffe, who had known her ten years or so earlier, thought the same. She was dark, tiny, with a very prominent nose on which she perched large, forbidding dark glasses, and a sharp chin that encased a mouth which shed its irregular teeth over the years. Her pouter-pigeon figure and thrust-forward chin had a combative look. She was about the same age when I met her as I was when she died – early fifties.

Since Simon's death the movie of *Trottie True* had come out, causing a considerable splash but little joy for the co-author of the novel. She was, as usual, displeased that the director, Brian Desmond Hurst, had engaged another script writer, C. Denis Freeman, who had made a lack-lustre job of a high-spirited book. She was more wryly amused when a very young Diana Dors, who was not in the picture, stole the limelight at the première in Leicester Square in 1949. One photograph of Diana, slim and brunette, in a low-cut, tight, scalloped, black neckline, survives from her *Evening Standard* cutting. However, the notices were better than those for previous Brahms-Simon films.

Caryl had published *Away Went Polly* and *A Seat at the Ballet*; her cuttings books remind me that she was also writing occasional ballet notices – she was always irritated to get letters complaining of ballet critiques signed 'C.B.' which were the work of the fledgling Clive Barnes and not hers. With some embarrassment she was still turning out regular child-verses for *My Home*, meticulously pasted up in special cuttings albums until they peter out in July 1960. She had seen many of her novels with Skid go into paperback. 'Brilliant,' she clipped the *Socialist Leader*, which judged one 'not to be missed'. She made occasional appearances on television (*Talk Yourself Out Of This*, 'a game to test the wits and the imagination', produced by her old friend 'Maestro Piffard'); on panels at Oxford (reluctantly cross-questioned by Michael Codron, the future impresario. She later recalled that she finally quelled him with an imperious, 'give that young man a cigarette'. The *Isis* reports that she 'smoked a chain of Abdullahs while sprinkling wit and wisdom over the undergraduates'); or in public rooms ('Ballet: Is It Effeminate for Men?'). And she wrote more pieces for *Picture Post*.

A year after Simon's death an Australian review of *To Hell With Hedda* judges that Brahms and Simon are 'rapidly becoming an institution', and another cutting proclaims that *Trottie True* was the latest proud purchase of the Tamworth Public Library. Rumours of a movie of *A Bullet in the Ballet* were tantalizingly frequent. In 1950 Edward Dryhurst had acquired it – £5,000 was the sum mentioned, none of which, of course, went to the author – and it was to be directed by Edward Greville whose latest successes were *Noose* and *Romantic Ages*. By 1952 other names were being bandied about.

As I remember it, she was concentrating at this time on moving sideways towards opera and especially theatre journalism and criticism. She had written for *Music and Musicians* as well as for *Dance and Dancers*: *John Bull* and *Time and Tide* gave her regular commissions for theatre reviews, but she was concentrating on *Plays and Players*. She especially enjoyed spotting emerging performers and picking out their strong points and their weak ones. 'What a first rate Shylock Eileen Herlie would make,' she wrote of the actress's Medea. 'The thickened utterance, the rolling orbs, the clotted locks, the quivering claws . . . but where is the terror that has squeezed the heart of the playgoer for twenty-five centuries? . . . Mr Jeffers' [the translator's] freedoms, Mr Gielgud's polite production and Miss Herlie's immaturity have reduced immensities of horror to the ragings of a displaced female person over the defection of an ungrateful careerist.' This was for the *Evening Standard*, a paper she was proud to have been sacked from three times, holding Charles Wintour, the last editor to do the deed, in scant respect.

But the early spotting of talent remained a source of particular pride. When we started to work on *No Bed*, she recalled one such critical assessment which she later included in her memoirs.

CB I had known Alec Guinness slightly but affectionately for some years. Esteem had grown in them; but it grew from unlikely roots. World War II was over, but only just. Yvonne Mitchell, lovely, elegant, imperious, highly talented and *en pleine beauté*, friend and actress, had been reading the Brahms-Simon *No Bed For Bacon*.

'You should send the novel straight to Alec Guinness,' she said; 'he would be the perfect Shakespeare and it would make a perfect film.'

So I sent the book to Guinness with what I felt would make an irresistible sales pitch. It went something like this:

'Dear Mr Guinness, I am sorry to burden you with one of my own books, but if you would leaf through it you could do so much for one character, Shakespeare.'

I sat back and read it over. A sure sale, I decided; and waited for the grateful Guinness to grab.

But the stars decided otherwise – so did Alec Guinness. Back came my comeuppance:

> 'Dear Miss Brahms, I could never forgive you for telling my public that I have a face like a dispirited haddock.'

When I came out of shock there was only one thought in my mind, and this was not 'Did I say it?' but 'Where did I say it?' I flew to the files and there it was, in all its raw brashness, embedded in a piece I had called *New Faces*, which had appeared in one of our shiniest magazines. It has long since vanished but I must have written about talented Pamela Brown, already beginning to coat her acting with mannerisms, Eileen Herlie, a cut-and-come again actress like a goodly cake of Windsor soap, Noel Wilman, a stylist if ever there was one, and one or two other good players; among them, though by no means a new face, was that of Donald Wolfit which I suggested was lined probably by touring so frequently the outer circle. (This had drawn a note from Wolfit, whom I did not at that time know, to the effect that possibly I was mistaking the lines on his face for his make-up in *King Lear*.)

As to Guinness, certainly I had written that he had a face like a dispirited haddock but I had not left it there. I went on to describe his excellence in half a dozen parts. I forced myself to read what I had written about Guinness. I found that, but for that unfortunate description, I had written a near-rave.

'See,' I had advised, 'his Fool in *Lear*, where the marvellously swift and dramatic gesture of tightening of the noose of rope sent him to his rendezvous with death.' Then there was Guinness's Richard II, who sat with his little nervous twitch of a smile that came and went and said all that needed to be said about this, the weakest of the English kings. Self-mockery was his first defence. I noted also that Guinness had played the King of France 'and probably his wheelchair too'. And, taking heart, I remembered praising, in the London *Evening Standard*, Guinness's apothecary Abel Drugger in Ben Jonson's *The Alchemist*, 'capering heartbreakingly like a very young monkey at the end of an organ-grinder's string'.

Thus fortified, I returned to the attack:

'Dear Mr Guinness, Just which are you disputing: "dispirited" or "haddock"?'

A few days later I was summoned by bell – the telephone bell – and a cultured voice announced: 'This is Mr Haddock Guinness. Would you be free for lunch on Thursday?'

Thus began my acquaintance with Alec Guinness, which was also notable for my first acquaintance with an avocado . . .

NS Guinness enjoyed *No Bed*, but failed to persuade Ealing to film it. There is an odd symmetry in the reference to the avocado which I had failed to notice. After I met Caryl in the eyrie to which she moved in Regent's Park – two glasses of dry sherry, some black olives, and a skirmishing conversation – we arranged to have lunch at the Ivy the next Saturday to plan our attack on the novel. My first artichoke . . .

When Guinness played T. E. Lawrence in Terence Rattigan's play *Ross*, we went to it, partly because Caryl wanted to see how much she could recognize of 'the man in the raincoat' whom she had met in Bumpus's Bookshop in the '30s.

CB The Lawrence legend is a mystery and it is in the nature of a mystery that there must seem to be more than one answer to it. Guinness gave us an eloquent and many-sided picture of T. E. Lawrence, a most impressive performance, gentle as a tear, and swift and kind and authoritative. It held the play, which is fragmentary, together. We saw a man small in stature but of great authority. A fastidious man. A proud man. A cunning man. And, following the flogging scene, a broken man, a limping, gasping man, his tears and blood together on his cheeks, his pride broken. We saw that he was insolent and compassionate. In fact, Guinness seemed to be most things that we believe the legend to have been, in a performance in which his extraordinary technique was informed and governed always by his heart. Still in search of T. E. Lawrence or Alec Guinness (they had by then so coalesced that I could not have said which) I went backstage to see him – or, of course, him. Or was it them? 'Will the real Mr Lawrence please stand up?'

Two young men, American, eager and offering, had been shown to his dressing-room before me. After a little disjointed and totally forgettable conversation, Guinness had said: 'Forgive me, but do I know you?'

'No, Sir.'

'Then how on earth did you get in?'

'Easy! We gave the stage-door keeper ten shillings each.'

'Only ten – I'd have thought I rated higher than that,' said Guinness, a saddened man.

'Each,' they reminded him, and passed out of his life.

At the Haymarket, Ned told us a story about the two Lawrences, T.E. and D.H., which, though it did not further my quest, has stayed in my memory. Eddie Marsh, he said, had lent T.E. an unexpurgated copy of *Lady Chatterley's Lover*. T.E. returned this with a note, saying that he felt privileged to read it, but he could not understand 'all that fuss about the sex business', because he'd 'never met more than half a dozen people who cared a biscuit for it'.

Guinness capped the story with another tale – of an encounter between Eddie Marsh and Lytton Strachey. It happened on the morning on which Marsh had first received and read Rupert Brooke's early poems. Charged with excitement, he rushed from Raymond Buildings to a neighbouring, sympathetic, Bloomsbury bookshop. Here he encountered Strachey, the one man in London whose voice might in moments of stress hit a falsetto note an octave above his own.

'A new poet,' he panted. 'His work is *steeped* in beauty!'

Only a superb technical comedian could have pitched Marsh's 'steeped' so high that it sounded unbeatable, and then judged Strachey's piercing answering shriek so that it topped it:

'STEEPED!'

I came away from the Haymarket theatre feeling I had seen an unwriteable play well written, an unactable play well acted, an undirectable play well directed.

But did I see the man in the raincoat with the hair like stubble? Hard to say – perhaps from time to time.

So much of our work together was in the musical theatre that I was very soon made aware of Caryl's independent and questioning attitude to composers.

I feel I should approach the subject of composers delicately.

The trouble about composers is that from the age of three, when they attack the family piano with the palms of their pinkies – *chm* –

chm – chm – their mothers tell them they are a second Mozart, only better, a definition with which they whole-heartedly concur. They are a breed of *monstre sacré* in a bracket all their own.

NS Just before I met Caryl she had adapted one of her short stories, *Under the Juniper Tree* (about a remote Spanish village awaiting the end of the world), as an opera, *Manyana*. Her libretto was the first opera commissioned by the BBC for television. The composer was Arthur Benjamin, whom she called 'Uncle Arthur'.

CB It was received reasonably politely at the time but it is not its critical reception which stays in my mind. One day Uncle Arthur, as I had rechristened him, called for an extra phrase: 'I need eight words, of one syllable each, expressing extreme rapture and passion!'
   The second, even more daunting incident came on the night of our live transmission. I was invited to Uncle Arthur's to watch, eat and enjoy. During the day a film company which had at one time owned an option on the short story, had sought an injunction to stop the broadcast. All had passed off smoothly; but I had thought it kinder not to worry my elderly colleague with the drama. That evening as we left the dining-table and settled ourselves in front of the screen, I began to wonder if I had made the right decision. We started with an announcement that there was a technical hitch. For ten horrible minutes we surveyed a blank screen, my certainty growing that the lawyers were at it again and that Uncle Arthur's glittering toy was not to be unwrapped for his delight. In the end it turned out that it was indeed a technical hitch, and *Manyana* was transmitted; but it is not an excitement which I recommend to the tyro-librettist.

NS We started work on *No Bed* and Caryl suggested Leslie Julian Jones as a principal composer. She also applied a divide-and-rule principle more common in the eclectic musicals of the '20s and '30s, enrolling Arthur Benjamin for a drinking song (always to her a 'Brindisi') and coaxing Larry Adler, who had just had a success with his film score for *Genevieve*, towards a setting for 'When Daisies Pied'.

CB I persuaded Ned that we should ask Leslie Julian Jones to compose some music for *No Bed*. Leslie had worked abortively with Brahms-Simon during the Blitz. He had also written and collated

[180]

the *Rise Above It* series of revues through which Hermione
Gingold glittered and Hermione Baddeley lovingly bumbled, at
the same period.

It so happened that Leslie J.J. was living in East Horsley, a
commuter belt community in Surrey, and that he and his second wife,
Hazel Gee (pronounced – by us – 'Ahzell Jay', because that was
how they pronounced her name when she choreographed for the
Folies Bergère), had joined a brave amateur dramatic group called
The Whips. From where it was but a whip-crack away to the try-out
of *No Bed For Bacon*, of which all that remains with me was an
unfortunate moment when the leading Whip converged upon my stall
with the obligatory bouquet, which I failed to see because my head
was turned the other way.

Inevitably a tape was made of a performance. Of course the
stockbroker who made the tape was enormously proud of his
achievement. He took it to Bernard Miles, a mere Mister in those
days. 'What d'ye think of *this* for a piece of recording?' the stockbroker
had swanked.

None of us knew of this enterprise. But one afternoon a
determinedly rustic voice telephoned: 'I'm Bernard Miles and I want
to open my theatre at Puddle Dock with a production of your musical
about Shakespeare.'

I did not believe him. All of Ned's generation left Oxford, if not
with a first-class honours degree, at least with a creditable
imitation of Edith Evans, John Gielgud, Ken Tynan; this had to be
some party-smartie doing his Bernard Miles.

'Oi doant want any of your music,' added Miles, carried away by
the rural rumble which from time to time takes over his Ben Jonsonian
personality. This – the rejection of Leslie J.J. in favour of a composer
of his own choice – had the ring of truth about it. 'Addison –
that's your man,' he was saying.

Jock Addison, John on our film screens, was and always has been
very much his own man. Indeed, I am still unable to persuade
him to compose the music for the opera I can see so clearly in *The
Three Sisters*. And this in spite of my acceding to his plea that I should
write a one-act opus for two contralti, a harp and a grand piano, for
a commission for an *avant garde* combo due to perform it in the
Wigmore Hall three weeks from yesterday when he was unable to
find me at home to answer my telephone. I settled on a one-act
farce by Feydeau; at least it had the benefit of no one else but me

introducing that frolicsome author to that usually staid concert-giving hall. This was the reason I found myself rising and bowing, in a mercifully all but empty Wigmore Hall, to what must have been the thinnest smatter of applause ever heard in it and a series of undoubted snores issuing from a revered critical nose.

Where was I?

Well, that – not the Wigmore Hall but the whimsically rustic accents of the future Lord Miles – was what started a regular pilgrimage to Puddle Dock for Brahms and Sherrin. We would go down to brood tenderly over the bricks and rubble that were to suffer a river change into something less than Shakespeare's rich and strange, but still a plain and reasonable, building in which to house the magic of the theatre. Lovingly we would breathe on a stone or pat a brick and tell each other unbelievingly – we were right there – that we were the Chosen People. Chosen, that is, by this great Man of the Theatre (old Bernard!) to write the musical that was to be played before the Queen and Prince Philip at the opening of the City of London's – and old Bernard's – own theatre.

'She'll come down by bloody barge' – old Bernard took on the gaze of a seer – 'and young Philip, he'll be sitting there beside her, and they'll come to anchor at Puddle Dock and she'll turn to him and say, "Philip, this is bloody marvellous."'

Ned and I exchanged dark looks. Somehow the royal dialogue failed to convince, but, as we said to one another afterwards, old Bernard was a Man of the Theatre, and possibly we were being obtuse.

These pilgrimages were threaded together between knots of pain that I have come to recognize as a play-writer's rosary, something akin to a string of worry-beads: the knots standing for pangs of indigestion, brought on in this case by old Bernard's sharp white wine and greasy cold sausages, which we suffered gladly from the hands of this Man of the Theatre.

These Mermaid working luncheons, moreover, supplied the perfect justification for Skid's favourite proverb: 'It is better to travel hopefully than to arrive.' It was – much! *No Bed For Bacon* told the story of Viola, a spirited girl banished in a fit of jealousy from the Court of Elizabeth I of England. Disguised as a boy, Viola was taken on in Burbage's Theatre, 'the great Globe itselffe', to become 'the first girl-boy player'. There she fell in love with Master Will Shakespob, Shikspar – he never could arrive at a decision on how his name should be spelled – and he with her. And if that is not 'all you know and all you need to know', go out and buy the book.

One of the first songs we wrote for this musical *No Bed* was a duet for Queen Elizabeth and her woolly-minded, elderly lady-in-waiting, Lady Meanwell, as they endeavoured to arrive at a firm decision on what gown she should wear to receive the Earl of Essex. It was one of few moments in our adaptation that 'old Bernard' approved, reading it aloud and with some relish in a voice as near Edith Evans's as he could manage.

Elizabeth (sforzando): Mean-Well!
Lady Meanwell puts her head round the door of the Queen's attiring closet.
Elizabeth: What did I wear at Tilbury the day I made that speech?
Meanwell: Ma'am, your peach.
Elizabeth: And what did I wear on the day we repelled the Armada?
Meanwell: I cannot remember, Ma'am.
Elizabeth: Think harder, Meanwell,
           The Armada, Meanwell,
           Now when did I wear that cloth of gold Drake brought
           back in the *Golden Hind*?
Meanwell: Ma'am, you didn't. You changed your mind.
Elizabeth: Me, change my mind? . . . And what did I wear at
           Barkingside?
Meanwell: The gown you wore at Bow.
Elizabeth: You let me wear it *twice*?
Meanwell: It looked so nice!
Elizabeth: Oh! And what did I wear at Ashridge House when my
           sister held me there?
Meanwell: Grey, Ma'am, your grey.
Elizabeth: Ah yes, my grey
           All day, all day . . .

Time went by, as time is wont, and the summonses to the Mermaid site continued – so did the indigestion. And each time we met, old Bernard topped his last preposterous idea with another even more preposterous suggestion, made in a variety of accents according to which role he was seeing himself in at the time – hayseed, nautical, riparian, Shakespearean (Prospero?) or Burbage. Did old Bernard require us to enlarge old Burbage? If so, it was only to cancel the order at our next meeting: 'No, no – I see I was mistaken then – but now I've got it . . .'

Came the day – and it was before the stage went topless – when the Man of the Theatre greeted us yet again with: 'Got it! Shakespeare says to the boy player, "Bare thy bloody breast!" and she can't because she's got *two* (descriptive gesture), you see!'

Only to greet us at our next meeting with the customary: 'No, no – I was wrong. I see it now. I don't want any words from you. Only quotations from *him* – the Bard – I see it clearly – what you must give me is an under-water, over-air tapestry of words from Shakespeare's plays.'

Our gazes took counsel of each other. Man of the Theatre was all very well, but there were limits. A Man of the Theatre could be wrong. It had been known. Next morning we took a step that must have staggered old Bernard. Skint at the time though we were, we sent back his option money. With it went a civil (he was, after all, a Man of the Theatre) explanation. Since we saw no way of writing the play he wanted we could only, in honesty, send his option money back. It was, I think, only £75 between the two of us.

And so the Mermaid arose – most un-Botticelli-like – out of its sea of rubble; happily starting with a success, *Lock Up Your Daughters*. Within its confines old Bernard trundled on a lot of plays, but only occasionally was a production I saw there cast and mounted adequately according to my own critical standards.

NS But the saga of *No Bed* was not over. We had lost Leslie Julian Jones and failed to gain Jock Addison. Meanwhile, we had written a kind of *Beggars' Opera*, *The Little Beggars*, first for radio under the careful direction of Charles Lefeux, the music arranged by Max Saunders, and the whole thing performed by kids (and Alec McCowen); and then for BBC Television with the same director. David Hemmings – along with Michael Crawford, one of the kids in the radio production – was already a veteran of the Aldeburgh Festival.

CB Then around choirboy age, he had a tendency to adenoids which in no way impeded the sweetness of his alto voice. He was a pupil of the Cone-Ripman Arts Educational School, and I kept interceding for him when the headmistress, an upright and charitable lady, pondered asking him to leave. I had been impressed with his musicianship, but in spite of my championship it was a near thing when she caught him standing at a bus stop with his arm round a Cone girl's waist. Useless for me to point out that it might have been worse – a boy. He had already appeared in the Aldeburgh Festival's *Albert Herring*, an amusing opera based on *Le Rosier de Madame Husson* by de Maupassant – a work I would still like to turn into a ballet. Britten and Pears, too, recognized the putative musician in the child. One day they said to him indulgently: 'Well, David, what do you want to do when you're grown up?'

'I want to be a doctor,' David replied without hesitation.

The two good gentlemen, their minds filled with thoughts of the services to humanity of a medical man and wondering how the high-minded boy would deal with the question, asked him why.

'So's I can see all those women naked,' he is reported to have replied.

To return to our ballad-opera, *Little Beggars* was highly regarded at the BBC. Eventually it was re-recorded in stereo as the Corporation's entry for the Italia Prize. We failed to win. As a sequel we wrote *Bigger Beggars* for an adult cast and sent it to RADA. John Fernald, at that time the Principal, agreed to stage it with his students, where it focused attention on a very young Tom Courtney. We put in a new song, 'Where Do We Go (To Make Love in the City)?', and changed the title to *Shut Up and Sing*. There was one snag – a big one. We needed a cello and RADA had no finance for this. So Brahms drew a deep breath and wrote to Mr Eddie Day of Francis, Day and Hunter, publishers of the new song, suggesting that if he would give them £100 RADA could provide a showcase for this certain hit. I daresay he smiled a grim smile, but like a paternal angel he paid up.

Denmark Street – Tin Pan Alley – the haunt of music publishers had a strange fascination for us. Was it not Denmark Street to which we were to take a nervous producer seeking backing for one of our revues? It was; and as we sat with him in the publisher's outer office, through the paper-thin walls we heard the object of our solicitation shouting: 'Money! He'll get no money out of me! All he's got is my name on a little piece of paper.' Our producer fled – we stayed to ponder whether this piece of effrontery was more or less sophisticated an argument than the famous: 'A gentleman's agreement isn't worth the paper it's written on.'

Denmark Street; the tune of 'Where Do We Go?' started out to

the American folk tune, 'Git Along, Little Dogies'. Brahms
hummed it to Sherrin, Sherrin baritoned it back to Brahms.
Sherrin's ear is unreliable, and as it winged its way to and fro, like an
inebriated shuttlecock, it became more and more debased. Finally,
Brahms said: 'Ned! We've got an original tune here.'

When they had finished laughing they went off in search of a
rehearsal pianist and sopranoed and baritoned it to him. He fitted it
out in arpeggios and twiddles. Now it so happened that the rehearsal
pianist had been twilighting: by day he worked as a song-plugger for
the old established and paternal firm of Francis, Day and Hunter
in Charing Cross Road. One day, unbeknown to its creators, he
played it over to Mr Eddie Day, who sent for them. The words of
the lyric were clear, simple and repetitive:

Where do we go to make love in a city?
Where do we go when we want to make love?
There's streets and there's walls in the heart of a city,
But you want somewhere soft when you want to make love.
So where do we go when we're making our loving?
Where do we go when we want to make love?

It seems to come down to us, in the age of stripping off, as a *cri de
cœur* of touching innocence.

Well, the song plugger got down to giving his boss what he felt
was a hard-sell performance and the boss bore down on the
song-plugger's shoulders: 'Cut out the twiddly bits,' the boss said
to the song plugger; 'give us a chance to hear what the tune really
is.'

Brahms and Sherrin exchanged dark looks. However, 'Little
Dogies' had got lost in their humming and baritoning, and the boss
seemed quite satisfied. But so far we had written only a chorus.
'What we need now,' Mr Eddie said sunnily, 'is a nice verse.
Something romantic, Lovers Lane – that sort of thing.'

For the first – and last – time since I've known him, Sherrin
looked alarmed – after all this was our first and only tune.
However, Brahms had a plan. She could see what they could do.
'We just take our tune and invert it,' she told the usually
resourceful Sherrin on the way back to the studio. Once more they
sopranoed and baritoned to the moonlighting song-plugger. He
sketched out a stave on the back of an envelope. The next afternoon

they went back to Mr Eddie's office, and the plugger played. 'We'll fit the words, if you like the tune,' they told him.

'Like it? I *know* it. I've published it. It's Julian's tune from *Salad Days* – Julian Slade – "I Sit in the Sun",' he croaked. So much for debasing and inverting.

A couple of years later we played with another folk song for our black Cinderella, *I Gotta Shoe*, and took it to another publisher a couple of doors down Denmark Street. He fidgeted as he listened.

'Hold on!' he said. 'I've published that tune.'

'Don't worry,' we replied, 'we'll drop it.'

'No, no! That's not the point,' he countered. 'I'm just wondering if I can sue!'

Fortunately, 'Nobody's Business', in its original folk version, is not in copyright. Saved by the bell! *Cindy Ella* or *I Gotta Shoe*, whether we were doing it on radio with Lis Welch, Bertice Reading, Cy Grant, and Lucille Mapp; in the theatre with Lis, Cleo Laine, Cy and George Browne; on television with the same cast; between hard-covers, in a novel beautifully illustrated by Tony Walton; or reviving it at the Criterion Theatre; in whatever its incarnation, *Cindy Ella* has always been one of my favourites.

Small wonder that I long to write a second pantomime – the first having been an all-black job. But if I ever do, how to equal the elegant, generous, stylish Elisabeth Welch – Lis to all the world – whose ageless singing has enchanted many generations of playgoers, and whose mutinous arguments have diverted many a rehearsal; or the wonderful Cleo Laine – who was the only Cinderella ever to go to the ball eight months gone with child, in an apricot maternity gown. (The child was to become a daughter, Jacqui Caryl.)

The pantomime I long to create differs from the norm in one respect: it will have a formidable Fairy Queen, caparisoned in a magenta velvet crinoline, of whom a timorous King Rat is clearly in a state of knee-knocking terror. Ned and I have discussed such an entertainment once or twice. The nearest we have got so far is a title, *Dick Whittington and his Dog*.

One of Caryl's quirkier ventures in the late '50s was an idea for a three-handed play featuring Diana Dors and two men (unspecified) who were to enact, in a confined space, a steamy drama which had no name but which she always referred to as *Lust in a Lighthouse*. Our working partnership was still young and, although I met with some disapproval, I was allowed to insist that this panting triangle at close quarters was not my meat. Undaunted, Caryl took John Osborne, fresh from his success with *Look Back in Anger*, out to lunch and tried to sell the idea to him. He, too, failed to rise to the bait; but endeared himself to Caryl by confessing that he was still getting a thrill from being able to afford to ride in a taxi.

By the beginning of the '60s our work together had fallen into a pattern. I was working in Birmingham for ATV, travelling north on Monday mornings and coming back on Thursday or Friday nights, depending on my schedule. On the night of my return we would invariably meet, usually seeing a play, a ballet or a film and having supper, in order to 'get our minds together'. We would then reckon to put in a couple of fairly solid days of work, starting with breakfast meetings and finishing with a last session at a coffee bar near Euston Station on the Monday morning before I set off again. Sunday lunch provided a break, as at this time Caryl invariably spent it with Charles Landon, her old fiancé.

As our working relationship developed, she became more demanding of time and commitment. Writing was never my principal interest, but it was her life. I could always guarantee an explosion by protesting that I was 'not really a writer'. While her own discipline in dragging herself to her crowded work table was firm, she harboured ambitions to produce or direct in whatever medium she was working. She inveigled herself on to a BBC training course for directors, argued herself into an associate producer's role for a music series on Associated Rediffusion TV; and she always tried to hold out for a director's contract on our stage ventures. She seemed oblivious of the fact that she was temperamentally ill-suited to any of these jobs. On the other hand, the enthusiasm which she could generate and the encouragement she could hand out to actors with whom she was working was impressive.

When I stopped commuting to Birmingham and joined the BBC (on her recommendation), our work pattern spread over the week as well as the weekend, often with Mondays and Thursdays as 'free nights'. By herself she adapted for radio *Trottie True*, *Away Went Polly*, and her unpublished novel *Look Back to Lyttletown*, a poetic portrait of a great house embracing life above and below stairs (her failure to find a publisher for the book was a major disappointment), as well as a frothy version of the Brahms-Simon fantasy *Titania Has A Mother*, starring Phyllis Neilson-Terry.

[188]

B Ned and I gave Phyll luncheon at Simpsons in Piccadilly when she was playing the lead in *Titania Has A Mother* in the studio next door. We were talking about Donald Wolfit with whom she had played her Lady in the Scottish Tragedy. Agate wrote that it was the best he had seen.

'I was playing an intimate scene with Donald,' she told us; 'it was after the murder of Duncan and I put my arm around his shoulder, to hearten the Thane. But Donald shrugged it off. "Don't touch me!" he said to me in the wings, and so,' she told us, 'I didn't. But I had to do something. I was his wife. If I couldn't support him physically, all I could do was listen.'

She cupped her ear in a generous gesture which stretched her long arms in a sort of salute, nothing abashed by the stares of the other diners.

'And that was Donald's mistake,' she emphasized, 'because when I listen, everybody looks at me!'

It must have been a riveting moment.

S Caryl wrote an amusing historical piece, *Tomorrow, Mr Tompion, and About Time Too*, for radio and television. Together we adapted a Brahms-Simon story about suffragettes, *The People in the Park*, for radio; we were commissioned to make a sound adaptation of Labiche's *The Italian Straw Hat* for radio, for the perverse reason that Val Gielgud, the Head of Drama, had such happy memories of the silent film; and we cobbled together an uncomfortable series of Light Entertainment shows called *Duchess Don't Allow*, which featured Caryl's old sparring partner from *A Bullet in the Ballet*, Ivy St Helier, as the owner of a decaying music hall in North London endeavouring to cope with the changing scene of strip shows and rock and roll. We spent a deal of time 'researching' at the old 'Met', the Chelsea Palace, and Collins's Music Hall in Islington, where we were shooed out of the wings by Peaches Page's aggrieved husband while she was singing her famous nude version of 'One Fine Day'.

We found radio a good way of subsidizing the first stages of writing and selling a stage show. *Cindy Ella* or *I Gotta Shoe* started in this way, and so did an entertainment called *Mr Tooley Tried*, woven around the Crippen case, which we were later to adapt for the theatre – only to be pipped at the post by a Wolf Mankowitz musical on the same subject called *Belle*. Our practice in such circumstances was to rework the

[189]

material as a novel. This one became an account of the crime and the year in which it took place, which we called *Rappel 1910*. We followed the same course with a piece about Admiral Benbow called *Benbow Was His Name* in which Sir Michael Hordern appeared on radio and Sir Donald Wolfit on television, his penultimate major screen performance.

Caryl had a particular admiration and fondness for Donald which led her to a comprehensive assessment of her relationship with him in her memoirs.

CB To speak of Sir Donald Wolfit is to think instantly of his Lear. He was in truth a very foolish fond old man; his majesty behind him, his human fallibility and the wretched infirmities of his old age upon him; and yet in everything a father and a King.

Gielgud has played his classical roles at Stratford-upon-Avon, on Broadway, the Old Vic, the National, and the Globe and Haymarket theatres. Olivier has played these theatres, and others, too; and both these leaders of the stage have been handsomely equipped. Wolfit has trundled Hamlets, Benedicks, Lears, Volpones, Othellos through the provinces.

Where is his great Othello now? A threadbare gown stained with greasepaint crushed in a mildewing theatre basket. But it has adorned a man who played the great ones, greatly; who has given the theatre, wherever it may have been, his Lear, Othello, Volpone, Malvolio, Benedick, Pastor Manders, Bottom, First Grave Digger, Iago, and a dozen or more characters, all of them infinitely men of gut and blood.

Poetry to Wolfit was drama. He could catch your heart between beats. When his Othello strode into the centre of clashing steel crying, 'Keep up your bright swords', his voice stilled the turning world; and the completion of the sentence, 'for the dew will rust them', fell into a silence deeper than plummets sound. I did not see his Hamlet, but I speculate that had I heard him speak the Prince's tender line to the ghost of his father, '*Rest, rest, perturbed spirit*', I would have found myself in tears.

But Wolfit, even when he recorded the sonnets, would not allow himself to be the Voice Beautiful spouting poetry. He would never let feeling dwindle into mere decoration. The agony in the cry of Volpone, the Fox of Venice, greeting the sentence of the Court of Justice with, '*This is called mortifying a fox*', has passed into theatre history. Already Wolfit's Volpone had no use for living and would be rid of breath. He gave up the ghost with the breath that left the swooning body of the Venetian prankster.

In an effort to convey to a new generation of playgoers the essence of what I found in the acting of Donald Wolfit, I shall have recourse to the profile of the actor and his work in my book about the theatre: *The Rest of the Evening's My Own*:

Wolfit is no nibble of an actor – he is a good blow-out, a cut-and-come-again, a chicken-soup-with-Mindel of a man. A man to step back from the canvas, assess the sitter, and fill the space with great bold strokes, to paint a character twice as large as life. And if I call him a stomach of a man, I do not allude to a certain elder-statesmanly rotundity which overtook his later years, but a man with a proper appetite, a gusto for a part.

His face? A round, broad-eyebrowed, histrionic moon. His body? Thick-set and serviceable. His voice? A passage played on an organ with, towards the end of his acting days, a certain roughness underlying it. His heart – and now we come to the root of the man – was the heart of King Lear. *Macbeth*, for poetry almost my favourite play within the canon, could never be my favourite rôle for Wolfit, with its nail-biting inglorious heart of one who would murder for his own advancement. But Othello – there is a different kettle of greasepaint – his heart bursting with the pity and pride of black Othello. The heart that would be limber with the rich-tongued rogue, Volpone. The withered heart of melancholy, pinched and frost-touched, aspiring only to over-topple, of his Malvolio. The heart, in short, to play comedy to crack the ribs and tragedy to rack the heart in us.

Then never doubt that this actor was all actor – a great actor. And that all these characters I have noted and many others, and all of them steeped deep in Drama, have only their broad eyebrows and his devotion to them in common; and, of course, the spotlight that pins them to our memory because to think of Wolfit in a play is to remember a giant in a spotlight by reason of his gigantic acting; not of course to everyone's taste, for he was no thrower-away of well-considered trifles. Nor was he good-taste-ridden. I have seen him play Giles Overreach with a painted-on moustachio – haste, perhaps, but much more probably the *enfoutism* which is so much in the rogue player's mind. Good

taste and Oedipus, even in decline, do not go hand in hand, and
Wolfit was a magnificent Oedipus. But a certain delicacy, born
of dedication and good sense, have combined to see to it that
I have never found him lewd, arch, sniggering or unsexed by
felinity.

CB Soon after the war a commission from *Picture Post* to create an
in-depth profile presented a built-in excuse to study the last of the
touring actor-managers at work in close quarters. This fascinating
exercise I could not refuse. In the late '40s Donald was presenting his
Company in his classical repertory in Camden Town at the Old
Bedford Theatre, as sanctified by the painter Sickert. On the telephone
he sounded wary. Obviously he was casting me as the West End foe
and fashionable spy, out to do a hatchet-job. So I decided to stalk my
prey with a Snark's thimble and care, and to choose the initial impact
in which to announce my presence with a hunter's skill. To this
end I haunted the house sedulously in careful anonymity.

I had heard about Wolfit's miserly thriftiness, his hogging of stage
and limelight, and the rest of the actor-laddie claptrap. But in all my
dealings with him I found the reverse. He was never miserly with
me, but treated me *en prince*.

I daresay I had seen him in two or three roles – Lear, Volpone,
Othello leap to mind; oh, and a dreadful Macbeth (although even his
Scottish Tragedy had its clarion moments). I remember in particular
Volpone's opening line, '*Good-morning to the day*', in which
'*Good-morning*' was separated by quite three minutes of business
before the closing words of the cue, '*to the day*'. And there was an
off-stage effect in his Master Builder of a crescendo of his footsteps
before his first entrance.* Very effective.

One night, doing my homework, I was sitting in the auditorium
for the first part of the Scottish Tragedy before going to the bar in
the interval to listen to what the sparse audience thought of Wolfit's
Macbeth. Behind me two formidable women, probably cleaning
ladies, were keeping up their own form of running commentary.

The Thane had been about to give his dagger speech. Wolfit's
way of giving the old warhorse rein was to advance upstage and give
the gates of the castle a good shaking, to turn, to advance to the
footlights to gather his audience in the strength of his gaze, to back

* cf. Peter Hall's *Diaries* – miked shoes for Richardson's Master Builder.

towards the o.p. side of the stage, to launch himself with a little run to the dread portal, to stagger, to halt, to descry the dagger in the air, and at last to go into the speech, '*Is this a dagger which I see before me, the handle towards my hand?*' – at which one of the good ladies sitting behind me observed to the other: 'Coo! 'E's seeing things!'

Armed with this endearing anecdote, I decided the time had come for me to introduce myself, and so, accordingly, I went back stage at the end of the piece and knocked on his dressing-room door.

'Come in,' said the star, as mellifluously as he could through the water into which his head was plunged. I announced my identity to his broad back. I told him how much I was enjoying that Camden Town season, and thus pleasingly prefaced I proceeded to my ''E's seeing things' bit, fondly imagining it would be received with gargantuan laughter. Not at all. Wolfit shook the last of the water from his head. He turned round to face me for the first time.

'Ah! Miss Brahms,' he intoned – almost sang – 'the *ill-u-s-i-on* of the Theatre!' From that time forth, through the weeks that followed and to the last days of his life, Donald Wolfit could not have been more of an ally to me.

It was much bandied about that the shoestring company with which he surrounded himself was chosen to set off his own performance, but what his critics discounted was Wolfit's way of extending the 'illusion of the Theatre'. He viewed life as we know it, if not through rose-coloured spectacles (for, make no mistake, his larger-than-life method of acting the classics reaped a rowdy audience at times), at least from the centre of a follow-spot.

He took me to his Holloway Road hide-out at which the company was rehearsing; it was a commodious eighteenth-century building called the Athenaeum, where they were rehearsing *The Taming of the Shrew*. Sitting on the side lines, he pointed out the merits of the cast. 'You see that fellow over by the door? He's going to be another Martin Harvey, Caryl.' I blinked. Martin Harvey to me was one of the Edwardian picture-postcards in my collection. There is no doubt in my mind that had Wolfit needed to define his own acting he would have said: 'You see that actor in the limelight stage-centre – he's another Henry Irving, but much better.' Since I could not have seen Irving for myself, I have no doubt that Wolfit would have been right.

Wolfit, when he had got a little used to my questioning, led me up to the loft of the Athenaeum of the North. 'This,' he said, 'is

the wardrobe.' He spread an arm. He opened a wicker
travelling-skip. How many times had it served to house Falstaff?
'And this,' he indicated the trunk, 'is where we keep it.'

'You do not have costumes designed for each production?'

'Designed, she says,' the actor-manager told the ceiling.
'Designed!' he repeated, infinitely pitying. 'This is a stock company.
We travel. The cast dives into this basket and fits up with any
costume suitable to the character.'

Then he fished out a once-white vest with a crimson heart
appliquéd on to its middle: 'This is worn by Rosalind in the Forest of
Arden. And this,' he pounced upon a stained and crumpled handful
of draped furnishing satin, 'is the costume worn by little Joan
Greenwood when she gave her Juliet – see, there are still pearls on
it. She sat and stitched them on all through rehearsals. When she
left the company she asked if she might keep it. Of course I would
not allow that. "I'll tell you what we'll do," I told the dear child, "you
shall wear it whenever you come to *us* to play Juliet."'

(I borrowed this situation when I wrote my book on Sarah
Siddons, *Enter A Dragon, Stage Centre*, in which there was a scene
where Sarah begged to be allowed to take a plum-coloured taffeta
costume, and Tate Wilkinson, 'The Wandering Patentee', would not
allow it.)

One of my happiest memories of Donald – but they are all happy
– was the afternoon he embarked on kitting-out an army among
my tea-cups – he had climbed up the endless stairs to my fourth-floor
Outer Circle, Regent's Park flat to discuss appearing on television in
our adaptation of our novel, *Benbow Was His Name*. And *en passant*
he described to us how to furnish forth an army in a single suit of mail
armour and a sufficiency of steel netting, on the lines of 'One man
wears a mailed glove – and don't forget there will be two of them.
Another carries a shield, and there'll be two knee-protectors, too –
that will be ample for a couple of soldiers . . . and there's the banner
holders!'

Drawing-room *politesse* in a performance was not for him. He was
born in the astrakhan collar of the actor-laddie, a little the worse
for wear on tour but nonetheless astrakhan – the imperial purple of
the stage.

When Ned and I dropped round to his dressing-room to ask if
he would give his blessing to our plan to invite his wife, Rosalind Iden,
to play Elizabeth I in the second mounting of our musical, *No Bed*

For Bacon, he shook an indulgent but nevertheless dissenting head. 'Rosalind,' he pronounced (with a long 'i'), 'has a curious Oriental disposition to sing in the minor key.'

I relished particularly his account of their two-handed *Othello* – a touring recital venture. 'Did it with Rosalind,' he said.

'And some wily cutting?' I hazarded.

'Gave 'em the man – and that's the play.'

But Rosalind Iden was not going to be ignored. 'And Desdemona,' she claimed with some of her rarely used firmness.

Donald indulged her. 'And Desdemona,' he acknowledged.

He returned to the drift of the story. 'Othello!'

He paused – Macready could not have timed that pause better – to let the full magnitude of the concept sink in.

'Othello! Cut out Iago – did the whole thing with lights.'

It was a sad, but proud task for me to write his BBC obituary programme with Michael Elliot, featuring Dame Sybil Thorndike, Richard Burton, Tom Courtney, Harold Pinter, Eric Porter, Ronnie Fraser, Ronald Harwood, Brian Rix and Tyrone Guthrie. To remember Wolfit, the most under-valued actor of his times, is to remember half a hundred moments of compelling magic and the other half of unsung kindnesses. This actor was a giant, stalking his stage. As Max Beerbohm said of Herbert Campbell: 'He always seemed to be the offspring of some mystic union between Beef and Thunder'.

We shall not look upon his like again.

s When we returned to *No Bed For Bacon*, picking up the pieces from the Mermaid débâcle, Caryl went on a short talent-spotting jag, looking for a replacement for the ditched Julian Jones and the barely involved Jock Addison.

b Composers? It is with a diffident pen that I approach the subject of the Master of the Queen's Music.

s Indeed, she paused for a paragraph before getting down to business.

b In fact, I shall put the distinguished, highly talented and bonhomous Malcolm Arnold between me and the cherub-like figure of that other Malcolm – Williamson. I suspect Malcolm Arnold of sending me up rotten but I think – and hope – affectionately. He composed the mellifluous score when Ned and I wrote a television adaptation of Schnitzler's *Anatol* which we called *Parasol*. One day we arrived at Ben Nesbit's office (Ben was Malcolm's publisher) to find that most generous-in-every-sense-of-the-word composer and his publisher tossing a toothsome secretary across the room into each other's arms. That plump little person flew through the air, if not with the greatest of ease, certainly with the squeakiest of protests.

NS Not even that endearing recollection of Malcolm Arnold could put off the evil day.

CB Well, now for it.

Our relationship with Malcolm Williamson, destined to compose the score for *No Bed For Bacon*, was full of surprises from the outset. Ned and I were skint – it can happen – and so, it soon turned out, was Malcolm Williamson, who immediately announced that he was an alcoholic. He may or may not have been, but that was his contention.

I found him by the simple expedient of telephoning Boosey and Hawkes, the music publishers, and asking them if they had on their books a young, educated musician with a gift for melody and an interest in musicals. They sent Malcolm. The first time we worked together we met in an empty BBC Television studio at Lime Grove – to save money on piano hire – and I admit that I had to pull my raised eyebrow back and attempt to take in my stride the fact that no sooner had he arrived than he strode behind the cyclorama already set for 'Tonight' (at that time the BBC's crack programme, on which Ned was working) where he relieved himself. A Bohemian, I explained to the arc lamps on high – it seemed the only safe place to look – and an Australian Bohemian at that!

Our masterpiece completed, we sent it to the beyond words beautiful Theatre Royal in King Street, which housed and still houses the Bristol Old Vic, and sat back, sure of success.

Back it came with a baffled note: Why, it demanded, had we written only one act? We raced to the files – they were right, for there in its pristine crispness was Act 2. We rushed to the post with it, forgetting in our enthusiasm that Act 1 was now with us.

Down at King Street, John Moody, the director of the theatre, said 'yes', to Act 2 – we were to be directed by Frank Dunlop. The waywardness of Williamson – perhaps a title for a melodrama of the Australian gold rush? – reached its climax after a Saturday morning rehearsal. There had been some disagreement between the collaborators. We went to a pub to talk it over. A miracle: Malcolm offered to buy a round of drinks. I should have scented danger. He bought his own drink last, a pint of Bristol beer which he proceeded to pour over my head. I was quick enough to stop Ned, a large man, from hitting him, and I got him and myself out into the street. It was a steaming hot day and the smell of beer filled the air. It was all right for Ned – he was going home to his parents, who lived nearby. I was staying with my cousin Pearl, now a magistrate. The smell of beer did not leave me all that sweltering weekend – but Pearl took it in her stride. Obviously this was how artists and Bohemians behaved.

The production did not transfer to London. Two further echoes from the past remain to be recounted. We tried *No Bed* again at Croydon and Golders Green some years later, with not one but two new composers – Dave Lee and John Scott. The day after the opening the notices were not good; and a wire arrived out of the blue from Leslie Julian Jones – voice from two pasts – with words to the effect that humiliating failure was no more than we deserved.

Ned dealt with it in his own way – he waited for three months, and then got his secretary to write apologizing for the oversight: 'Mr Sherrin is abroad. He has asked me to thank you for your kind telegram of good wishes which had been mislaid . . . he and Miss Brahms were so touched to hear that you were thinking of us . . . so kind, etc.'

I did not speak to our director, Frank Dunlop, for a very long time after Bristol; and I vowed that I would not review one of his productions, not trusting myself to be fair. However, one day some tickets arrived from the *Guardian* who wanted me to cover the London opening of *Joseph and His Amazing Technicolour Dreamcoat* at the Roundhouse. Off we went. Ned, who usually knows everything, said nothing. At the end of an enchanting evening, we hurried away so that I could write my piece.

'Who directed it?' I asked as an afterthought.

'Frank Dunlop,' said Ned.

'Oh my God!'

Well, it was a good production so he got a good notice. A week later I was at the Royal Court. Frank Dunlop came running up the steps after me.

'Caryl, Caryl,' he called, 'thank you so much for that notice. It was very generous.'

'Don't count on it again,' I heard myself saying coldly. 'My generosity is like Christmas. It comes and goes very quickly.'

NS Towards the end of her life Caryl had further occasion to animadvert on the eccentricities of Australians. She received a deal of fan mail from that country, but one particular approach had a more practical end in view:

CB I was entertained right royally by one of my Australian readers. The rickety table at her Battersea digs positively groaned under its load of goodies – only I was not hungry. I had put up a strong resistance to visiting the good lady at all. She must have been hint-proof, snub-proof, and deaf to social nuances over the telephone. It was soon made clear that I had been summoned to her bed-sitter to launch her protégé, a young Aussie with total recall and a one-man Dickens programme that she did not seem able to launch for herself.

'As I wrote to Emlyn Williams, he can't live forever,' she pointed out to me.

That must have endeared her to the splendid Dickensian no end.

NS It was after I had left Birmingham that Caryl's most concentrated activity in the musical theatre began. In her youth she had embraced the worlds of ballet, opera and classical theatre enthusiastically, but had despised the light musical theatre. Now, thrown into it and impressed by the new 'seriousness' of musical entertainment after *West Side Story* and *Gypsy*, she set herself to master a new form. While I was working on 'Tonight', she occasionally wrote topical parodies with me, or compiled medleys for special occasions with Peter Greenwell. Most often these were performed by Millicent Martin or David Kernan, or by both of them.

By the time I had moved on, via a brief stint with Light Entertainment during which we wrote the Schnitzler musical, *Anatol*, with Malcolm Arnold, she had begun to look on writing for television as her main source of income. She demanded to be included in these ventures and had an unrivalled ability to sulk if there was no place for her. She refused to visit the two stage musicals I directed which were put together by other hands – *Come Spy With Me* with Danny La Rue and *Only In America* with Bertice Reading. Indeed, we barely met during these episodes as she was quite unable to countenance any of my ventures in which she played no part. Most of our rows – which were not frequent, apart from regulation barbed sparring – occurred when she suspected some betrayal. For my part I held (more passionately as the years of collaboration yielded their own evidence) that I had proved my loyalty.

In her memoirs, Caryl picks up the theme of work in music in television.

My most sustained brush with song-writing took place around television studios – not theatres.

Far away and long ago, as Ira Gershwin with hindsight might have pinned it to time, there was this irreverent series of comment programmes. We who worked on them regularly never sought to raise their status by miscalling the songs and sketches which were their bone and sinew, 'Satire'. BBC1 mounted them and they owed their being to Donald Baverstock's optimistic foresight, Alasdair Milne's bulldog tenacity and his unfaltering loyalty to them, Ned Sherrin's ability to harness and drive on a complex of highly charged talents, and David Frost's hit-or-miss navigation of his personal pilgrimage to the top. Under their electric leadership, the rest of us tottered on. We emptied the pubs by 10.20 every Saturday night and we were taken off the air for going over the top so often that we sometimes felt we were the Board of Governors' nervous tic. Ned named the series 'That Was The Week That Was', 'Not So Much A Programme, More a Way of Life' and 'BBC 3', which had for a theme song 'It's All Been Done Before, But So Has Spring And Summer'.

For a long time TWTWTW was a hopeful expression on Donald Baverstock's rubicund countenance. He would catch Ned, who was directing cameras on the BBC's at that time crack programme 'Tonight', just as he was sloping off to work with me, with his 'Let's explore the new programme, boyo' – they don't come more Welsh from Welsh Wales than Baverstock.

At root, 'That Was The Week That Was' was a writer's programme. It created its own stars: Millicent Martin, David Frost, Bernard Levin, Willie Rushton, Lance Percival, Roy Kinnear and David Kernan for starters. Ned developed his writers. We were a close-knit team punctuated by *ad hoc* authors. A flag should have been hoist at the Television Centre each Saturday night (each Friday, Saturday and Sunday when 'Not So Much A

Programme' filled the slot) in a bright beam of white light, picking out the inscription 'In the beginning was the Word'.

We were a more or less fatalistic hard core, swinging on a pendulum somewhere between hope and fear according to whether our current offerings were still in or had been scrapped, the common enemy being time – and at times, I must confess, our artistes.

NS Caryl never took kindly to artistes who failed to see the possibilities in her material.

CB If an artiste took a dislike to the piece we had created, no amount of coaxing could make him or her comfortable in performance. Better to tuck it away for a bit, rejig for a different artiste if time and the topicality allowed. Sketches were easier – there would always be some clever guest-performer around the corner delighted to be invited to the programme. As Coral Browne said: 'It's like being invited to appear at Court.'

Bleary-brained and cotton-wool mouthed, we would browse through the Sunday papers – they would already have been briefly plundered on the air in the programme but there might be some disregarded paragraph which would serve for a line in our opener – Milly Martin singing a syncopated news-song, 'That Was The Week That Was'. A lyric was worked out over the telephone by Ned and me, with space left for Saturday's news story. Or maybe there might be some indication of a budding theme which would develop as the week flashed past. On Monday the hunt for writers was on.

NS In spite of her certainty that TWTWTW was a writer's programme, she became hugely admiring of the performers for whom she wrote and they, invariably thirty or forty years younger, were protective of her.

CB We had some splendid artistes before the cameras – Millicent Martin the perfect revue artiste, a singer who could dance and act anything that lay on the surface – no Lady Macbeth she; and Frost, whose skills in those, the earliest, days wobbled like a blancmange in an earth tremor. Frostie served as stand-up comedian, a role in which he fancied himself, why none of us knew; a political anchor man; also commentator and general utility. He wrote a lot of his own material and was never less than

courageous, to say the least of it; some would say to the point of
foolhardiness. But then we all had to find our form and in finding it
make fools of ourselves in those days – a habit which in the present
writer still holds, twenty years later.

My own rise from the ranks was by no means meteoric, though
for one of our initiating dry-runs Dave Lee (our regular musical
director) and I were told to weave the songs in Lionel Bart's 'Fings
Aint' Wot They Uster Be' with other similar tunes. Dave and I found
that four could be played simultaneously. But when first we went
on the air my sole brief was to write our opener over the telephone
with Ned for Milly Martin to sing:

> '*That was the week that was,*
> *It's over, let it go!*'

The music was by the Australian macrobioticist composer, Ron
Grainer. And that was it. This did not challenge or extend me at
all. So I bided my time. After all, it was a change of pace: wherever
we went we were fêted, altogether too much for the good of our souls.
I still smile sardonically when I recall the solid matron, old enough
to behave more sensibly, clutching at Ned's sleeve emoting: 'Let me
touch you, you marvellous man!'

Small wonder that at fifty-two he sometimes behaves like a spoilt
schoolboy who ought to be expelled.

I think that probably my first breakthrough arrived when I read
in one of the papers in the first week in 1963 that Madame
Tussaud's had melted down the wax of some personalities who had
slipped away from the public eye for a time. They included
Marilyn Monroe, Vivien Leigh, Lord Kilmuir, Marshall Voroshilov,
Lieutenant Colonel Harry Llewellyn, Selwyn Lloyd and the boxer
Terry Spinks. Their wax was re-processed for James Hanratty, the
M6 murderer. This made me very angry indeed. I find it so much
easier to write my kinds of occasional verse – news-condition verse
written not for the page but for the voice – when I am angry. This
is what came out:

> *Flames whisper now their threnody*
> *O'er Voroshilov and Vivien Leigh;*
> *Flames disrespectful, not for quelling*
> *Melt Lord Kilmuir and Colonel Llewellyn;*

And the consuming flame now shrinks
The waxwork form of Terry Spinks;
Flames are the cradle, flames the lace
That frame sweet Marilyn's radiant face

Ashes to ashes,
Wax to flame;
Selwyn and Marilyn the same.

Furnaceman, as you stir the pot,
Ponder a moment on this lot –
Brave travellers on Fame's golden tracks
Reduced, now, to amorphous wax.
Beauty, brains, brawn and personal symmetry
Boiled in your cauldron to anonymity,
The cheaper to achieve the morrow's
Attraction in the Chamber of Horrors.

Ashes to ashes,
Wax to flame;
Selwyn and Terry Spinks the same.
Spare, friend, a sigh for Vivien there,
But for sweet Marilyn a prayer.

In a voice quivering with rage I read those lines to Ned over the telephone. 'I'll ask Michael Redgrave for Saturday,' he said.

Michael Redgrave – so intelligent, so sensitive – I knew if he would come to the programme I would be home and dry. And so it was. From this moment on the lowly Caryl Brahms was allowed to lend a pen to anyone who could tolerate her, or who needed a little extra zip or a touch of elegance.

Michael Redgrave, Edith Evans, Max Adrian; it was in his invitations to the idols of the contemporary stage that Ned showed his great strength as an impresario, and I have a recording made by George Martin, the Beatles' recordist, to prove it. Ned even invited that very great lady of the stage, Dame Sybil Thorndike, to speak some of my verses. Many and endearing are the stories of Sybil. It is my loss that I saw her not in the high days of her acting, but only in trivia. She best describes those high days in a phrase of her own: 'I like to go bang-splash like the Greeks!' Continually on her lips was: 'I'm locking Lewis [Sir Lewis Casson] in his dressing-room until he has learned his lines.'

This was an action in which Ned resembled her strongly when the late Stephen Vinaver, the brilliant American writer, who imported into TWTWTW the form previously pioneered by Annie Ross which we called 'the Jazzer' – in which convoluted jazz rhythms were reflected in intricate words – returned unexpectedly to the States. He left in a hurry for reasons of health, and with no time to let Ned know, and Ned said to me: 'I'm locking you in a room until you've written the Saturday Jazzer for Milly.'

'But Ned, I can't!'

'No one else can, so you'll have to. And mind you get it done in time for her to learn it.'

That gave me two and a half days to produce a whole new art-form – new to me, that is – and Milly what time she could scrabble out of the day and a half in which she would be learning and rehearsing half a dozen sketches and the Brahms-Sherrin topical opener, before our band-call on Saturday night. And they talk of pressures! But then Milly was and is as able and remarkable in her own way as Ned and David Frost are in theirs.

Sybil Thorndike had worked with Ned and me earlier and, perhaps even more unexpectedly in those days, with John Dankworth in a radio play we had written, *The Sunday Market*, in which she took the part of an upper-crust antique lady selling off the treasures of the family home. The papers were full of photographs of Dame Sybil ostensibly playing John Dankworth's saxophone – an exercise in which certainly she was not required to indulge during the play. Most of them were captioned, 'Thorndike sings Dankworth'. Some years later I was asked by the Dankworths to decant the Dame at the church in Wavendon where she was to read some poems as a part of their All-Music Festival. She armed herself with a shelf-full of books and we drove down to the outskirts of Milton Keynes together. I was astonished that, waiting to enter the church from the platform end, she clutched my hand to give her confidence. I should, of course, have known that like the true artist she was, she would be nervous no matter how often she had given recitals of poetry. After all, Mrs Hookham once told me that Fonteyn was always nervous before she danced a classical role at her home base, the Royal Opera House. The two Dames, Sybil and Edith, appeared together in the long run of the comedy *The Waters of the*

Moon in the '50s under the aegis of H. M. Tennant: and it is Dame Edith who speaks my lines on the recording of 'Lay Waste the Lilies', verses written on hearing of plans to redevelop Pavlova's old London home:

Must they lay waste the lilies?
Where once Pavlova's swans went swanning by
Set up their glass-walled tower in the sky;
Uproot Pavlova's garden? Banish the blackbird –
From Golders Hill to Greenwich none is heard.
Fill in the lake where sunning swan could preen
To the attentive dancer on the green.
Obliterate, now that her swan-song's done,
The Ballerina, pausing in the sun.

City-builders, who dream crystal and steel,
Dream high, build high, sail high,
And snatch a new dimension from the sky,
And London has sprouted a thin forest of glass –
Stiff cubic trees; hutches for humans.
But what can a hutch say to the heart? Reiterate
A steep steel right to dominate,
Where on a lawn that's gone
Pavlova, in a green world, watched a swan.

Typical of Ned under pressure – when is he not? – that he placed my dedication to Christopher Hassall in the TWTWTW book under the wrong set of verses.

I can no longer recall just what it was that provoked a letter accusing Bernard Levin and me of anti-semitism. It was, suggested the writer, people like us who make people who do not like Jews write rude comments about them on walls. But I do remember Bernard's comment: 'Tell the writer Caryl and I slip out at night and write the insults ourselves.'

Anyway, Bernard dealt with the matter very strongly in a piece on the programme and Ned told me to write a song as an endpiece. I decided that a parody could best do this.

And did those feet in ancient time
Walk upon Israel's mountains green?

And was the swarthy lamb of God
On Israel's pleasant pastures seen?
And did the countenance divine
Shine forth, hook-nosed, from Zion's hills;
And was Jerusalem builded there
In Tel Aviv's satanic mills?

Bring me the laws by Moses told
Bring me my arrows of desire
Bring me no spear, no gawds, no gold,
Bring me no chariot of fire.

I will not cease from mental fight
Until the world give him his due,
Christ who was born in Bethlehem
A humble, poor, and honest Jew.

Heather Harper sang it that Saturday to considerable effect, and honour was satisfied.

The branch railway lines with their quiet rural stations and halts came under the shadow of Dr Beeching's axe throughout the year and TWTWTW took up their cause with a dirge from me, beautifully set by John Dankworth and eloquently spoken by Michael Redgrave. It seems that not even Beccles, the Suffolk home of the Widow Paradine Frost, mother to David, was exempt from threat, which made the whole thing all the more personal and pressing.

Travellers and train spotters made our cause theirs and snowed us under with letters, one of which read, pathetically: 'I travelled on the last passenger train and bought the last dog-ticket from Watermoor to South Cerney, and all the railway men were in Best Boots with smart buttons.'

That settled it. Off sounded Dankworth's unaccompanied choir;

Withington Halt, Chedworth Halt, Alvercot,
Chelmscott, Longford and *Lechlade,*
Bourton-on-the-Water, Stow-on-the-Wold,
Brize Norton . . . Norton . . . Norton . . . *
Burbage and *Bourne.*

* Could one ever forget the gentle echo of Norton with its dying fall?

[205]

(Passenger, spoken by Redgrave):
Spare, Woodman, spare the Beeching branch
From Hayward's Heath to Horstead Keynes,
Spare, too, the eleven fifty-four
To trundle down its iron lanes,
Be merciful to railway stations,
To Lewes, all change here for Glynde,
Where we have waited for relations
On platforms open to the wind.
People in fields at Chipping Norton,
How will they know the time of day
Should the twelve-twenty cease to run
Eight minutes late down Didcot Way?
And oh the anguish of the deep heart's core
The milk train will not stop here any more!

Good Doctor, have you never dawdled
Where the down train should have been,
Breathed in the unforgettable, unforgotten
Station smell, part dust, part kerosene?
Let your degree, your Ph.D., earned in the field of electronics,
Prove to the world man's proper study is viable Railway
Economics.

(Singers *a capella*):
Walsingham, Snettisham,
Halesworth and *Beccles . . . Beccles . . . Beccles . . .*
Burbage and *Bourne.*

(Passenger):
Old engines with their primal anger gone,
Their fire and fury rusted quite away
No longer chuffing into Platform One
Butchered to make a scrapyard holiday;
Don't think they will not take it hard at *Hatch*
Thorn Falcon, Donyatt, Chard,
Their summary despatch.
Back to the pack, old dragons! No one cares,
For galleons, balloons, stage coaches, sedan chairs.
And oh the silence when the stations die,
In *Tewkesbury, Ripple, Brill, Fairfold* and *Ardingley.*

[206]

(Singers):
Eastleigh, Romsey, Andover and *Savernake,*
Bowers Gifford, Benfleet, Laindon and *Leigh,*
Wickford, Shoebury, Swaffham and *Saxmundham,*
Stanford-le-hope . . . hope . . . hope . . .
Burbage and *Bourne.*

(Passenger):
And oh the silence when the stations die,
In *Tewkesbury, Ripple, Brill, Fairfold* and *Ardingley.*

Composers! Of course some – but not many – are as delightful to
work with as John Dankworth – called by Ned and me 'Inigo', for no
very clear reason. His wife, Cleo Laine, sang the theme song of
'Not So Much A Programme', which won us the Ivor Novello
Award for the best screen song of that year. That subsequently it
fell from my desk and broke my toe can hardly be blamed on the
kindly and generous Variety Club of Great Britain, but rather to the
fact that I was using it as a bookend at the time.

I think of Inigo Dankworth's honest face as permanently a pale
shade of green, partly from the fatigue of working far into the
night, but even more from migraine, from which he suffered untold
agony until he found a migraine centre. Now he is a pale shade
of pink. I wonder if his diet sheet allows the tins of Heinz tomato
soup which is (or was) his favourite form of food? Inigo has his
own kind of rather rueful wit, much in evidence when, as so often,
he is telling anecdotes with himself as the fall-guy.

Cleo is an experience all to herself. A unique jazz and pop singer
who has come into her kingdom, which is world-wide. I was lucky
enough to write a song to some perfect music by John Scott, called
'Woman Talk', for Cleo Laine and Milly Martin on, I think, 'That
Was The Week That Was'. Subsequently Cleo took it over as a solo
and called an album *Woman Talk*. This found its way to America
where another magnificent singer, Carmen Macrae, adopted it –
she called her album *Woman Talk* too. It was interesting to hear it in
the voices of two such different artistes – Cleo who sings it with a
silver filigree of notes and Carmen whose sound is as a deep bronze
gong – each superb after her own fashion.

One night the Dankworths came to dine in my kitchen where I
feed my friends, irrespective of rank. On this occasion Sir David

Webster, then Artistic Administrator of the Royal Opera House at Covent Garden, and his side-kick, Jimmie Cleveland Bell, Ned Sherrin and Norman St John Stevas were at table, discussing the behaviour of teenagers, until Cleo astounded all present by announcing: 'I'm just an ordinary Mum.'

Composers?

And so, with as many twists and turns and divergencies as the river on the banks on which it stands, to Greenwich, scene of our best musical venture. There in the theatre on Maze Hill where Sarah Siddons sawed the air, clutched her bosom, gave voice, and reduced the good wives of Blackheath to swoonings and their good men to resounding blowings of the nose; there, not a couple of poop decks from the *Cutty Sark* at permanent anchorage, I saw or rather felt, the presence of the old barnstormer, come back to comfort me. Let me recount the circumstances.

Sing A Rude Song, our Marie Lloyd musical, was being staged at Greenwich. The usual bumpy approach through not-enough-production-money, through auditioning to Robert Stigwood, through Barbara Windsor's stubborn refusal to take singing lessons, through her loss of voice on the eve of the first night, through a terrible and sleepless Friday night coaching an understudy in her songs, through to a hasty briefing in the morning with Ned to compère, Robin Phillips in polo sweater and jeans reading Marie, the choreographer doing the dances and the understudy singing the songs. Through my – I hope disguised – despair. It was while I was sitting alone in a row of seats midway down that the comforting ghost of Sarah Siddons sat behind me. She lent me her strength.

Yvonne Mitchell had come upon her before me at the Bristol Theatre Royal and emerged not in the least disturbed; but then Yvonne was a lady of high courage.

Long before this I had had a strange experience in Norwich. I was staying at the vast and ancient inn in a honeycomb of corridors to be with Richard Berkeley Sutcliffe, then a private soldier in a division of artists working on camouflage under Oliver Messel. The hotel, suitably enough, stood in the precincts called Doomland. One of the corridors was intensely cold and Richard and I would run through it holding hands to give each other courage. At night, in the corridor outside my room, I heard a great groaning and a clanking of chains, and even under the quilt and blankets my limbs were frozen, ice-cold.

[208]

Then there was an occasion on a hot afternoon in June. I was standing in Charing Cross Road on the opposite pavement from the Wyndham's Theatre. Suddenly the busy street turned ice-cold as a wind whipped up from nowhere and a whirling cone of dust went spinning across the road and in through the gallery door. The traffic resumed and warmth came back.

Before this I had been staying, again to be near Richard, at an old mill at Farnham dating from 1100. It was a grey day, and as I talked to Grace-Mary Grace who ran it I chanced to look idly out through the window. A cone of dust blew by and brought with it an air so icy that Grace-Mary and I wordlessly shivered.

From Farnham ghosts back to the Greenwich variety. Greenwich is my Shangri-la. I used it as an escape hatch all through the war and even when my playground turned into my workshop, when Ned and I became Governors of the Greenwich Theatre, it remained a sanctuary.

I first came to Greenwich when my chum, Nina Tarakanova, the soubrette ballerina, moved there with her husband, Neil Maclaren. (Nina it was, who once coined the definitive description: 'She dwindled down the street.') It was returning from spending a few days with Nina during the Blitz that I found myself at Clapham Junction one night with all London on fire before me as far as the eye could see. One afternoon, Nina, Neil and I were returning from a walk in Greenwich Park. We paused at the open gate of a walled garden surrounding the dark keep I was soon to learn was Vanburgh Castle.

'How green that grass is,' I remarked; 'I've never seen grass so green.'

'I dare you to go right in,' said Nina.

In went I, followed closely by Nina and Neil. Suddenly we found ourselves surrounded by small boys; they must have dropped from the skies or the trees or the Carolian chimney pots, for we had not noticed them before. It was a boys' school, then. Before we could bow out, the Headmaster appeared. Desperately I longed to beat a rapid retreat from what I thought would be the displeasure he would visit on three adult trespassers. The Headmaster, however, was a genial man.

'Come in and let me show you round,' he said.

'Neil Maclaren and Nina, my wife,' announced Neil.

'Webb-Jones,' said the Headmaster.

[209]

They all looked at me. 'Caryl Brahms,' I mumbled, 'and I'd love to see round.'

'Not *the* Caryl Brahms?' said the Headmaster.

For the first time I used what has since become a formula. 'Well, *a* Caryl Brahms,' I admitted.

Vanburgh Castle, it seemed, was an RAF Benevolent School. The boys sang in the choir of the Royal Naval College chapel. 'I'd love to hear them sing,' I said.

'Come down one evening when the little wretches are in bed,' said the Headmaster. 'Boys become more like human beings then.'

It was a date. I determined to enter this new world within a world. To begin with I would visit each dormitory and leave it singing – the boys, of course, not me! Late in the afternoon on the given day, I reported at Vanburgh Castle. Before this I had collected a commission to write about it in the *Daily Telegraph*, the fee for which I intended to give to the school amenities fund. 'By the time you're half-way through you'll be in need of a gin,' said the enlightened Headmaster. He grinned like one of his own pupils.

'I do not anticipate having any trouble,' I told him; I dug my chin in the air. He grinned again.

So off set I for the smallest boys. They were not reluctant to chat away to me, sitting at the end of each bed in turn. Nor were they loath to sing, particularly as it put off the evil hour of lights out. Word flew round the dormitories that 'a lady' was going the rounds to hear them sing. All the small boys sang willingly – I left the choice of song to them, and there in the corridor, half-way round, stood my faithful James Webb-Jones with a glass of gin in his hand, which, though gin has never been my drink, I put back gratefully, for by now I had joined battle with the between-agers who flatly refused to 'make fools of themselves'. They, lacking the ready friendliness of the smalls and the poise of the prefects, were at the self-conscious age.

So I accepted defeat and went down to dine with the Headmaster. Half-way through dinner a message came down from the rebels. They'd practised a song, so would 'the lady' come back to hear them? I left the delicious Irish stew and dumplings, and rushed upstairs before they could change their minds.

This experience was richly to bless my life. I met the Padre of the Royal Naval Chapel and would sometimes go on Sundays and take

luncheon as his guest in the magnificent Painted Hall.* We would
go there by bus (for petrol was rationed at that time and one could
not run one's car – in my case a disreputable jalopy) and amuse
ourselves noting the chatter of the upstairs passengers ranging
from the getters-on at the National Gallery, through the Old Kent
Road, to the decantering at Greenwich Park.

One snatch I overheard, passing a badly blitzed building, which
comes back to me in hours of gloom and anxiety: One daily cleaner
to another: 'It's going to be a lovely world after the war is over' –
deep sigh – 'lovely!'

I would go, sometimes with Nina but mostly without her, taking
my writing-pad with me. I always sat beside the same bed of roses
– Alexandra roses – where the gardeners would keep a deck chair
for 'the lady from Regent's Park'. After a time they would give
me tomatoes, and eggs which were still on ration; and at the Pavilion
tea-rooms the manageress would set aside the kind of sandwiches I
liked, and once – it was her birthday – invited me to take tea with
her.

Down the hill, but still in the park, Ned and I were to make the
acquaintance of Fred and Mabel, the lavatory attendants,
separated by a hedge over which Mabel would hand Fred a mug of
tea. They so entranced us that we put them in our novel *Rappel 1910*
as a running gag.

It was *Sing A Rude Song* which turned my Greenwich Shangri-la
into Workshop Corner. It contained some of the best songs Brahms/
Sherrin have written and the music was by Ron Grainer. In the
beginning were the words and we had the usual bumpy time early
on with our composer.

Some years before this, new caretakers had come to Number 3
Cambridge Gate, where I had moved (from Furzecroft) after Skid's
death. They were a family of three – a mother, a father and his
stepchild, Rel, Rell or Relle. The first time the Family Grainer
impinged upon my consciousness was, to say the least of it, bizarre.
I had been about to descend to the lower depths on some sober
domestic matter when, at ground-floor level, I came upon a strange
stout-ish vision – our new caretaker, no grey grim matron of the
usual kind, but a brassy-headed figure wearing black tights and an

* I was told by a friend who went with Mrs Roosevelt on a visit to the Painted Hall,
that the moment came when she put a most important question to the Admiral of the
Fleet: 'What do you use to polish your silver, Admiral?'

abbreviated black tutu, flicking at the banisters with a sugar-pink dusting-brush.

'Er,' I said.

'Grainer,' said the vision, 'Mrs Ron Grainer.'

The 'Mrs' sounded respectable, but the accent was definitely Australian. It seemed that the vision had a husband who was a composer – surely I must have seen him scrubbing the stairs – and a daughter – Rel, Rell, Relle – who needed a violin.

Time passed. The Family Grainer, caretakers, ceased to take care – technically, that is – and we lost touch with them. Then a music publisher, keen to play us one composer's music, put on the wrong tape. What I heard delighted me. Reluctantly the publisher confessed the name – not of his protégé but of . . . Ron Grainer.

Soon, another happy coincidence. Someone, for some reason, held a Sunday evening of ballet at a West End theatre. Ned and I arrived in the foyer at the same time as John Neville, the popular man's Hamlet. He looked round the chattering throng: 'They all look so young,' he exclaimed disconsolately.

We were delayed by friend after friend on our way to our seats and reached them too late to look at our progammes. A small jazz combo was playing meticulous jazz. The ballet began. The music was by Ron Grainer.

I wrote to congratulate him next day and sent it to Dr Dick Alexander, the medico round the corner, who I knew treated both of us. The Grainers entered my life again. It seemed that the vision in the ballet skirt was now 'managing' her man: 'There's nothing wrong with Ron the Lover,' she assured me, 'it's Ron the composer who is the problem.'

Sing A Rude Song still had to sail through some choppy seas on its voyage to a berth in the theatre just above the *Cutty Sark*. The musical – which Harold Hobson has said 'calls for as radical a modification of criteria as *Waiting for Godot* did 15 years ago' – began in 1961 as Lord Ted Willis's idea for a sort of biographical *Black and White Ministrel Show*, without the Black and White. The life was to be Marie Lloyd's. The songs in Lord Ted's mind were Marie Lloyd's. Having just failed to sell Lord Ted our musical of *No Bed For Bacon* (for Peter Sellers), the idea of a certain production of anything in the immediate future, even at Bromley, seemed attractive. But most of all we were attracted to the idea of slipping a few of our own songs past Lord Ted.

[212]

By 1962 we had read the two biographies and a great many books about the music halls of the period; we had had tea (and Gentleman's Relish) with Mander and Mitchenson, the theatre historians; had lunched with Clarice Mayne, whose famous impersonation of Marie made lunchers at neighbouring tables at the Ivy look up, and with Ada Reeve at the Hoop in Notting Hill Gate. Her stentorian and caustic comments brought an equally elderly lady creaking across the room to the defence of her heroine. We had talked to Marie Kendal, who created *Just Like The Ivy*, and to Mr C. Denier Warren who came to tea and left his umbrella behind. They all had one thing in common: they leant forward and their voices dropped to a conspiratorial hiss when they got to those incidents in the story that had been considered shocking at the time. Sixty years later, one had the feeling that they were still living the scandal.

Act One

We produced an enormously long script called *Don't Dilly Dally*, covering most of Marie Lloyd's life and all three husbands, incorporating practically every song she had ever sung as well as a large number we had written with Ron Grainer. By now Lord Ted had visions of the show having a life beyond Bromley, and he asked us to increase the cast and make it 'a big production'.

We recorded a tape of the new songs with two extremely kind ladies who sang with spirit and heavy colds in the nose. We played the lot to Lord Ted and a new backer, and after four and a half hours we all went away and heard no more. We were about a hundred pounds up on the commissioning, and about a couple of hundred down on expenses.

Act Two – 1963

Henry Hall was looking for a subject for his son Mike to present in the theatre. We looked over the four scripts we had written for Lord Ted; worked on another four drafts with Henry and Ron, and produced an entirely new version called *Cleo Laine Meets Marie Lloyd*. By now Mike Hall thought the best thing would be for him to take all the versions away with scissors and paste and produce a definitive edition to be called *My Old Man*.

After some months he confessed that it had been too much for him, and we heard no more. We were about a hundred pounds up on this commission, and a couple of hundred more down on expenses.

Interval – 1964

Oscar Loewenstein arranged for Joan Littlewood to hear the music.

Once again, the tape was spooled out, the familiar story reeled off, and Miss Littlewood, unmoved, stumped away down the stairs into Curzon Street.

Act Three

In 1965 we produced a television musical, *Take A Sapphire*, starring Georgia Brown. During rehearsals she saw a script which we left lying about, carefully casual. By now it was called *The One and Only*, a song which still survives on the LP if not in the show. The idea appealed to her. We gave lunch to Peter Bridge, a director, in the hope of bringing them together. However, the two ends never met.

This time we finished up the cost of lunch at The Garden down, and on 24 August 1966 a letter from Peter Bridge said '. . . I find it very difficult indeed to take such a decisive step and plonk down a somewhat hefty royalty right now . . . there are no less than four period musical biographies being launched in the West End momentarily . . . and who knows what will happen to the shows about Houdini and Grimaldi and Jorrocks and Barnardo?' By now, we all know.

Act Four

Now Marie Lloyd Junior appeared on our scene, a lady who had much of her mother's determination and also, she assured us, many of her mother's props and band parts, as well as the full copyright in her mother's life, 'left by will'. We were working with Peter Wood, the director, on a few more drafts, under the benevolent but uncontracted wing of Hugh Beaumont of H. M. Tennant.

Peter's idea was that as this was a musical, we should start by trying to tell the story entirely in terms of the songs and that we should not add dialogue until we knew what gaps there were between the songs. The musical structure established, we asked Alan Bennett to help with the book. On 15 March 1967 we predicted that we would rehearse in December to open in Manchester in February 1968.

By July, Alan had come up with several scenes and two apologies. 'I am sorry about this typewriter. Jonathan [Miller] always thinks when I write to him on this, that they are spirit messages typed *en planchette* by some ectoplasmic being,' and, 'Again naught much for Marie. It just doesn't seem to flow. Perhaps you'd better start following Coral Browne about with a tape recorder and use her as a model. Or Miriam Karlin.'

With a show assembled and a leading lady straining at the slips, a barrage of letters from Marie Junior hit us at the same time as rumours of rival shows. We wanted to be sure that Marie Junior

[214]

approved our treatment, and paid her £200 to work in what she liked to call 'an advisory capasory'. Marie Junior was not keen on the rival versions. Her letters are full of phrases like 'Joan Littlewood will make mother a coster-monger – to coincide with Stratford'; Dan Farson, Joan's collaborator, became 'that cheeky fellow'; and her letters were invariably signed *'sincerely yours, Marie Aylin, Marie Lloyd II, "Junior" as known professionally'*.

She had her own ideas about casting. 'I am now looking at Georgia Brown on TV and I think she would be most unsuitable for the part . . . her eyes are very dark, and my mother had fair skin and blue eyes. My choice would be Petula Clark who has lovely mannerisms, wink of the eye, etc, etc, etc. But I suppose she would want too much money.'

It was not to be. On the night we were due to play our new songs to Binkie Beaumont, Joan Littlewood announced an opening date for her Stratford production, and the benevolent wing was withdrawn.

No Palace, Manchester: no commission and a few hundred pounds expenses.

Act Five – 1968

We sold a television version of what had now become *Sing A Rude Song* (after a brief life for a few more auditions as *Hey! Cockie*) to Yorkshire Television. Joan Kemp Welch was to direct it. But Yorkshire lost their TV mast and we lost our production. Marie Lloyd Junior died on Boxing Day of this year.

Act Six – 1969

We realized that the next year would be 1970, Marie Lloyd's Centenary Year. And so to the new Greenwith Theatre which had a tradition of music hall and a playhouse which had served Marie Lloyd as well as Mrs Siddons. Once more we found ourselves auditioning, this time to a delighted Ewan Hooper, who stipulated only that we must bring some backing.

At first it was to be £1,000, and a manager was quickly found to put it up, but as quickly withdrew. Ten more auditions in seven days and another manager found, the production requirements had gone up to £3,000. By the time the admirable Robert Stigwood came to our rescue, the estimate was more like £5,000, and motherhood had claimed Georgia Brown.

The play has produced a splendid shower of reminiscent correspondence. There was the grand-daughter of Marie Lloyd's first agent, George Ware, who wrote 'The Boy I Love is up in the Gallery', who remembered her grandfather as 'tall and slim, ginger beard and liked gin'. There is a delightful correspondent who met Houdini, the Great Lafayette, and many other of their kind and helped to tuck up Chirgwin, the white-eyed Kaffir, in his grave at Streatham . . .

After the alarms and excursions of the first week of the run, we had a triumphant house-full season at Greenwich. Then we languished, awaiting a West End home. By the time we came to the Garrick in June 1970 we competed with a heat wave, a General Election, a World Cup, Wimbledon, and a test match – and lost.

After *Sing A Rude Song*, Ned and I became Governors of the Greenwich Theatre. These were still the days of Ewan Hooper's administration, and we gave him as bumpy a time as our composers gave us. The oustanding episode took place without our actual presence. Ewan's Nevada Street office looked down upon Dustbin Row and there, to Ewan's amazement, a young man in the cast of our next musical, *Liberty Ranch*, and a member of his secretariat were having sex, she sitting esoterically on the actor's lap. Ewan could scarcely believe the evidence of his own eyes. The father of five children, he had not known that the sexual experience could be shared in that way.

We did one more play for Greenwich – a Feydeau translation directed by Peter Coe in a manner which I can only describe as 'the less said the better'; Ewan's face, confronted by the broadening of his sexual horizons, remains a happier memory.

NS Feydeau became a staple of our life in the later '60s and '70s. We translated most of his one-act plays and many full-length ones for television (where they were dashingly played by Patrick Cargill) or for the theatre; and we published two collections of short stories based on them, *Ooh la la!* and *After You, Mr Feydeau*. Caryl also wrote *No Castanets*, a novel derived from our Braganza musical, *Take a Sapphire*. In 1964 W. H. Allen published an anthology of her theatre criticism, *The Rest of the Evening's my Own*, and ten years later she negotiated a delicate deal with Weidenfeld and Nicolson to bring out her book on the four major Chekhov plays, *Reflections in a Lake*. George Weidenfeld had asked her to write a book about Gilbert and Sullivan, a commission she did not relish. However, she agreed in return for a promise to

publish her Chekhov. In fact, as she read and wrote more about the
Victorian team, she warmed to them:

B   As Gilbert and Sullivan grew older and more impossible (and I,
week by week, with them) it seemed not, as I had supposed before
I started out, that it all happened a long time ago, but that, indeed,
they lived and squabbled only yesterday. And it became clear to
me that I must have invented them in one of the novels I wrote with
S. J. Simon – particularly Gilbert.

S   Her own skirmishes with composers continued to echo the friction
between Gilbert and Sullivan.

B   Composers! We had a nail-biting time with the aged American
composer, Arthur Schwartz (*That's Entertainment, Dancing in the Dark*),
whom we met in New York and with whom we wrote an early draft
of the Brahms-Sherrin (and ultimately Ron Grainer and Herbert
Chappell) *Nickleby and Me*.
    Arthur was understandably coy to commit to us. We ploughed
our furrow trustingly, thoro' bush thoro' briar, until we had written
enough songs; but one was terribly conscious of working with a
venerable volcano whose fires were by no means extinct and were
dangerously likely to erupt any old time and cover us in red-hot
lava. Arthur had come to live in London with Mary, his lovely,
domestically many-talented wife, and his genius younger son,
called by me Thunderfingers because of the way he punished
the piano.
    Arthur Schwartz, with his bright black tinted hair, was in a
splendid position for legal skirmishes as he was a lawyer as well
as a composer of songs. Walton Street and Manhattan re-echoed
to his vengeful threats. But for the time being none was levelled
against us. We went through the usual traumas of playing to artistes
and managements and each civilly worded retreat by them was followed
by a muffled thunder of 'Nobody does *that* to Arthur Schwartz.'
    I recall one desperate occasion when Ned and I joined him in
New York for a flying visit of twenty-four hours, into which we
managed to fit an audition, a supper party, a night at the Algonquin,
a working breakfast, a second audition (the lordly Sherrin has never
allowed the penitent Brahms to forget that, jet-lagged, she fell asleep
at the second audition of her own work), a luncheon at Sardi's, a

matinée, and one act of *Jesus Christ, Superstar*, before catching the night plane home (and mercifully falling asleep again on that).

The crunch came after we had auditioned in this country rather often and to no effect – it can happen. The management to whom we looked most hopefully – Harold Fielding – wrote a letter to us addressed to Ned. When I arrived at his house, he said: 'Sit, Caryl, and hold on tight.' Like one of Barbara Woodhouse's dogs, I *sat*.

The letter disclosed the fact that Arthur, our composer, had written his own version of the play *Nickleby and Me*, and had sent it to our putative management. Mr Fielding wanted to know about which version we were inquiring.

Brahms and Sherrin wrote a dignified and, they felt, definite withdrawal of their lyrics from Schwartz's music. In replying, the old volcano disclosed that all the time we had been working together he had kept a diary. The plum entry was: *'Ned looked at the ceiling!'* We still use the phrase as a shorthand for exhausted patience.

We went back to the drawing board for a composer (Ron Grainer) and produced a version which Ned directed at Stratford E15 in 1976. The facilities of the theatre were not all we could have wished – like no scenery or costumes for the first night – but in the winter of 1981/2, with nice and clever Lindsay Dolan staging the musical numbers, we got it on at Chichester as a Christmas attraction.

Even our enemies could not deny we were an attraction – did we not attract snow, hail, rain, easterly winds and ice that bitter season of good cheer, as well as all manner of pantomime buffs from seven to seventy? Alfred Marks starred, doubling Vincent Crummles and Wackford Squeers. One evening Alfred, in the character of Crummles, hanging on to The Infant Phenomenon's sagging arabesque, remarked: 'The talent of this child is not to be imagined. Her *entrechat un . . .*' he kissed his fingers!

I am not usually in favour of improvisation, but I wish I had thought of an *'entrechat un'*.

Side By Side By Sondheim started as a kernel in David Kernan's mind. He had worked with Ned on 'That Was The Week That Was', and on various Sunday sorties which Ned had devised along the same lines as *Side By Side* and for which Peter Greenwell and I had created our medleys as a new, or at least different, humour-form.

Millicent Martin had been our star on TWTWTW. That was in her little Black period – i.e. the little black dresses which complemented her red hair and white skin and, incidentally, cost about two guineas a go. David K. brilliantly co-opted Milly and the gifted Julia McKenzie, two pianists (Ray Cook and Stuart Peddlar), with the somewhat puzzled blessings of Stephen Sondheim; and Ned co-opted me with a brief to create a Sondheim medley. Until then I had only worked on medleys with Peter Greenwell, which means I interfered with his polite piano renderings no end. But for *Side By Side* I had to work with Peddlar and that was a very different and less experienced kettle of semi-quavers.

The billing of the two ladies, known to me as Goneril and Regan, took place under an unexpectedly tranquil star, since alphabetically the 'Ma' of Martin comes before the 'Mc' of McKenzie. And *Side By Side* found Milly at her most generous and offering, though Julia in the beginning was (quite unnecessarily, as things turned out) a little defensive. But they made themselves into a co-operative, called ingeniously Incomes Company, from the line in a Sondheim song, 'In Comes Company'. Both brilliant Milly and gifted Julia were in shows on Shaftesbury Avenue, so in the beginning the co-operative co-operated publicly solely on Sundays. They gave their show at Wavendon, the Dankworths' music base, at Brighton, in the lovely little Georgian theatre at Bury St Edmunds, and at the Greenwood Theatre of Guy's Hospital. I missed the first performance as I was in Canada visiting Robin Phillips's company at Stratford, Ontario. Ned reported that the girls had acquired two leaf-green dresses off an Oxford Street peg, so Milly's Little Black became Milly's Little Green. Before long Julia's beautifully moulded back became as well-known as Milly's much-exposed front . . . she always has been a generous and offering girl – particularly in the matter of her front. The two girls became bosom friends.

The time came when they all wanted to turn odd one-night stands into a permanent home. Ned and David looked about for a management to front the co-operative. After several false dawns the lot fell on Helen Montague and Cameron Mackintosh.

Helen Montague; at that time her attractive youngest daughter was a self-contained and sturdy two- or three-year-old, who sat herself down on a rehearsal-room floor to draw in a large exercise book. I think her name is Louisa, but she would demand that the family should change it every few days. Once she came up with 'Furniture': 'Call me Furniture, today.'

'Of course, darling, but why?'

It seemed that when guests saw her mother's sitting-room they would exclaim, 'Pretty furniture!' Reason enough, do admit.

She is, as it happens, fortunate to have a name at all. For a long time Helen pendulumed between Louisa and Victoria, but eventually the clock chimed: 'Victoria'. However, her husband went to register the infant and could not recall this, the nearest he could get being 'something old-fashioned'. So he entered the infant as Emma Jane Anne Jenny Beth Louisa.

No sooner opened in London than a hit, is the history of *Side By Side By Sondheim*. Eventually Broadway beckoned; the first night was a dream but its aftermath contained, for me, a hiccup.

I was staying for the first and last time, at the New York Hilton. It was a steamy New York summer. Deke and Jill Arlon who manage Ned, and sometimes out of kindness me too, were staying there as well. Passionate gardener that I am, I felt the earth in which the azaleas at the Four Seasons (where Donald Erickson, Editor of *Esquire*, was regaling me) were growing, and found it dry, sent for the bemused manager, and complained on behalf of the flowers.

Back at the Hilton, I changed some travellers' cheques, placed the dollar notes on the top of the square handbag I was carrying, intending to put them in my notecase later, took out my keys and attempted to unlock my door. While I was fumbling, a man I took to be a hotel strong-man in what seemed to be a uniform, came down the corridor.

'Can I do it for you?' he asked, and fumbled a bit, too.

Finally, the door relented and the strong-arm dwindled down the corridor. I fell asleep as my head touched the pillow.

Next morning when I awoke expecting to find my bag in its accustomed place, it wasn't. Uselessly I searched and searched. Finally I raised the house phone and awoke Deke. Together we went through the same routine, with the same lack of success. We telephoned Ned. We sent for the house detective – I did not know a man could be so fat. Some two hours later the bag was found at the back of the corridor ice-dispenser, minus the dollar notes and the credit cards. I felt deeply outraged that a thief had entered my room while I slept. The dark horror of what would have happened had I woken up, still haunts me.

To coax my mind away from shock and horror, a friend, Tom Megdall, took Ned and me to the newly opened Tavern on the Green, sibling restaurant to the highly decorated Maxwell's Plum. Here, we were told, the head chef from the Connaught in London was installed. This was how I came, still dazed, to dig my spoon into the basinful of white, creamy vichysoisse thoughtfully ordered as the most soothing antidote to near-mugging yet invented. I tasted it. I stopped.

'Does American vichysoisse have a cheese flavour?' I enquired meekly.

My cohort of strong men pooh-poohed the little woman's taste-buds and then, tasting a spoonful, climbed down.

Our host sent for the head waiter and pointed out the error. The head waiter denied the soft impeachment: 'It's vichysoisse,' he said.

'Taste it', I ordered, brandishing a spoon.

Somewhat loath, the head waiter tasted. He whisked the glutinous mess of potage away. It was blue cheese dressing. It had been stacked on a cooler next door to my hoped-for vichysoisse, and I hate to think of the effect on my already shocked stomach had I politely consumed it.

I've made a fool of myself in, or on the way to, American restaurants in my time. The occasion which leaps to mind coincided with the next occasion on which I bumped into John Neville. Diligent readers will remember that our last encounter was at a Sunday ballet performance – music by Ron Grainer. Now the scene changes to Boston, Mass.

Ned and I had flown in from New York to catch a preview of Stephen Sondheim's *Follies*. Neither of us had been in Boston before and I had asked Peter Bull for the name of a good restaurant. Bullie suggested one called, I thought, 'Pierrefours', a fabulous fish place. The Boston experience was bizarre. We had booked into a Boston Sheraton because Stephen and Hal Prince were also staying there. Two single rooms, our docket defined. However, when we signed in we were told neither room had been vacated, so off we went to lunch. We hailed a cab and directed him to 'Pierrefours'. On the way there we were regaled by a Lebanese driver, who had been in the US only five years, with fiercely patriotic anti-British anecdotes. 'Here we shot the first British,' he gloated as he turned one corner. 'Here's where we shot some more,' at the next. Then he leaned out of the cab window and spat into history.

We came to a jetty.

'Oh, look, Ned – what a coincidence, 'Pierrefours' is on Pier 4.'

Ned shook a pitying head at me.

On our return from 'Pier Four' (seafood up to expectations), we were shown to our rooms, mine on the third floor, Ned's on the second – beds still unmade. We pointed the fact out to Reception. Reception sent a page to conduct us to approximately the same rooms on floors 4 and 5, with approximately the same unmade beds. Our complaints were a bit crisper. They sent us higher up – floors 6 and 7. The unmade beds were becoming monotonous. We sent for the Floor Housekeeper. She apologized and sent us up two floors. By degrees we were escalated from floor to floor and from housekeeper to housekeeper, until it seemed that there was no made-up bed at the inn. At last, at last, on the top floor I found such a room. I flung myself on the house telephone.

'Tea,' I gasped, 'a pot of tea . . . please!' I remembered.

'That will be half a dollar extra for serving it on the top floor,' said Room Service.

And we had booked our rooms! I could not forbear from wondering what would have happened had we just dropped by on the off-chance.

Refreshed by a shower and a pot of tea, and the poorer for it, I sallied forth with Ned for the Stephen Sondheim-Hal Prince try-out in another cab, to be pulled up at some traffic lights. John Neville had been having problems (which were to prove insoluble) with a try-out of the Alan Lerner-John Barry *Lolita* at another theatre. He was about to cross before the lights turned. He pulled up at the sight of us, aghast.

'Oh, my God!' he gasped at me, 'not you?'

NS The two years which I spent in America proved a strain for Caryl. She had arranged her life to concentrate on our stage work, and the problems of collaborating across the Atlantic were complicated. She received a royalty for her work on the Sondheim medley and now, in her late seventies, she drummed up a deal of journalism – both reviews and profiles. Over some two or three years she wrote her last novel, *Enter a Dragon, Stage Centre*, a story in the old Brahms-Simon manner around the life of Sarah Siddons. Its structure suffered from the long period of time over which it was written, but it contains some backstage scenes of strolling players written with gusto. In spite of her experience at the Hilton she became devoted to the pace and excitement of New York and allowed herself to be flown over on any pretext, usually one invented by her – especially if she could hole up at her favourite Algonquin.

She greatly regretted not having visited Los Angeles and complained long and loud about this deprivation. However, when she was invited to San Francisco by her friend Gerald Asher, apart from enjoying the company of her host and a reunion with Hermione Gingold, she was not enthusiastic. She also made annual visits to the Stratford, Ontario Shakespeare Festival to monitor and review the productions of its director, Robin Phillips, whose work she much admired. (Her original relationship with Robin had been tense, for initially he had been more a friend of mine than hers and she was characteristically possessive and jealous. However, equally characteristically, once she had adopted him as her close friend, she was equally possessive of him and closed her mind firmly on the earlier period.) Michael Billington wrote vividly of her Canadian trips in an obituary essay in the *Guardian*:

'She was, in every way, an extraordinary woman; a seemingly ageless figure viewing the world from behind tinted glasses with amused affection ... but what I chiefly remember about Caryl Brahms is her indomitable spirit and endless encouragement. I had the good fortune to travel with her a few years ago to the Shakespeare Festival at Stratford, Ontario ... and was amazed at her tireless readiness to roam the province in search of drama in a juddering bus.'

Somehow we managed to compile a one-man show about Noel Coward, commissioned by Roddy McDowall who turned out in the end not to have the rights to the material he was ambitious to perform. We worked on a musical based on Anouilh's *Colombe* with the American composer Mike Valenti, which has not seen the stage; and we embarked on a book of essays about great lyric writers which was not published (as *Song By Song*) until after Caryl's death. When I came back from America work became easier. We dramatized a detective novel under the title *Hush and Hide*, and revised our Beecham play for Timothy West. Caryl also threw herself into devising, with Peter Greenwell, a series of medleys for the Yorkshire Television *Song By Song* series.

As Patrick Garland took over the Chichester Festival we started to research and write *The Mitford Girls*.

[223]

CB But to return to our own hard-tried, and at times very trying,
composers. Any suggestion that Brahms and Sherrin coaxed,
cajoled, bullied or drove Peter Greenwell, skilled pasticheur and
tuneful composer of elegant scores, to take refuge in a couple of
heart-flutters after working with them on *The Mitford Girls*, is refuted
strenuously and frequently.

The Mitford Girls – what a vista nicely poised between hope and
heartache this extraordinary family of English eccentrics conjures
up for me. But before I can share it I must set down certain facts
of life about setting up a musical.

Large-scale musicals can cost so much these days that only
millionaires such as Andrew Lloyd Webber (*Jesus Christ, Superstar*
and *Cats*) or Michael Codron (taste, energy, and careful choice of
impresage) or Robert Stigwood (*Jesus Christ, Superstar, Evita* and the
Bee Gees) can afford to mount one, and even they could need
support from American alliances – or come to think of it, do they?
These days, the Western trend, understandably, is for more modest
casts, solo performances, two-handers, quartets being the order
of our times; that is, when they are not wooing the playgoer with
proven successes such as *Oliver!* or *Oklahoma* or *My Fair Lady*.
With vast sums at stake, then, it is hardly surprising that West End
managements no longer nurse their shows for those dangerous first
six to eight weeks, since a sizeable musical costs between £200,000
and £400,000. Even a good cast album, essential for plugging a
show on radio, can cost £20,000 or more.

NS These estimates were, of course, written in 1981.

CB Patrick Garland, who directed the Brahms-Sherrin two-man play
Beecham for the Salisbury Playhouse and later for the Apollo Theatre,
Shaftesbury Avenue so skilfully and smoothly, has the great gift of
creating an ambience in which happiness and work grow side by
side. When he invited Ned and me to create a musical – *The Mitford
Girls* – it was normal for us to include in the package Peter Greenwell,
for we would need both music in pastiche arrangements of evocative
standard songs and tuneful music for our original lyrics to stand
alongside them. We took as our theme Julian Jebb's brilliant
television programme in which the four surviving Mitford sisters talked
of their sister Nancy. Their leader in all things was the Duchess of
Devonshire – later Ned was to liken Debo Devonshire (in fact the

youngest Mitford sister) to a Jewish Momma holding her headlong family of older sisters together, come what may, in an embrace of steel.

Julian started the ducal ball rolling by asking Debo to give Ned luncheon at Chatsworth and she bravely – in my estimation – agreed to hear what he proposed, which, incidentally, was to cannibalize Decca's *Hons and Rebels*, all Nancy's books, and anything and everything anyone had written about the family. Debo sent Ned a list of nine assorted dates on which she would be lunching at Chatsworth, to which Ned replied that, of course, he would have liked to lunch at Chatsworth on all of them but as it was he would arrive on . . . In the meantime, Ned invited the Duke to one of his radio programmes. Andrew Devonshire has become one of my favourite off-stage characters for, to my great regret, I have not met him, though Rory Fraser told me that at the luncheon table at Chatsworth (lovingly christened The Dump by the Duchess) my name was mentioned, whereupon the Duke observed: 'Did you say Caryl Brahms? She wrote the funniest book I have ever read, *A Bullet in the Ballet.*'

Which is flattering but not entirely accurate, for I wrote this send-up of the ballet with that great humorist S. J. Simon. Andrew Devonshire, however, won my heart when he christened our musical *The Mitford Girls* 'La Triviata' without having seen it. He also announced in one of the Sunday papers that he went to John Wells's political farce *Anyone for Dennis?* three times because his own name was dropped into a conversation: 'My name is the Duke of Devonshire, not Mitford.' Even the print in the newspaper took on a defiant aspect.

Controversy surrounded the production of *The Mitford Girls* – inescapable with the introduction of Unity Mitford, Diana and Oswald Mosley and Adolf Hitler as characters, however peripheral. Caryl's cousin, Professor Anthony Levi, has written in his book *Changing Faiths*: 'as a Jew, I found it a little hard to stomach'. In a piece for the *Sunday Times* called 'Swingtime for Hitler', Jessica Mitford reported: 'Caryl Brahms, Sherrin's co-author, would like to see the Hitler sequence cut out, "I feel very strongly – it would be unnatural if I didn't." As she spoke,' adds Decca, 'I sensed the shades of six million holocaust victims invading her thoughts.' Decca and Caryl quickly established a rapport but Decca's exemplary muckraking over-emphasized Caryl's objection to a two-line scene, though she *was* unhappy about the way it was played.

Both of us embarked on *The Mitford Girls* as an exercise in style, reckoning – perhaps wrongly – that the minefield through which we were treading would make our balancing act, as we attempted to cross it, the more spectacular. In effect, the production, though charming and principally performed by seven of the cleverest actors in the country, was not as severe as we had envisaged. Had it been, it might not have been as popular. However, we both of us regretted one aspect of the critical response, which was expressed by Francis King in stronger prose than it is his wont to use: 'There remains a flinty bedrock, which, underestimating their subjects as much as their audience, these authors never touch.' Our feeling was that we had not been writing a show about that bedrock and that had we been invited to do so, we would have declined. (But we have all been guilty as critics of writing about the show we saw in our heads and not the one the authors put up for our delight.) Caryl was certainly uneasy about the effect of the Hitler moment and it was cut from the London production. My own feeling was that a more rigorous attitude to the material would not have created the ambiguous effect which was seen on stage.

In a programme note for the Chichester production, Caryl conjured up a nostalgic echo of the period in which her professional life began, which I include here since it seemed to bring her career full circle:

CB For me, the joys of working on the Mitfords were many. The warm, enveloping welcome of Clinch's Hotel, the six virtuoso girls, Patricia Hodge, Liz Robertson, Patricia Michael, Julia Sutton, Colette Gleeson and Gay Soper, with Oz Clarke as all the men in their lives, wicked Pat Dolin and inspired Lindsay Dolan, who did the choreography . . . and the songs – our own and those we borrowed – all of which sent me tumbling back into the Twenties and Thirties, like Vivian Ellis's

> 'I'm on a see-saw
> You throw me up and you throw me down
> I don't know whether I'm here or there.'

Back in those carefree Twenties our whole world seemed to be on a see-saw, alternating between the high of putting the first 'war to end war' behind us and the dark, fast-approaching low of the next

[226]

'war to end war' in the Thirties. The contrast between the
Twenties, when the newly released girls and boys frisked out to play
at being Bright Young Things sporting baby clothes, whizzing one
another up and down our grander thoroughfares in go-carts and
wheelbarrows, and the Thirties – the one decade in history that
was to last only nine years, since war overtook it in September and
we realized, however reluctantly, that the holocaust was inevitable.

Central to our see-saw, which acted as a European kingpin, was
the American recession. But that was going on a long way away;
it couldn't happen here, we comforted ourselves, and returned
smartly to the gold standard. That was in 1925, of course. *Punch*
published a cartoon in which the pound sterling looked the mighty
dollar defiantly in the eye.

In the Twenties, should we have been born girls, we would
probably have been called Bobby or Billy or Bubbles, Babs or Jo. Had
we been boys they might have named us Eustace or Aubrey or
Edwin or Archie. Not a Samantha or Gary in sight.

We erected the Cenotaph in Whitehall in the Twenties. How
white and new it looked when our griefs were fresh. Still in the
Twenties, we abandoned the poems of Rupert Brooke and took to
quoting the more abstruse Sitwells.

We all went to the ballet – the Diaghilev Ballet of course – as
often as our parents' purse would allow. We scampered home to
re-cover our cushions to accord with the bright palettes of Bakst
and Goncharova and tried to sing the tunes correctly in *Petroushka*
and throw the accents in the right places in the esoteric names of
our favourite dancers until, in 1928, suddenly our Ballets Russes were
no more, having ceased upon the midnight with their talented and
cultured impresario leaving us to hurry off to the latest Cochran Revue
– probably by that new young man called Coward. We hurried back
to paint our pianos white and pickle our furniture to the stripped
pine beloved of Syrie Maugham, and somewhere along the line we
banished Culbertson from our bidding at bridge and argued with one
another in the light of the rules of the Acol system.

The end of the Twenties found us breathless with the urgency
of it all. They marked the passing of the taffeta-clad and
limp-of-limb Pierrot doll that could have been the symbol of the
age. And then, just as we had become accustomed to the fact that we
had won the very last War in the World – or so they told us – there
we were in the Thirties, with only just time to idolize Colonel de

Basil's Baby Ballerinas, Baronova, Toumanova and Riabouchinska.
The age of irresponsibility had passed, and for good or ill we were
swept into the Thirties to face a war in Spain that was none of our
making, with our bright and beautiful world in pieces at our feet.

Life, it seemed from now on, in the words of Longfellow, was
going to be real – horribly real, and earnest – boringly earnest.
Our cartoonists, quick to realize the way events had taken us over,
tore the gossamer from before our eyes.

Hail and Farewell were in the air we breathed. Facing the future
with what equanimity we could muster, our fashions changed. By
day our street suits resembled uniforms with padded shoulders. At
night we floated in our clouds of glamour. And at formal luncheons
we retained our hats. Cocteau, Dali, Berard dictated our fashions
just as Franco, Hitler, Mussolini re-defined our boundaries – or
tried to do so. They shouted and strutted and gesticulated, those
monstrous little men, and refused to allow us to ignore them. It
was as though our *Train Bleu* had left Waterloo station, carrying us
into Europe with it, silencing our protests by its speed and inevitability.

As though for every dictator the Axis could throw on to the board
– the bloated Mussolini, Hitler, the shrill hysteric Franco in the
shadow of Mozart's Commendatore – we could counter with Fate's
statesmen of our own: Baldwin – his lips were sealed – Chamberlain
who 'would have made a good Lord Mayor of Birmingham in a
poor year'. We knew we were at a disadvantage – we could not
speak to those foreign fellows in our straight-forward, brash if you
like, British way and say, 'Look here old man . . .' The closest we
could come to it was through some clumsy and verbose interpreter.

Because my personal obsession has always been, and probably
always will be, with theatre in all its manifestations – its many-coloured
coats – I think of those two decades in terms of the comedies and
dramas of the day, its ballets and seasons of operas. For our
delight Beecham spent a fortune on them. Toscanini conducted our
orchestras, and for the *haute couture* of a Chanel or a Paquin we had
our own Norman Hartnell who could turn out our duchesses and
our royals like tea-cosy ladies in tulle and sequin-snowed crinolines.

And of course we passed through fashion fads – our paper-bag
cookery, our 'It' girl, our 'wireless', our bigger, but not necessarily
better, cars. Television started transmissions from Alexandra Palace.
The Crystal Palace at Sydenham met its doom – just in time, they
said, to prevent it acting as a land-mark to enemy aircraft should

they have the temerity to have a go at us. We tried on gas masks. We kept a sharp look-out for Russians travelling on our trains with snow on their boots, and 'just in case' we took the names off our railway stations. We cultivated our allotments and lost our shirts at the greyhounds. We practised biting every mouthful twenty times, and started sending our saucepans to Lord Beaverbook, hoping he would make good use of them. There were Anderson shelters at the bottom of our gardens.

One good lady, I remember her well, dropped into our ARP post to get her gas mask adjusted and shook a lot of sand out on the floor I had just swept. 'It's from the desert,' she said. Very telling.

Soon we were to abandon our comfortable, common-sense slogan 'Safety First', perhaps forever.

This was the ambience in which Lord and Lady Redesdale's six daughters, Nancy, Pamela, Diana, Unity, Jessica and Deborah grew up, and these were the events which conspired, as the dancing mood of the Twenties darkened into the ominous Thirties, to separate them, seemingly for ever . . .

Caryl wrote no more about *The Mitfords*, musicals or composers. It is, perhaps, worth pointing out – though she preferred not to dwell on the fact – that she was nearly seventy when she collaborated on *Sing A Rude Song*; in her seventies when we wrote *Liberty Ranch*; and nearly eighty when we worked on *The Mitford Girls*. Her friend Dorothy Fields, the great American lyricist who died in 1974 at the age of seventy after her two last shows, *Sweet Charity* and *See-Saw*, is the nearest comparison I can think of in terms of longevity. I suggested once, when the London box-office returns from *The Mitfords* were dwindling, that we should advertise 'Lyrics by the oldest living lady lyric-writer in captivity'. The suggestion was not adopted.

8

A view from the balcony

Caryl's move to Regent's Park – No 3, Cambridge Gate – had occurred a couple of years before I met her. It was at about that time that she took to wearing the dark glasses which were one of her trademarks in later years. No one seems exactly sure when she made the change – they were omnipresent by the time I arrived on the scene. Cambridge Gate was a pleasant flat with a large kitchen, a cluttered sitting-room, and a balcony over the Park which she packed with plants with whom she conducted long and encouraging conversations.

A clutch of profiles appeared in newspapers and magazines during the last decade of her life which gave a fair picture of some of her eccentricities and of her style of life.

Janet Watts of the *Guardian* came upon her in 1976; by then she was long established in her eyrie:

> Caryl Brahms lives in a flat in Regent's Park within barricades of books and under the benediction of several winged cupids. Literary paraphernalia and lush green indoor plants sprawl over the solid formal furniture (one mass of leaves entirely embraces a bookcase: a hop, explains Miss Brahms); on the balcony outside, ranks of bright begonias beam in the sun; inside, amid cool shadows, Caryl Brahms is imperious in sunglasses, anecdote and reminiscence . . .

Sheridan Morley, despatched to interview her for the *Radio Times* a year later, found much the same scene. He refers to the many flights of stone steps up which she slogged, often several times a day, in spite of a bad back. (She was often in pain from the back and could not walk long distances. In an unsettling encounter during the war, she had been 'taught on' to a group of students by a distinguished back specialist in a North London hospital. Impersonally addressing the potential doctors, he pointed at the anonymous little figure in the hospital shift.

'Of course,' he said briskly, 'this poor woman will never walk again.' His patient waylaid him after the lecture and gave him one of her own on the subject of tact and insensitivity. She managed to move about for the rest of her life, helped by frequent visits to a variety of osteopaths.) Morley opens his piece with a perennial question:

One of the middling mysteries of the universe (perched roughly half-way between 'Is there a God?' and 'When will the National Theatre really open?') is the precise age of Caryl Brahms. *Who's Who* is unusually discreet on the subject, noting merely that she was born in Surrey and had her first book published in 1930, though it does add that her hobby is collecting glass walking-sticks and she lives in Regent's Park.

It was there (in a top-floor, no-lift flat which resembles nothing so much as a very good secondhand-book shop where the owner has a great affection for the kind of plants which look as though they are about to strangle you) that I went to talk to her, primarily about herself but initially about *Variations on Themes by Chekhov*.

These are short stories by Chekhov, though he didn't actually write them; Miss Brahms did. Being a brilliant researcher, currently engaged on a book about Chekhov's four great comedies, she explains: 'I came across his notebooks, and in them are one or two very brief entries outlining characters whom he'd noticed in his travels and whom he evidently thought might fit into a plot or be worth building a plot around. Only he never managed to fit them into any of his stories, so I thought I would.'

It must take a certain amount of courage to write short stories by Chekhov if you don't happen to be Chekhov, but then courage is not something Miss Brahms has ever lacked; among many legendary stories about her there is one which recalls a morning in the mid-1950s when she went into the office of Malcolm Muggeridge, then editing *Punch*, to apply for the job of ballet critic. 'Your present man may be very good-looking and adequate and all that,' she reputedly told him, 'and I know I'm only a short Jewess of Portuguese extraction, but I do happen to be rather better at the job.' I don't, in fact, know if she got the job there and then on the strength of this, but history does relate that between 1940 and 1970 she held a series of ballet and drama critic positions on a vast range of papers from the *Daily Telegraph* to *Time and Tide*.

Yet criticism has only ever been a part of her life: on her passport

[231]

she puts 'novelist and critic' as her occupation, and it is presumably only the lack of space which prevents her adding 'songwriter, satirist, playwright, translator and show-jumping fanatic'.

Since those halcyon days Miss Brahms has been involved in an epic biography of Gilbert and Sullivan (out last autumn, glowing reviews) and in countless continuing theatrical projects with Sherrin: 'People ask how our partnership works, and the answer is bumpily. But it works. We battle our way towards each other from a series of stubborn individual starting-points. Everything emerges from a wrangle, but the great thing, you know, in a partnership, is to sit facing each other. Except when you're writing songs. Then we go for a drive in my car and Ned gets nervous about my driving, but the songs do seem to get finished more quickly.'

Regrets?

'One or two: I've never visited China, but then again I'm not altogether sure that I want to. I wish I were a better writer, and that perhaps I could have settled for just one kind of writing, but the great thing about chopping and changing a lot is that however bad it may be for a career, it is awfully refreshing for a life. I've just gone where work has led me.'

Marriage? 'No, never; I was engaged a lot, but somehow never got around to it, and by the time I was too old to consider it I was really rather glad to be single.'

As I left to start the long journey downstairs, I happened to mention that I'd been surprised to realize at the beginning of our interview how much I knew about Caryl Brahms's work and how little I knew about her life. 'Life? What life? With all that work, there really hasn't been very much time for a life, has there?'

In the *Ham and High* in 1981, Ruth Gorb captures something of her individual style of entertaining at home:

Laughter has always been the most important thing in her life, and after that, the theatre. Her own stage-set is a flat looking over the trees of Regent's Park which, she says with mild surprise, seems to have grown up around her. Plaster cherubs cling to the striped walls, a climbing plant of jungle proportions threatens to engulf the windows, and everywhere there are pictures and footstools, trinkets and artificial flowers, bibelots and glass walking-sticks and hundreds of books.

In a voice redolent of Hermione Gingold at her most outrageous she will offer guests not tea, but ginger and honey ice-cream: 'What else can one have a three o'clock in the afternoon?'

Inconsequential and sharp at the same time, she wickedly only hears what suits her. Tantalizingly she starts to reminisce, then says she can remember nothing, and the past is past: 'I have lived so many different lives that time and age are immaterial to me.'

At the time of the Ruth Gorb interview we were working on *The Mitford Girls*. 'Debo, the Duchess of Devonshire, couldn't have been more helpful about it all,' said Caryl. 'She calls the whole Mitford thing "the industry". They all call me little Miss Brahms – not to my face, of course.'

Caryl, with her own Mitfordian instinct for nicknames, could never quite find the correct one for Debo. She had long reserved 'the Little Duchess' for the Duchess of York, now the Queen Mother, and Debo was also too tall and striding to qualify. The nearest Caryl got to a character label for Debo was 'a witty, well-meaning girl who deserved to go up in the world'.

Ruth Gorb continues with Little Miss Brahms:

Little Miss Brahms has plunged with glee into the '20s glamour and the zany idiosyncrasies of the Mitfords, a bitter-sweet subject wich had instant appeal to her. 'I'm rotten, heavy as lead, if something isn't right for me. I look for the sparkle of things, for sequinned stories and glittering people. I like everything to have about it a feeling of the theatre, a feeling of ballet. And I would like to feel that my words dance, too.'

Her words have been dancing for many years. She will not have it that she is a wit, but says that she is a cause of wit in others. She attributes her humour to her Sephardic Jewish blood, and her inspiration simply to listening to people talk in theatre bars. She doesn't look back, because lovely things are forever about to surprise her. 'And now,' she says, 'the nicest thing of all has just happened to me. I've been made a governor of the National Theatre. Absolutely marvellous, because it gives me a chance to pay back to the theatre some of the joy it has given me for so long.'

Pauline Peters, for the *Sunday Express*, came upon Caryl in one of her favourite haunts – the Grill Room at the Café Royal:

[233]

'I will take out grandmama's eyeglass,' said Caryl Brahms, delving into her handbag for a lorgnette through which to read the menu. In the dull glow of the *fin de siècle* gilt of the Café Royal the waiter hung on her desire, addressing her obsequiously if imprecisely as 'Milady Caryl Brahms'.

Milady was hiding most of her face behind violet-framed dark glasses, blanking out her eyes and so focusing attention on the determined set of her chin, the ropes of amethysts cascading down her front, her vermilion lipstick; she looked game for anything.

She exclaimed at the prettiness of her glass of hock and seltzer, her tongue rolling round the penetrating cadences of aristocratic English. This accent is one thing she has in common with the Mitford sisters, the subject of her latest musical play.

Her driving has a certain individuality. 'My driving is superb,' she maintains. 'I can manage with traffic which is moving but not with great big coal lorries which suddenly stop. In fact anything quietly, peacefully, parked is in danger of getting a butt from me.' It is with her at the wheel that Ned Sherrin and she compose most of their songs. The action speeds up their thought-processes. 'Ned says he gets more by me if I'm driving. I'll agree to anything when approaching a roundabout.'

They do have rows, but only about words, never about money or percentage or credits, a great feat for a writing partnership. 'I have a terrible fear of writing, I sweat in the palms of my hands through sheer fright, and when a proof copy of a new book arrives from the publisher I am much too frightened to open the parcel. I sit and look at it.'

She lives in a flat in Regent's Park, cared for by a housekeeper who is told if she dares to interrupt the flow of words: 'Go away. I'm earning your next week's cheque.'

Occasionally in the afternoon she indulges herself by watching the racing on television. 'I never have the slightest inclination to place a bet. Why should I? My whole life is a gamble, utterly precarious.'

NS Back in 1970, writing about *Sing A Rude Song*, Philip Oakes was more concerned with the mechanics of collaboration:

The team of Sherrin and Brahms may not seem as inevitable as, say, Laurel and Hardy or fish and chips; but it's a show-business fixture

[234]

which has weathered the turbulence of radio, TV and the theatre, and ticks along now as cosily as a carriage-clock.

They wouldn't do for everyone. A great deal of their time is spent in chat, with Sherrin jotting down whatever seems relevant. They also argue a great deal, with Miss Brahms reaching for the adjectives ('If I can't find one, it's the end of the world'), and Sherrin plucking them out. They are both sentimental, shrewd, and utterly dogged. Jointly, they have the stamina of a team of oxen. What some critics have tended to dismiss as their 'light-weight charm' veils a lot of muscle.

Caryl Brahms has been in the business for a good many years. Her age, she says, is her own business, but she's over twenty-one. In 1930 she's on record as having written a poem about King Canute attending a party in his bathing suit. ('Why,' she inquires, a bit peevishly, 'does everyone remember the ghastly things?')

She's formidably built and accoutred, with immense blue spectacles like a racing-driver's goggles, and a fistful of rings which she wears like knuckle-dusters. Her favourite is a massive amethyst which once belonged to Edith Sitwell. She trained at the Royal Academy of Music, dabbled in ballet, and settled finally for writing about it. When Sherrin first phoned her, she says, her first reaction was to brush him off. Instead of which, she asked him round for sherry and discovered they had a lot in common, namely a taste for working in tandem. She's assiduously flamboyant, an act which Sherrin fondly applauds.

They're both intensely loyal to their old shows. *Cindy Ella*, a saccharin retelling of the Cinderella story which was first produced in London in 1964, has just been staged by the National Theatre of Jamaica. And, says Sherrin, they've received a cheque for £24. 'Each,' says Miss Brahms firmly. It's the togetherness, one feels, which keeps them going.

Maureen Cleave, in the *Observer* in July 1981, was sharply observant, in a profile she wrote of me, of Caryl back on home ground:

Somewhere near rock bottom in an appraisal of Sherrin's character must lie his relationship with Miss Caryl Brahms with whom he writes most of his original work. He wrote to her when he left Oxford and they embarked on a partnership which survives, to the mystification of everybody, to this day.

'It's deeply psychological,' said a friend, 'a relationship that would defeat the layman. We would all like to get to the bottom of it.'

NS I have always wondered who said that. The answer is very uncomplicated. When I met Caryl I found a perfect launching pad for a half-hearted writing career and a very steadfast friend. She could, of course, like most of us, be jealous, possessive and obstructive – indeed her ability to make waves was probably greater than that of most of us. However, she had a unique ability to draw things out of a collaborator which were his own, but would not have surfaced without her husbandry. In addition, it would be foolish to deny that as she grew older I felt a responsibility for her. I believe that she, in her turn, found someone whom she could trust, as far as she trusted anyone, whose company she could enjoy, and who challenged her into new fields which she would not otherwise have entered.

Although I think her preference in men had always been for the prototypical tall, British, if possible blond, and public-school escort, she had, I am sure, closed that chapter of her life by the time I met her. She used to say that Dutch men were her ideal: 'Always ready with an umbrella if it rains.' She talked readily of her followers in her young days and offered freely, especially to comfort and reassure young women in difficulties, the story of her abortion in the Hotel Martinez in Cannes in the '30s. She was also frank in her dislike of Dr Edith Summerskill, whose politics she dismissed because she thought that Dr Edith was unwarrantably brusque when fitting her with a coil in Hampstead during the same decade. Back to Ms Cleave:

> Miss Brahms could be thirty years his senior, and to meet her is the complete theatrical experience. She is tiny – everybody has to look up to Ned Sherrin and Miss Brahms has to crane her neck at all times. She wore an astrakhan coat and huge spectacles with dangerously glinting frames. She has a marvellously scoffing laugh and does everything in the grand manner, even for an audience of one.
>
> A typical story begins: 'And Ned led me into Sardi's . . .' Her favourite is where he was a defence witness for a soldier accused of careless driving and the judge dismissed his evidence, saying: 'I am disinclined to trust this witness.' And her second favourite is that for many years his only appearance in *Who's Who* was as a footnote to herself.

[236]

'There is a dichotomy in that boy,' said Miss Brahms in richly reflective vein, 'a lot of Ned is lovely but there is one part of him which is loathsome. Ned's loathsomeness is the one thing I can call my own. A brilliantly able boy but self-destructive, destroys everything as he goes along. I've done my best for him but he won't allow me into his mind. Ned is Narcissus who looks in the lake and says: "I am perfect . . ."'

Ned was making tea; Miss Brahms was making the most of the situation to behave badly.

'I do hope,' she continued, 'that my affection, love and admiration and, oh, everything, does come through in all my terrible strictures. I would like to say that I try to keep a couple of hundred pounds on tap in case Ned fell ill in America and I could rush to him immediately . . .'

Ned came in with the tea; he'd heard all this before.

When he is in England they work together most weekends, sitting in opposite chairs fighting over each sentence . . . [Ned said] that he was terribly fond of her when he wasn't being terribly unfond of her.

Caryl and Shirley Mowbray, her part-time secretary for a while, both wrote books about the Braganzas in Brazil. Shirley's was written before she joined Caryl. Shirley is dismissive of her own book. Caryl's *No Castanets*, based on our musical *Take a Sapphire*, though amusing, was not a success. Shirley writes:

As for my book about Brazil, I didn't want Caryl to read it, but she insisted, and wrote on a postcard: 'Too bad to be good, too good to be bad, Too Bad!' which I thought was vintage Caryl. She then told me, in two sentences, the two things I must remember about writing. She was absolutely right, and if I had been able to follow her advice I would be a really good writer now; but it meant taking trouble, and writing a different sort of book which I knew (having spent years as a book editor) wouldn't make so much money. She took infinite trouble herself, as you of course know. She once asked me how much money I made from writing and I did wish I hadn't told her; she was utterly taken aback, and it seems monstrously unfair that craftsmanship like hers should be less well rewarded than rubbish like mine.

I still miss her. One of my daughters sent me an invitation to a

Purple Party at Cambridge last week ('Wear something purple') and my immediate reaction was 'Must take Caryl.'

NS I have asked Shirley Mowbray's permission to quote her letter. I add her formal observation of Caryl at work:

Caryl was the most generous person I have ever met. Every morning, as soon as I had settled the tyepwriter and myself opposite the portrait of Mrs Siddons, her first words would be, 'Now, who needs help today?' And before anything else was done, off would go the cheques, the postcards, the bunches of flowers, the cheering letters, to everyone from theatrical knights to the children of the porter of the hotel where she often stayed in Brighton. Nobody was too unimportant, too peripheral, or too boring to be helped; her compassion was huge and universal. Once I needed cheering up myself, I forget why. The memory of the disaster, whatever it was, is completely submerged, but time after time since then I have had cause to remember gratefully the comfort she gave me. 'When one door shuts, another opens,' she said. 'Again and again in my own life, my own experience, I have proved that this is true.' Her wit and her style were unique and well-known; but her kindnesses were often done in secret, and nobody but her secretaries and assistants can have had any idea of their extent.

NS Caryl's last secretary, Charlotte Darwin, saw her in all her later moods – at her most frail and tired and at her most beleaguered: but also in periods of great hope, energy and happiness. Ms Darwin writes:

Miss Brahms – I would never have dreamed of calling her Caryl, and always experienced slightly disapproving shock when I heard anyone else referring to her as Caryl, or even addressing her as such – Miss Brahms and I had, perhaps remarkably, a very fruitful relationship. She always said I was a literary ignoramus (she was right), but that being a dull and somewhat earthbound person I was well qualified to look after the boring business of life. (I was not insulted by her judgement, as there was never, in fact, a dull moment.) In terms of our working relationship, this meant that I filled in official forms, wrote to the bank managers (though these letters were always phrased by Miss Brahms who, as far as I could make out, had been doing the most courteous battle with them for decades, and always

Caryl and Joyce Weiner, her agent at the time, at the Akropolis – 'full of
colleagues and editors and publishers'

Caryl on the balcony of her ne
– and last – flat in Regent's Pa
in the early 1950s

The Levi brothers, Caryl's
cousins: Peter (left) and
Anthony (right), at the time bo
Jesuit priests

Caryl and Ned: (left) in a garden on the way to Chichester, and (below) eating oysters in Whitstable

Caryl and Ned, during a rehearsal of *Beecham*

Caryl with 'wicked' Anton Dolin
– a lifelong friendship

ryl at work on her memoirs

Caryl and Ned (right) with a line-up from *I Gotta Shoe*: left to right, David Toguri,
Brian Kirk, Deke Arlon, Jill Arlon

The *Song by Song* team, with Caryl in the foreground. The others are, left to right: Elizabeth Counsell, Elisabeth Welch, Nancy Dussault, Ned Sherrin, David Barnes, Tony Roberts, Diane Langton, Polly James, David Kernan, Elaine Stritch, Linda Lewis, Deke Arlon, Vernon Lawrence, Teddy Holmes, Irving Davies

Caryl in her Regent's Park flat, 'under the benediction of several winged cupids'

winning, despite odds which often became distinctly long), I found us both the best buys in Berwick Street market, kept her well stocked with forbidden Newberry Fruits and Callard and Bowser butterscotch, and did the usual things that secretaries do for busy writers.

One bank manager arrived to apply the ultimate sanction. Having buoyed herself up with a stiff brandy before he arrived, I watched Miss Brahms ply him with tea and crumpets and be rewarded by a peck on the cheek and an increased overdraft before he descended the stairs and she collapsed on the sofa.

Every Friday morning I would ascend those endless stairs at Cambridge Gate (I think there were eighty from the street level), urged on by the seductive aroma of fresh coffee. I was usually met at the flat door by my employer swathed in a magnificent, hooded, white towelling bath-robe (which I coveted dreadfully), wearing what I used to think of as her Morning Smell of post-bath eau de cologne, watering can in one hand, and an excited 'Just come and *look* at my strawberries/slugs/lilies-of-the-valley before we have coffee.' Coffee was an event in itself, subject to much experimentation and discussion. It was made in a *cafetière*, having progressed from the jug method, which simply meant that you didn't have to strain the coffee into the cups. The beans were ground in the Mouli mill to a count of twenty, and, even more important, the coffee was stirred exactly forty-two times before being permitted to brew. Coffee made, we plotted the day's business, and if possible we galloped through the dull bits so that we could start on the book review, or the next chapter of '*Fred*' – the autobiography's working title. 'Trottie darling, I'm sorry about these dull bits, but I've got a treat in store for us.' The morning was punctuated with the arrival of Lolly (Jessica Pearce), Miss Brahms's devoted Welsh housekeeper who exercised considerable and so-gentle authority, cooked like a dream, and did far, far more for the maintenance of the household than she originally had intended when she first started her 'light duties four hours a week' for Miss Brahms upon retiring from full-time work ten years earlier. Lolly and I were not permitted to chat while there were most important things to do, and caught up on each other's news in stage whispers behind the closed kitchen door.

Book reviews and articles were always typed in double spacing and on yellow paper (easier for the eyes), letters never had typed beginnings and endings. Almost everyone had a nickname, and I was often hard-pressed to remember people's real names when addressing envelopes. A skill I perforce developed very early on was balancing the typewriter on a rickety gate-legged table which was loaded with teetering piles of books, files, 'Darling Robert's' file (her accountant), and press-cutting folders. I once tried to clear this table, and was threatened with the sack. The trick was to counterbalance the largest pile of books with the typewriter, and then to remember to adjust the balance before putting the typewriter away when work was finished.

Last October I got us each an amaryllis bulb, one pink, one red, and we had bets on which one would flower first. Miss Brahms kept hers in the drinks cupboard, hidden under a sort of silver dunce's cap, and murmured constant encouragement to it. Sure enough, it started to respond to this tender loving care, and I conceded defeat. When I was helping with the clearing of the flat after Miss Brahms died, I found the bulb, with its beautiful green shoot, still in the cupboard, and took it home. Strangely, it went into a sad decline, while mine took off like a week, flowering brilliantly in February. It was another two months before Red Lion Amaryllis Hippeastrum recovered and followed suit.

NS The view of Regent's Park from Caryl's balcony was spectacular. 'On a clear day,' she used to say, 'you can hear the lions or Robert Atkins.' It is here that her last reminiscences start.

CB If you happen to be abroad at 6.30 a.m. and in the neighbourhood of my Regent's Park fourth-floor balcony, I am to be found in my bathrobe, a glass of red wine in my lily-white, from which I shall be quaffing while doing my spring and summer gardening.

How do I come to be wine-bibbing so early in the morning?

Many years ago Ned Sherrin and I set out from London to spend the weekend with Major Alan Rooke and his cosy crony, Dennis Woodford, who were then living at Wooton, known to irreverent Brahms-Sherrin as Rookery Nook, the same Midland rugged keep that imprisoned Oswald and Diana Mosley, the fascists, in the war. We set out after Ned had finished his office-boy chores on a Friday around 6 p.m. in one of the ancient jalopies I drive while rich women run sports cars.

What with a breakdown or so, what with losing our way, what with a rest at Northampton, although we were expected to dinner, it was nearly twelve o'clock midnight by the time the jalopy finally chugged round the circular drive of the pre-Cromwellian pile. Our hosts were models of hospitality. They batted not an eyelid. We sat down to dine in a leisurely style. Time has no meaning in an old English country house. Before long it was 5 a.m. They lit my candle and bade me sleep well.

Being a good guest Caryl thought it inappropriate to ask for the cup of tea without which she was unused to rising. She clutched her glass of port and faced . . .

. . . an historic four-poster with a pair of gleaming mahogany library steps to ease my way into the nest of curtains, crimson damask lined with heavy saffron silk. Placing my glass of port carefully on the bedside table, I fell asleep. In the morning I awoke in the suffused light of saffron and crimson. No early morning tea. Ah, but I had my glass of port – that would usher me into day nicely. This was how I contracted the taste for red wine to introduce me to the day.

I owe to Alan Rooke the advice never to drink an expensive wine if I do not know the cellar – better to order the restaurant plonk. (Douglas Bunn added to my wine lore by telling me to order a bad year of a good wine for my own 'cellar' – a corner of the kitchen.)

Alan Rooke now has grown his own white wine, Lincoln Imp, at Stragglethorpe, for he sold Wooton, lock, stock and wooded acre after acre. It was, however, while he was still at Wooton that I had the fascinating experience of watching Pamela Vandyke-Price perform a perfect piece of wine detection, following clue after clue precisely until she had unearthed the district, even the vineyard, where a rare wine was grown.

Caryl had an extraordinary roster of secretaries. At one time in the '60s her regular advertisement for new stocks in *The Times* became a welcome joke. She was not a good hirer, and she hated the word. However, she prided herself on being an acute judge of character and each favoured candidate was (for hours, days, a week . . .) a paragon. The good lasted, but even then there came a time when the relationship exploded. In such cases the good ex-secretary became a friend and was called to sort out debts, filing systems, income-tax claims.

Margaret Ramsay, the great reader and literary agent who represented us for years (often against her considerable will and better judgement) once rang Caryl in response to one of her advertisements to suggest a male secretary. The man was Joe Orton's lover and, subsequently, his murderer, Kenneth Halliwell. Caryl had just engaged a girl after endless 'auditions'; the post was no longer vacant. Halliwell killed Orton a few months later. There was, I am sure, no cause and effect. Caryl had had male secretaries before. David Robinson, the film critic of *The Times* and biographer of Chaplin, did some research for her. Then there was an actor whose billing in the casting directory, *Spotlight*, was 'Charles, formerly Percy'. Charles, a successful restaurateur after his brief stint, was always to Caryl 'Formerly Percy'.

Certainly the secretaries who, with the succession of 'Lollies' – housekeepers – were her only daily companions for the last thirty years of her life, saw her hardest struggles at close quarters. She gave most of them an impossible time and showed most of them great kindness. Grey was not a colour she inhabited.

CB As I grew up my series of governesses turned into a series of secretaries with a similar set of functions – to see that my bills did not turn into summonses; to ensure that I signed and dated cheques; to pick up stitches in my prose, dropped by my pen in haste or excitement; to know where I put my spectacles; and generally to keep an eye on me.

Many of these should-be life-belts have become my good friends. One in particular, the wife of a vicar and mother of five, remains my haven and sure shield in times of trial, like yesterday and probably tomorrow. Some were so bizarre that I think they must be characters from my books. Which distracted Damozel was she who lost a section of my novel *Away Went Polly* on her way to the typist, with no name, address or other means of identification on it? Next morning she arrived on my doorstep in tears and I had to staunch my own the better to comfort her. Later that day the telephone rang. A reader had found a chunk of pages in a telephone booth and had recognized the style. 'It had to be yours,' he said.

(But then I have wonderful readers who loom up from out of the blue when most I am in need of help. There was that English accent which materialized from out of the mist on a foothill of an Italian snow-alp, took in me, my car and my predicament in the fall of a snow-flake, called out, 'Well met, Miss Brahms! I can fix this for you,' and conjured out of the thin air some snow-chains. 'Saw you in a box at the Scala the other night,' he told me. 'It was just like being back at Covent Garden and I stopped feeling homesick.')

[242]

Another good lady I could never forget ran into a stationary car in the drive on her first morning, collected a parking ticket on an errand to Victoria Street, and at the end of the afternoon greeted me, on my return from the Open Air Theatre in Regent's Park, with 'I've taken out a lot of the silly jokes in your script – I suppose that's what you meant me to do.'

Speechless, I gasped 'Tea!' and set about repairing the damage before I left for the evening's theatre. I returned three hours later to find she'd left the kettle on the gas and the room was full of fumes. I hate to chronicle that I telephoned her before she left the house next day to tell her that I did not think she was going to enjoy working with me: 'Find a job in the middle of a field,' I advised.

The law exerted a fascination for Caryl who chronicled her brushes with the police and the judiciary. Soon after she moved 'to what Norman St John Stevas insists on calling "The Regent's Park", I was pottering about doing a little "gardening" on my postage-stamp balcony overlooking it, when I noticed a policeman on a motor-cycle crouching in our drive the better to pounce on the unwary motorist and serve a summons.' She fired off a letter to *The Times*, I suspect as much as a change-of-address notice to the world at large as to lodge a deeply felt protest, and was rewarded by a minor rash of stories on the lines of 'Author of *A Bullet in the Ballet* finds a Bobby in the Bushes'.

The new landlady of her Crown Estate flat was a formidable woman who looked like Bette Davis in one of her more aggressive down-and-out roles. 'A *soi-disante* Englishwoman who, I was told by Scotland Yard, was in fact a Pole. Mrs Carter-Bowman recruited caretakers from homeless people she found wandering in the Park. One particularly cold winter, having enlisted an Irishwoman with a son of twelve in her usual manner and, finding the Irishwoman nearly as fiery as she was herself, she smashed their basement window and refused to have it mended. The wind whistled through the house. The boy looked ill. The tenants had no hot water.' The tenants banded together and agreed to retain Caryl's solicitor. Luckily, the landlady's opening gambit was to strike him – so he had her up on an assault charge. Caryl enjoyed having her letters to her landlady read out in court especially her last which suggested that it was too cold for her to sit and write in the flat – 'I hope it is warm where you are,' she concluded. The magistrate sent down a note asking for a list of her novels. She scribbled back in reply that she was contemplating *A Bullet in the Landlady*.

In a different league, she strayed into the world of '50s drugs. She had abandoned her balcony and dropped in on a mainly Russian restaurant in Hampstead. At the next table two men were deep in conversation. Caryl was an inveterate eavesdropper and very soon she heard the name of a Festival Ballet executive. Subsequent conversation convinced her that the men were exploiting dancers to smuggle drugs and that the unrepealed homosexual laws of the day gave them a chance to blackmail members of the ballet company into going along with their plans. She was not keen that such boys should be put at risk. She paid her bill and hurried home to telephone the police.

CB It was while I was speaking to Scotland Yard that my door-bell rang. I broke off my conversation to answer its summons. There, teetering on high heels and swaying from wedding-reception champagne, blinked a friend. She followed me in and I continued my exposition to the police. They asked me to call at the Yard and have a chat in person. So I propped up sozzled chum – shall we call her Ophelia? – who was by now enlivening the afternoon with snatches of song, in the back of my jalopy, and off we drove to Scotland Yard. Any thought of leaving Ophelia in the car while I coped with the constabulary was out like a flame, for she set up a wail of 'Wait for me!' that could be heard from the Thames Embankment to the holy wall of Jerusalem. So out I bundled her and together we waited in a reception room, very bare with only a wooden table and four wooden chairs. Soon a plain-clothes policeman, probably a detective, appeared. He surveyed us. 'Miss Brahms?' he enquired.

'Yes,' Ophelia piped up before I could speak. And for the rest of the interview he showed a strong tendency to address his remarks to her. Finally, I was handed over to the custodian of the police files, a large book was taken from the shelves and opened before me.

'Can you,' said the custodian, 'recognize the man you saw here?' I could. I was told that a man from the drug squad would call at my flat to take down some details. When I collected Ophelia I found her slumped over the table, snoring, with a police matron who had brought her a mug of hot black coffee, shaking her gently: 'Miss Brahms, Miss Brahms! Wake up!' she was saying.

NS A few days later Caryl was given a conducted tour of the sleazier parts of the West End in a police car – pushers and pick-up places pointed out. 'Heady stuff,' she commented. Reading that account, I could not help recalling the incident when she had her one brush with marijuana, some decades later. An American friend was smoking grass. Caryl, eager to experience a new sensation, asked if she might have a joint to take home. Jonathan gave her one and she drove off. I called in the morning to find out if she had enjoyed her experience. 'Didn't feel a thing,' she said sharply. 'I took it out on to my balcony so that the smell would not be so incriminating if there was a police raid, and I lit it sitting there looking out over the Park. It was a lovely night but I felt absolutely nothing.' It was some months before I remembered that she never inhaled!

Another brush with the law occurred on the way back from an opening night at the Chichester Festival. We had some memorable journeys through the countryside in search of memorable theatre. One such, Canterbury and a matinée of *Macbeth* with a TV star as the Thane getting wolf-whistles from eager little girls as his Lady unzipped the front of her gown intoning, 'Come to my woman's breasts and take my milk for gall,' was followed by oysters at Wheeler's Bar in Whitstable. After Joan Greenwood's great Hedda at Oxford we skidded over a hedge and a ditch, and I came to surrounded by helpful villagers, to hear Caryl saying firmly, 'Ask that black gentleman to put my car down.' After Peter Wyngarde's fine Cyrano at the Bristol Old Vic, she went to sleep at the wheel and I went to sleep in the passenger seat. We awoke on the wrong side of the road with glaring headlights rushing towards us. Then again:

B We had been to Chichester to see *The Magistrate* by Pinero. We were discussing, as I drove along the narrow and then not particularly familiar Sussex lane, the nature of farce and how farce is really tragedy turned upside-down. I had registered that a car was following us on the winding road. 'I wish,' I observed to Ned, 'that car would overtake – it's rather too close for comfort.'

No sooner wished than bingo! – with the unsought addition of that unmistakable police-car bell, the blue light blinking on the roof, the dread word *Police* popping up, and the hand signal to stop. Two police officers came over to inspect us; one a smoothie, the other saturnine and smouldering who remained a tacit threat throughout, the lowering cloud before the flash of lightning. Smoothie leaned over the driver's window the better to sniff out alcohol on my breath. There was none. What were we doing so late in that dark Sussex lane? I explained that we were returning to town after an indifferent performance of a classic farce. Smoothie was not impressed. They had been following me for some time (they had indeed, and too close at that) – did I know my car had been weaving?

'We have been discussing the essence of farce and tragedy, and I kept pulling in to let you overtake,' I told him helpfully. Smoothie was not convinced. Had I taken any alcohol that night?

'A brandy in the Press Room before the performance and a half glass of the house red over supper,' I said crisply. They remained unconvinced, in fact positively dubious. They produced a breathalyser. 'Is that . . . that *thing* sanitary, Ned?' I asked icily.

'Perfectly, Madam,' Smoothie interposed.

What kind of person used it last? Had it been breathed into by an alcoholic, for instance? No.

Finally I agreed, and blew hard into the horrid bag. After several failures they were satisfied. They took it to the front of the car to examine it in the headlights. Ned got out to see fair play. When they came back to me they said that I had gone past the mark. Ned said I had not. A chink was appearing in their armour. Ned pressed home the advantage: wasn't there another test? Couldn't we go to a police station and let me walk along a white line? What about the Leith police? Backtracking, Smoothie asked if we could not stay the night locally?

No!

Could Ned not drive the car home?

'Certainly not,' said Ned, 'I'm pissed.'

They gave up and we set off for London, and half a mile or so on Ned went into a reflective mood.

'Do you know,' he said finally, coming out of it, 'you had two brandies in the Press Room before the play; one in the interval; half a carafe of red wine in the restaurant; and a brandy before we left?'

NS We got home safely; but the incident remained a warning to Caryl to say 'No' in future if she suspected she might be about to follow a drink with a drive. When she drafted her first account for her memories, she told the story as it appears here. I pointed out that if she published it that way it would be a wonderful weapon in the hands of the prosecution if she were ever hauled up again. She removed the paragraph about her actual intake. Since she is beyond the reach of the law it seems proper to restore it.

A view from the balcony

On a trip to Stratford-upon-Avon with the director, Colin Graham, she was in a pile-up on the A40, a highway she often chose for a crash. On learning his patient's destination, the ambulance attendant insisted on reciting 'To be or not to be' in English and then in Welsh.

Taxi-drivers were Caryl's great favourites and she, often correctly, imagined herself to be a favourite of theirs. This blithe confidence led to some hiccups.

We took a taxi back to my parked car and I went on ahead to open the sunshine roof and start the engine running. When telling this story, which I might add Ned does at the drop of a parking meter, invariably he says ruefully at this point: 'Off went Caryl leaving me to pay for the taxi – of course.' It brings the house down, bless him.

'What's her name?' the driver asked him. Now, my relationship with my taxi-drivers is very special. They will ask me about the new plays or about Ned, whose television exposures have made him known to a lot of viewers. One once said to me: 'Well, have you come out without opening your letters, borrowed your fare from the porter, and are you late?' So when the driver asked Ned who I was, it was all Lombard Street to a china orange, thought Ned, that he would hear some affectionate remark about me.

'Brahms,' said Sherrin.

'Who?'

'Brahms – Miss Caryl Brahms.' He waited expectantly. 'The writer,' he added helpfully.

'H'mmm,' grunted the driver, 'I've had bloody ructions with her before.'

She had a reputation for wit, but, she wrote, 'over the years I have acquired a reputation for *faux pas*. It used to be a reputation for bitchery; but time mellows and now people often charitably assume that I have simply made a mistake.' Sometimes she emerged the loser. Reluctantly visiting Mary Morris backstage, an actress she had often criticized, she was rewarded with, 'Ah, Miss Brahms, still writing?' On the other hand at Covent Garden a woman bore down on her in the Crush Bar:

She was at her most regal, like an Ironclad on royal duty as she came to anchor in a space beside me. 'I have just read your book about the passage to India,' she said.

[247]

Me and E. M. Forster, I thought. It seemed unlikely, and she was speaking again. 'What did you call it?'

What had I called it, and which book? Only one title came to mind and it was out before I could suppress it: 'Barnaby Rudge,' I heard myself say. All the wrong things in all the right places.

NS Then there was the first night of *Hay Fever* at the National Theatre.

CB Time: the first interval. The foyer was filling, and Noel Coward stopped his hasty exit to exchange a few words with me. Ned was talking to Adrienne Corri, who was being squired by a thin, dark-haired man. 'Oh, Caryl,' said Ned who is about twice as high as I am. 'You know . . .', and the rest of his sentence drifted away into the babble way above my head. One name only floated down to me: 'Vidal.'

I was astonished. I remembered Gore Vidal from the sequel to TWTWTW, when he had appeared as a speaker. I looked closer at Adrienne's dapper escort. He wasn't as tall as I expected. He was considerably thinner than I remembered, and his hair – usually a ruffled greying mess – was well-brushed and the colour of a raven's wing. Clearly a new leaf had been turned, or something. That 'something' should have given me pause, but no – on I rushed, addressing myself to fellow author, Gore Vidal:

'How is your book going?'

Adrienne's escort swallowed.

'Well, I hope,' I hurried on; 'we two have a lonely furrow to plough.'

'Er,' said Adrienne's chum. A little doubtfully, I thought.

I turned to Ned for help; that lordly one was looking definitely quizzical. He led me away as one might an idiot child. 'I know who you thought you were speaking to,' he crowed. 'You thought he was Gore Vidal.'

'And wasn't he?'

'Of course not. He's Vidal Sassoon.'

NS One very hot Sunday morning we went to a drinks party in Chelsea given by Timothy West and Prunella Scales soon after their wedding. Sitting on a window-seat with his back to the light was an actor Caryl thought she knew.

Well, I went over to speak to the actor. We were in quite a small room and the lunch-time was sun-filled. Soon it became evident to me that the actor did not remember me. I ploughed on. The room grew warmer, smaller, the general conversation louder. I felt a bead of sweat on my forehead. I mopped. I sent a pleading look over to the lordly Ned. He was standing watching my struggle with amusement. I threw in the sponge and rejoined him.

'I've just been talking to the most difficult man in Chelsea,' I told Ned, still mopping. 'You might have come across to rescue me.'

'That,' said our hostess crisply, 'was my father-in-law.'

Hissing names to Caryl as people approached was a risky venture. Either she got it wrong as in the 'Vidal' confusion, or she did not hear at all and was later aggrieved and complained bitterly of not having been warned. She did it once at a BBC party to celebrate the retirement of Mrs Reynolds, a particular favourite of hers who had long presided over the hospitality room at the TV Centre. Most of the professional talkers were on parade.

I found myself standing beside Russell Harty, who seemed to be taller than I remembered and must, I decided, have had a very rough luncheon.

'For a moment,' I said, 'I thought you were that awful Michael Parkinson. Such dull programmes.'

He affected not to hear, so I gave up.

Later I said to Ned: 'Russell Harty looks a bit under the weather.'

'Russell isn't here.'

'Yes he is – over by Alasdair Milne.'

'That,' Ned said at his most severe, 'is not Russell – it's Michael Parkinson.'

On one occasion, soliciting financial help for a child actress whose work she admired, she wrote a long charming letter to Robert Donat, asking him for a contribution and finishing off with an elaborate compliment on his current performance at the Cambridge Theatre. Unfortunately, the actor in the play at the Cambridge Theatre was Brian Aherne.

She hated the musical version of *The Canterbury Tales*, and since she was not reviewing it she left at half-time. Some years later she turned up at a theatre for a first night, and was surprised to see none of the usual first-night faces as she took her seat in the centre of a crowded row. She had not had time to get a programme, and as the curtain rose was dismayed to find that she was condemned to sit through the first act of *The Canterbury Tales* all over again. She never knew how the second half ended.

Perhaps the excitement of first nights added to her aptitude for confusion.

CB John Gielgud was leading a company in a classical repertory at the Palace. Tonight *Much Ado*; tomorrow *King Lear*. I had taken refuge in one of the many foyers. Towards me came Claire Bloom, beautiful and polite as always. We exchanged the kind of remarks that the wise drama critic invariably adopts to hide his thoughts, and to which the young actress replies in the same guarded fashion. I said, infinitely condescending, I fear: 'And what are you doing, Claire?'

'I'm playing Cordelia here,' she said, 'tomorrow night.'

She drove it home in deadly fashion, but still politely. Her name was up in lights outside the theatre.

NS Much to her surprise, Caryl became obsessed by horses in the 1970s. Partly this was due to her disenchantment with the current crop of ballerinas and her surely held belief that the jumpers she was watching more and more frequently on television were more graceful. Still, it came as a surprise.

CB I had learned to ride the hard way, on a donkey. That is to say, when I was a child, they plonked me on Nancy, our aged moke, and told me to copy my Cousin Tana who was into the rise and fall of stirrup-riding. That later I progressed to Kitty, our Welsh pony, was due less to improved horsemanship than to the demise of Nancy. I was never allowed to ride Beauty, our white station-going mare. Not that I demurred against this, for I was even terrified of diminutive Kitty. Every time she refused a planked bridge over a dike she won her own way without further effort; and as there were as many dikes in our part of Essex as there are stars in the night sky and all of them bridged by planks, it will be seen that my neighing quadruped and I spent some exceedingly isolated outings together.

NS Fortunately, I was broadcasting on 'Any Questions' as her horse-fever reached its peak. Another panellist was the late Dorian Williams. I asked him how I could most easily introduce Caryl to Hickstead – by now her burning ambition. 'Nothing simpler,' he said. 'Just write to Douglas Bunn – he'll love to fix it.' I did, and it proved one of the most rewarding friendships of Caryl's later and Douglas's middle years. Her Hickstead subscription became my annual Christmas present.

Hickstead is the Sussex Glyndebourne for horses. From the four quarters of the globe they come, the elegant, well-schooled riders, to what David Coleman, the television commentator, has called 'the best equine arena in Europe'. From the outset Douglas Bunn foresaw that his jigsaws of jumps were what was needed to get the post-war British show-jumping scene back up on its hooves and prancing; and since with Douglas to have a vision is to get down forthwith to creating it, his emerald-green equine arena has come to pass.

The first time I went to the all-England show-jumping course on the Brighton road, I was more scared of the prospect of the company assembled on the Master of Hickstead's balcony than the horses safely penned off from the spectators below.

We decided on that first occasion that my best card would be to stay *shtum*, confine my comments to a plain 'yes', 'no' and, in an emergency, a cautious 'maybe'. All Douglas Bunn's other guests were quite naturally at home with race-cards in one hand and a glass of champagne in the other. No need for them to pick their words as neatly as the accomplished quadrupeds negotiated their hurdles.

After the first impact on conversational stilts I wonder the Master ever asked me to luncheon on his balcony again. Having *shtummed* my way to live another day, I soon became foolhardy with the horses. They are surely the most highly disciplined creatures to be seen outside the ballet and I experienced something of the delight with which I watch a good ballet company in class – predicaments, catastrophes, sweat and all. And it is this hard-won discipline that makes the dressage display, so dull to uninstructed eyes, so absorbing to the connoisseur of *haute école* in any of its forms.

Before my next visit to watch the jumping I went to Hickstead to interview Douglas for the *Guardian*.

The Master of Hickstead keeps open house. That is to say that on the morning I called at Hickstead Palace, the great door was not locked. 'It never is,' said Douglas.

[251]

'Have you any idea how many horses you own?'
'Fifty, I suppose. Maybe sixty.'
I tried again.
'Have you any idea how many people you have on your staff?'
'No. And I dare not let myself find out.'
Mrs Pamela Carruthers, a course builder of international
distinction, once said: 'I love working at Hickstead. We get such
splendid ingredients there!' Like everyone else who works there,
she has Douglas peering over her shoulder, which, were he less
friendly, could be an intimidating experience.

Hickstead Palace, an ancient and amiable citadel of a manor
house, is a couple of arrow-flights away from the show-grounds: 'I
believe in living over the shop,' says The Master, cheerfully. For
the four-day meetings Bunn, who used to captain England and act as
chef d'équipe to the team as well, fills his ample home with the
German and American teams. It is a continuing gesture of gratitude
'because they were such splendid supporters of Hickstead when we
first got started'. The feeling for the high theatricality of the show-ring
that is bone of the Bunn bone caused the establishment to be
mistrustful, almost abrasive, in Hickstead's contumacious salad days;
but now that the need to fight for survival in terms of the gate
(sixteen to twenty thousand spectators, Coleman estimates) and
riders is over, Douglas has wisely put the rough with the lethally
smooth behind him.

Ned has called me a show-jumping groupie – and I suppose there
is some truth in the canard. I once asked Douglas to introduce
me to Harvey Smith. He was summoned to the balcony. I was
presented as a writer: 'Good,' said Mr Smith, brightening, 'a
writer – then you can write me a dirty monologue for my
nightclub act. Something like "Eskimo Nell".' (Too dirty for
the Windmill?)

To be with Douglas on a show-day is to be with a burly piece of
human quick-silver; everywhere and nowhere to be found. One
moment he will be talking to you, but even as he completes the
sentence, he will be down at the ring-side, or at the observers' platform
in the centre of the green area. And suddenly back to the balcony
and on the telephone, like one of the little silver balls one strives
to slant into a hole in a fair-ground puzzle. 'I believe in delegation,'
he has the effrontery to declare, 'But,' and here the naked truth
rears its rarely totally comfortable head, 'all my work is done before

the show starts. When it's on, my job is to sit there and wait for something to go wrong – or go wrong in an hour's time.'

From which I gather that while it is a jumpy sort of occupation to be an impresario of human beings of genius, to be an impresario of horses of genius is to be confronted by hurdles and hazards at every turn and water-jump.

Bunn had been called to the Bar, and practised for a time.

'Why did you give up?'

'Because I could earn millions there,' he said.

On my second visit to a meeting, the going got tougher. Douglas said confidently to Ned: 'I'm going to take Caryl down to the ring, she'll enjoy that.' While the riders lined up their horses to receive their rosettes, I was still hoof-happy, safe on the spectators' side of the course. But what was that set in the middle of the hedge to which the Master was guiding me? A gate! A gate that opened! A gate through which the Master was expecting me to pass. Clearly non-noblesse obleeged. I dug my chin in the air. It was going to be total confrontation before a multitude of people, and doubtless a jeering Ned, with the steaming horses breathing fire as the Master escorted me down the line. In a lucky flash I saw the best place to pat the horse's neck where he could neither bite me nor kick me. I had to reach up on my toes to achieve it. A word to the rider and on to the next knee-knocking – mine, not the horse's – encounter. After this, my equine baptism, Douglas Bunn's balcony became home from home to me, and I was to find the Hickstead balcony the friendliest place in the world.

Before long Ned and I were asked to present the rosettes for one of the events. This is an honour I prize dearly and had done nothing to deserve. I hope I was adequate. I know I was proud. And, of course, we all know what pride comes before – in my case, literally. For out there with the BBC television cameras turning, an ominous crack came from the regions of my waist. Through my country suit I clutched at my descending knickers. The BBC television cameras were recording but could I trust them to cut away from my predicament? Yes. So there were only several thousand spectators to witness my disgrace. Not for the first time at Hickstead I dug my chin in the air, and with one hand clutching my clothing I patted, congratulated, left-handed passed up the rosette, and continued on down the line.

But my near-disaster at Hickstead was not the first time the elastic of my knickers had snapped – that occurred crossing to the Casino gardens at Monte Carlo with Massine, the distinguished choreographer, in broad daylight, with the unmistakable garment descending around my ankles. I stepped out, neat as a show-jumper. Massine bent to whip them up and gravely hand the wretched garment back to me with a bow, feet in faultless third position. And the rest of Monte Carlo sipped its elevenses champagne, too well-bred to notice.

Do Hickstead and Monte Carlo make me eligible for the *Guinness Book of Records*? A Lady would ignore the, to me totally irresistible, question.

Enough that Hickstead sits in my heart and memory with its maze of hurdles, banks and water-jumps. Its open draughty balcony, now fenced off (courtesy of Everest Double Glazing), its great oval dining-table, its friendly waitress pressing a brandy on me on the chilliest spring or autumn days, Douglas and his sons and daughters and, more recently, smiling, spirited and beautiful Lorna, his young wife – pointing sympathetically when Ned goes off into drowsy sleep after lunch when everyone else's heart is in their mouth as horse and rider risk everything on the terrifying Derby Bank.

NS Undoubtedly, the greatest pleasure of the last years of Caryl's life was her appointment as a Governor of the National Theatre. This imaginative gesture was Norman St John Stevas's; and if Peter Hall viewed her arrival with some foreboding he did not let on. Her memoirs record:

CB The first time I went to the National Theatre as a Governor, I was required to meet and talk to the Financial Administrator and two of his minions, a daunting prospect. But I don't daunt all that easily.
'I've come here to work,' I announced.
They looked at me with strong disfavour. 'Miss Brahms,' said the senior spokesman, 'Governors of the National Theatre do not work – they meet!'
'And between meetings,' I told them firmly, 'I shall work.'

NS Her immediate ambition on joining the governing body was to improve the food served in the actors' canteen. She was very disappointed to find that it was so good and so inexpensive that there was barely any room for improvement.

I sometimes think – usually at around four a.m., when my spirit of optimism is at its lowest ebb – that the only tangible thing I have accomplished during the two and a half years of my governorship of the National Theatre has been to improve the sandwiches served in the Governors' parlour, and no one knows what a struggle that has been.

Her concern for the National was fierce, her attendance at Governors' meetings eager. Her object, after a long career on the press side of the theatre, was to improve relations between the National and its critics. To this end she took to inviting her critical colleagues to have a drink in the Governors' guest room on first nights. I think she rather resented the theatre's well-staffed Press Room whose express duty it was to smooth the path she had chosen to level. However, she decided that she needed a role, and so she defined it. She was highly delighted when her term of office was extended by a year. She did not live to serve it all but she was as much encouraged by the gesture of confidence as by her favourite piece of National gossip. When one of the National's actors appeared naked in the Howard Brenton play, *The Romans*, a nude photograph of him was published in a Sunday newspaper. The actor was embarrassed when his mother telephoned. 'I've seen your photograph,' she announced.

'Yes?' he replied, apprehensively.

'You're not eating enough,' she said, 'you're too thin.' Caryl also joined the large gallery of people connected with the arts to be painted by John Bratby.

Have you ever felt like an onion in the process of being peeled? Layer after layer of your hidden self exposed as the white rings are forcibly unfurled? You haven't? Then you cannot have been painted by John Bratby, the lay-it-on-thick-painter – in the civil sense – and so your experience of life will be a little less rich for that reason.

'Would you say that Christ had charisma?' was one of the questions shot at me while he applied a thumbful of orange paint to the canvas, when I underwent a four-hour analysis by paint and painter called 'sitting to him'. Until then, I knew Mr Bratby's work only through his designs for Sir Alec Guinness's film *The Horse's Mouth*, which I decided were generous – a safe word, and fair with it, I felt.

Never an enthusiastic sitter, Ned Sherrin tried to comfort me. 'You won't know yourself when Bratby's finished with you.'

He sounded confident. Thus fortified, I looked immediately on my arrival at a largish canvas on an easel: Tom Stoppard, the dramatist, instantly recognizable and clearly blazing with talent. Propped up against a stack of smaller canvases, I spotted a demented Jeremy Thorpe. Donald Pleasence was a sinister egg on the eastern slopes, with Arthur Lowe, hard-boiled on the foothills of canvases, to the west. Nearby in the Counting House – or was it Bratby's conservatory? – Michael Codron, the canny impresario, was brooding – had he got into his eighth million in profit or his seventh? What, merely his fifth? Hell! He could count them on the fingers of one hand.

Bratby unwittingly explained the peeled onion method to me: 'My interest is in people. What it is that gives them the drive to emerge from the crowd.'

I looked about me. Assorted flowers painted on kitchen mugs. Rampant sunflowers; even the mop-head petals looked rebellious. If he were to paint a lily, it would surely turn out a tiger lily.

John Bratby, RA, ARCA, RBA, FIAL, FRSA, Failed Intermediate Arts & Crafts, must have been one of the students most determined not to succeed to come out of Kingston Art School, to which he had been given a grant. Fortunately he insisted on painting his world his way, and so he was bound to emerge from it in the end. They grabbed back his grant when he flunked in arts and crafts, so he worked for a time in a factory. Subsequently, a brewery and then a wharf furnished a kind of livelihood. He kept his brush in by painting his rebellious sunflowers and the domestic objects he collected around him, tables, chairs, bottles, and tins, very much like the French painters at the time of Cézanne, though infinitely unlike their works. He painted them on murals, walls being less costly than canvas. Necessity became a choice.

At the Royal College of Art, which finally he joined (preferring it to The Slade), he collected dustbins from the boiler rooms and ecstatically painted them in groups. Later he was to become unpopular with the mother-in-law of his first marriage – a sorely tried lady, one assumes – by 'borrowing' her groceries and spiriting them away to paint. His painting in the thick, 'the unnatural look of vigour in a painting', made it imperative to demand an extra allowance of artist's material. Awarded a travelling scholarship, he went to Rome to study the art of Michelangelo and Raphael. The visit was not a success – more a culinary disaster. He hated the taste of garlic, and the foreign cooking upset his diet.

While Bratby paints, he keeps up a barrage of questions. One of them hit home. I sought to change the subject lightly but definitely: 'Has it occurred to you,' I asked, 'that while you study me, I may be studying you?'

She became very attached to Bratby and they corresponded regularly after the sitting; but she never bought the painting. It was outside her price range and she never displayed pictures of herself, though her ormolu desk was stuffed with old photographs. Whatever her attitude to her appearance in earlier years, she was self-conscious, particularly about her teeth, during the last decade. Few remained, and although there were times when she might have been able to afford to replace them she was, in truth, a physical coward and would not risk the pain and discomfort. In spite of her enormous moral fortitude and the heroic battle she waged to keep creditors and bank managers from the door, she could not bear tiny physical mishaps. A bruise, a cut, a pinched finger, provoked a wail of complaint, when a threat to bankrupt her would turn her into a stag magnificently at bay. After a nervous illness in the early '70s a mild diabetes was diagnosed, and she followed her treatment with morbid apprehension for the rest of her life, keeping it easily in check.

Another of her obsessions was spotting promise – an early glimpse of Tom Courtenay's quality at RADA or Hywel Bennett on tour with Donald Wolfit at Golders Green or Rosemary Harris outstanding among an afternoon of Juliets in the old manner of RADA productions. Letters after her death reminded me of the flurry of imaginatively phrased, encouraging postcards which poured out of Cambridge Gate whenever she saw performances which she admired. Two prodigy protégés – Simon Mulligan and Roy Theaker – played the Beethoven 'Minuet in G' on piano and violin at her memorial service at St Paul's, Covent Garden. She wrote:

I have a string of little geniuses. I seem to collect them as rich women collect a string of horses. Simon Mulligan begins with all the advantages. First, his commitment to his music at the age of ten which is equalled only by his mother's commitment to his music. He

wins every competition in sight and has just been awarded a
scholarship at Colet Court, the prep school for St Paul's.

NS Simon Mulligan is still racing ahead with his musical career.

CB My second small genius, Roy Theaker, is a musician also, nudging
nine.
'When will Roy be nine?' Simon's Mum asked, keenly.
'In September 1982,' I told her.
'Younger than Simon, then.'
I have come upon this intense concern about age among other
prodigies. Peter Brook, the brilliant stage director, frequently asked
'How old is he?' when a new and young luminary burst upon the
scene. After his much discussed Dali *Salome* at the Royal Opera
House, I christened him the *enfant terrible* of Covent Garden. Later
in the same year I was talking to the future brilliant drama critic
Kenneth Tynan who announced his intention of staging an all-black
Macbeth: 'Another *enfant terrible*,' I commented.
'I thought that was Peter Brook,' Ken observed.
'He's the Grand Old *enfant terrible*,' I suggested.
Retournons à nos génies.
Roy Theaker has a thatch of thick but cropped hair. He is as
sturdily as fair-haired Simon is delicately moulded. I discovered
him while we were rehearsing *Nickleby and Me* for the Chichester
Festival's Easter show. His Mum is a part-time nurse for the mentally
retarded. Dad is a lorry driver. They have two other sons, both
musicians, both some years older than Roy, who have
distinguished themselves while at Christ's Hospital, the blue-coat
school. Now Roy has been offered two scholarships; one at the
Chichester Prebendal School, which is the Cathedral choir prep
school, the other at Christ's Hospital, which would take care of him
until he is eighteen.
I dream of two tiny boys, fair-head and ginger thatch, playing
Mozart on two concert grands on the large stage of the enormous
space of the Chichester Festival Theatre.

NS Jamie Arlon, the older of two sons of Deke and Jill Arlon (the other is
Timmy), endeared himself to Caryl by announcing to his mother after
we had spent a day at their farmhouse, 'Mummy, Miss Brahms is older
than any of us, but she seems the youngest of us all. She's got (pause

for thought) personality. (Pause for more thought.) How can I grow personality?' At the time Jamie was shyer than his younger brother, and he and Caryl embarked on a correspondence about writing, and in particular about words which both relished and which has had a marked effect on the boy.

'I can rarely resist a cacophony of adjectives,' Caryl wrote. 'I consider it one of the greatest failings in my own writing – though humour has its own poetry and words should be made to work for a humorist as they do for any other poet.'

The boy was unsure of how to address her: 'Dear Caryl, or should I say, Dear Miss Brahms, but to make it simple, Dear Caryl Brahms?'

She replied:

Dear Jamie,
As you suggest, 'Dear Caryl Brahms' is simple, but 'Dear Caryl' would be even more simple, so let us be Caryl and Jamie. I am delighted that you have found your way to poetry. You choose two very good examples in Wilfred Owen and Dylan Thomas. So you can see for yourself what I mean by making a word work for you.

I myself have a cousin named Peter Levi and he is no mean poet, so I'll write him (that is the Edwardian manner of saying 'write to him') to ask which of his poems I should send you, though you may think them a little abstract and philosophical, yet somehow I think you should grow into them as you grow older. Have you read the poetry of Rupert Brooke? A marvellously simple poet. I will see if I can get you a copy. I am enclosing a postcard of Shakespeare's tomb. It was sent to me by the son of a writer called Cyril Connolly who is nudging ten years old, and addressed to me by his step-father, my cousin Peter, the poet. Have you ever visited Stratford-upon-Avon and seen the bust for yourself? They make a small charge to see it, which I do not approve because I think people would give some small gift in the money-box without being extorted, but the whole little town of Stratford-upon-Avon is living on the crumbs from Shakespeare's table so I suppose one should expect the tourists to be fleeced by that beautiful church.

You need not answer this letter because it is in answer to yours, but of course you may if you want to write.

My love to your parents and Timmy,
Your friend, Caryl.

[259]

NS A postscript advised: 'The best bedside book for a writer is *The Oxford Dictionary*.'

By now she had recommended Dickens and Alan Coren, *The Oxford Book of English Verse*, Rupert Brooke, *The Tailor of Gloucester* and Philip Howard's piece on words in *The Times*. Jamie was keen at that age to become a journalist – a breed viewed by his show-biz parents with understandable suspicion. Caryl was determined to direct him to the paths of good journalism. He got the next letter along with a book by Virginia Woolf.

CB ... a most distinguished writer, because I think you will relish the words which she has chosen – at least I hope so ... Of the two sorts of journalism, the kind I would like you to think about is the better kind – very good journalists often become foreign correspondents for their papers; they deal in facts and their work is better and more important than the hack journalists who centre on show-business and other kinds of publicity.

There are also two kinds of writing; one kind of writer uses every adjective he can think of, and of this kind Charles Dickens is an example. The other kind selects carefully the word that will best project his thought, and makes his words work for him, because he uses fewer but almost always more powerful words: this is the kind of writing I try to do, but both kinds are acceptable.

I am looking forward to having a long talk with you and your mother about writing: perhaps in your next holidays. Enjoy the book with all its rich words, and give my love to Timmy, your Mamma and Father. Blessings ...

NS And a month before she died she had the passage from *Don't, Mr Disraeli* in which the young John Masefield finds Whiteley's Toy Bazaar out of tall ships, typed out and sent to him. He already had the poem. It was the last letter in their correspondence. Her handwriting by now was becoming disconcertingly frail and spidery but the batch of letters and postcards continued to wing out from Cambridge Gate – a couple, almost indecipherable to Terry Sheppard, a friend who was then staying in Los Angeles, and of whom she writes in her memoirs:

CB Moving a little up the age-scale, we arrive at Little T, a good-looking young dancer-actor with an 'Enquire Within' for a mind, who is Ned Sherrin's house-guest, on and off. He came by his sobriquet in the odd way nicknames are generated. Terry Sheppard was appearing in *The Mitford Girls* at the Chichester Festival and in it is a character, Decca Mitford, whom her mother calls Little D. So, as is the way of such things, Terry became Little T. He looks on Ned and me as mentors in all things social. A friend, an older man, was taking him to see *Another Country*. Little T came down wearing a pair of denim jeans and a faded denim jacket. 'You cannot possibly go to an evening at the theatre in that outfit,' Ned told him sternly, so up he went and changed into a striped blazer, which made twenty-four-year-old Little T look about fifteen. 'You certainly cannot wear *that* at this particular play – stop and think what it would imply,' said Ned, sterner than ever.

Finally, Little T settled for a reasonable suit.

Later, I lectured Little T on his reprehensible attitude to the theatre, he unwarily having told me that he would pursue a feud with a young woman in the cast of *The Boy Friend* in which he was about to play at Farnham in Surrey. 'I'll get even with her, like putting itchy powder in her wig, or a laxative in her coffee on the first night.'

'Little T, you are to do no such thing.'

'You've never been in the chorus, Caryl.'

'That has nothing to do with it. You owe the theatre so much. We all do – you must develop a responsible attitude to it – a proper attitude. You should put the play before your private feuding. Stop behaving like a naughty school boy. Be professional.'

'I shall put the laxative in her tea and *she* will be terrible. And *I* shall be professional.'

In fact he was promoted from the chorus to the leading part, and decided to behave well.

There is something attractive for an older person about closing the generation gap across some three or four generations. It may work the other way round but I can no longer remember. Caryl delighted to tell the story of her old editor on the Arts page of *The Times*, John Lawrence, a frail figure whom she described as 'the best arts editor I ever had' and who had recently been confronted by an apparently dangerous gang of punks. 'Go away,' he said, 'you are frightening the ladies hereabouts.' One produced a flick-knife. 'Do put that thing away,' said John, adding improbably, 'How do you know I am not in MI5?' They slipped away. A week later he was vainly trying to catch a bus, which declined to stop. His previous assailants materialized and stood, their backs to the bus, on a zebra crossing. They held their ground. John clambered majestically on to the bus and then they bowed and waved – 'It's all yours, Guv.'

Caryl's similar succour came after we had driven up Shaftesbury Avenue so that she could see *The Mitford Girls* sign on the Globe Theatre in lights for the first time. She dropped me at Cambridge Circus and set off towards the Tottenham Court Road where she plunged her car down a deep road-excavation. It was perched precariously 'at a rakish angle, half in and half out'. Her rescuers were at first her principal panic. An apparently fearsome group of punks, whom she thought had come to jeer, stayed to heave the car out of the hole, make sure she was all right (even if the car was really not), insist that any girl who was a contemporary of theirs would have been in screaming hysterics, and wave her on her damaged way.

Towards the end of the war, Guy Ramsay told Caryl a tale of his grandmother. It took her nearly forty years to turn it into a story. It did the rounds of her favourite editors and was firmly rejected. I have included it here because she was particularly proud of it, and I find it warm, economical and moving. It was her last piece of fiction.

Guy's Grandmother

Guy's Grandmother was Irish, and extravagant with it. Opulent in June; skint in July. It was July. It was, too, the turn of the century.

Guy's Grandmother was going into Dublin by public transport, her brougham being temporarily in hock in the yard at the back of the pawnshop. Now it so happened that travelling by the same horse-drawn brake was an old, old lady, an ancient crone, a scrawny old woman, a distraught old scarecrow. Describe the old bag as you will, she was rooting among a multitude of tattered petticoats for a couple of coppers for the fare. Guy's Grandmother bought two tickets, gave one to the old lady, and handed her a book which had slipped to the floor while she fumbled. The old witch thanked Guy's Grandmother in accents so cultured that, stirred to interest and pity, she fell to chatting with the poor old bundle, and before their journey's end she had discovered her name – Mrs Thackragh, 'pronounced Thackeray; a direct descendant' – and her address, Liffey Buildings.

Time passed and before you could say 'William Makepeace' it had become August. Opulent once again, Guy's Grandmother drove forth in the brougham – out of hock once more – drawn by a pair of somewhat lean bays, to call on Miss Thackragh, taking with her a hamper laden with comforts for the poor old lady. The hamper contained a chicken, several slices of ham, a dozen eggs, butter, tea and sugar, a bottle of good red wine, a corkscrew – an afterthought – and a few peaches.

Liffey Buildings was a tenement, bleak and tall. At the very top in a damp, peeling, bare, icy attic, Guy's Grandmother settled herself to enjoy a nice chat with her new friend. Miss Thackragh, on her side, produced her Thackeray. 'I always have it with me, my dear, in case,' she said.

It was the first of many visits. When the good months came round, out would drive Guy's Grandmother and never without a hamper of good things, and up those old cold stone tenement steps she lugged it while her brougham and bays waited below.

However, one day the caretaker sent for Guy's Grandmother. This time she went into town by public transport and took no hamper with her. Miss Thackragh had passed on. Her death had been caused by a splinter of oyster shell she, incontinently, had swallowed. There, in a dark corner of the icy attic, stood a little barrel of oysters sent to Miss Thackragh by Guy's Grandmother a few days earlier. There, too, was Miss Thackragh's last will and testament. She must have been regaling herself while pausing for thought.

Miss Thackragh had bequeathed forty thousand pounds, stitched to the bottom of the mattress, to Guy's Grandmother: 'The only person ever to have shown me kindess' – a purple spider could have written the words – 'together with the volume written by that master of irony from whom I am directly descended.'

Here Miss Thackragh must have put aside her pen, and, by way of punctuation, partaken of her last oyster. Her will was never to be signed. Miss Thackragh's money went to her next of kin, so infinitely less than kind.

As for Guy's Grandmother, she caught the public horse-brake home – it was September; not the month to be extravagant. And on the journey back she read *Vanity Fair*. Evening papers cost money.

A late passage in Caryl's memoir reads:

As I write these words, it happens to be one of those Lents (1982). Strictly speaking, I suppose it has nothing to do with me, a Sephardic Jewess. But in another sense it has everything to do with me, I

suppose. So Lent it is, and my always Lenten effort for some
years has been 'Be nice to Ned'. I need hardly add that Ned has no
such resolve to be kind to Caryl. He has been known to put up his
arm, bent at the elbow as though to fend off blows which I have
never rained on him, calling out, 'Lent, Caryl, Lent!'

NS So at the end, as in the beginning, we return to her ambivalent attitude
to religion; the unswerving way in which she clung to her Jewish faith
while not going with it to Synagogue, and the fascination which the
Church of England and the Roman Church held for her. She always
emphasized that she was a Sephardic Jew – as opposed to the Ashkenazi
of Eastern European origin. Although her father, Henry Abrahams,
was Ashkenazi, the dominant influence at home was her mother. Apart
from her penchant for collecting C of E bishops, she was particularly
proud of, fascinated by, and concerned for, her three Catholic cousins.
Anthony and Peter Levi had been Jesuits and their sister Gillian is a
nun – they were the children of the second marriage of Caryl's Uncle
Bert. By an odd irony she re-established contact with Peter when he
met Malcolm Williamson at Mass while we were working on *No Bed
For Bacon*. (Peter Levi doubts that the meeting was *at Mass*. He only
remembers a vinous lunch at Dom Moraes' in Chelsea.)

Her agent for many years, Joyce Weiner, has pointed out the autobiographical way in which she anatomized this dichotomy in one of her
last short stories, *Hear!*, published in her collection, *Stroganoff in
Company*, in 1980. Two sisters are at home in London, in the story. In
an overfurnished room, in an Italian Renaissance bed, Ventura Digbye
is dying. It is no accident that the clutter of the room reflects to some
extent Caryl's own surroundings and the family background of antiques,
rich carpets and *objets d'art*. As Ventura grows weaker, Pearle her sister
sits and prays. Through the window competing gramophones make

> . . . an unexacting background to the Shemah, the Hebrew prayer
> that Pearle was muttering. The prayer that is said by practising Jews
> in the morning and at night, and which is spoken at their deathbeds.
> 'Hear, O Israel, The Lord Thy God, The Lord is One . . .'
>
> Pearle finished the Shemah but she did not straighten up. Her
> hands still screened her face.
>
> 'Lord God of Israel,' she extemporized, 'I've said the Shemah but
> it's not for me, it's for Ventura. You know what she is – too proud
> to say it for herself. But there! You made her, Lord, and so you

understand her. She's a Jew all right, for all her Christianity. You can't change your race any more than you can change the colour of your eyes. I told her so at the time. But she wouldn't listen then and she won't listen now. Her florist's bill alone! And all this useless furniture! But now the poor soul's time has come. Be with her, Lord. Into Thy hand I commend her spirit, and with her spirit her body also. The Lord is with her, she shall not fear . . .'

'*Ours is a Nice House, Ours Is!*' the gramophone re-affirmed.

I asked Mervyn Stockwood, Caryl's second Bishop – 'the third if you count Trinidad' – if he had sensed a fascination for Christian forms and philosophy. He replied (18 March 1985):

I find it a difficult question to answer. I met Caryl at the Palace at Wells in the early '50s when I was still in Bristol – thirty years ago or more. I have a vivid recollection of our meeting which was unexpected . . . I remember she asked me many questions about the things that bishops did . . . In addition she was interested in my work in Bristol and in the ups and downs of a fairly tough parish in East Bristol. She was clearly curious with regard to the motives of a young man entering the ministry. Again, she wondered how we spent our days. I think she had had little experience of parsons and church life, and when she met Bradfield and me, who appeared to be fairly reasonable human beings, her curiosity was awakened.

I do not recall any 'religious' conversations with her, though we had quite a talk when Peter Levi retired from the Roman Catholic priesthood. And . . . [when she came to Bishop's House] . . . she appeared to enjoy meeting some of the lively clergy – especially my succession of chaplains. It is only a guess, but I think in those rather troublesome years when so much was in the melting pot, this apparently archaic institution, the church, witnessed to values which were precious to her and was still capable of influencing many people. At any rate the church was something to be respected for the right reasons and not just as an article in the national junk-shop.

Caryl certainly felt an interest in and concern for Mervyn. The very theatricality of his manner appliquéd on to a belief which held its own fascination, was irresistible. That he was a devoted host to interesting guests, and a bishop, no doubt played its part. 'Good Fridays come and go like white butterflies over the cabbage patch,' she wrote, and went on to include 'those many, many Good Fridays when Mervyn Stockwood, then the Bishop of Southwark, was staggering down the aisle of his South Bank Cathedral, bearing the great wooden cross over his shoulder'.

CB   I had been commissioned by the *Guardian* to write a profile in depth of Mervyn for their columns. 'Can you put me in touch with some of your incumbents?' I asked him. 'Friends and foes,' I laid it on the table.

'Yes,' Mervyn agreed cheerfully.

It did not take me long to discover that, be it foe or friend, they had one fact in common which they were all keen to offer. The great wooden cross under the weight of which the Bishop of Southwark tottered on Good Fridays – was hollow! The whole staggering scene was a superb and effective piece of play-acting.

Ned and I looked forward always to Mervyn's Mid-Lent parties. So many different sorts of people, and we were among those always asked to stay on for luncheon, after the drinks. John Betjeman would be there with Elizabeth Cavendish, Norman Hartnell, Hywel Bennett and his wife, Cathy McGowan – Mervyn married them – Jennie Lee, David Owen. Cathy told me that as a teenager she used to pass Mervyn's official residence on the top of a bus and crane her head to peep into his walled garden, convinced that Bishop's House, Tooting Bec, was a brothel.

I first met Mervyn when he was a priest in Bristol. His bishop was Bishop Bradfield of Bath and Wells. In those days I still used to think of the Church of England as a kind of ecclesiastical Harrods, with its vicars and priests salesmen – not very expert salesmen, it seems, for there they stand, vast churches in cities and perhaps particularly in London with equally vast stocks of religion left on the shelves owing to consumer resistance, a likely average for many a London church attendance being a congregation of twenty. Even if the incumbent is a man of more than usually vital personality and doubles church attendances over two years, his parish will still yield merely a meagre forty customers. Its vicars, in short, are the salesmen of its empty echoing premises, its bishops branch managers, with God the Chairman of the Board *in absentia*.

Acquainted now with two bishops – not counting Trinidad – my questions were growing more sceptical. I was fascinated by

Mervyn's politics. 'Mervyn isn't really a Socialist,' said his Tory opponent on the Bristol City Council. 'He's a good old-fashioned Radical with Conservative parachutes to keep his jet from over-shooting the runway.' And the man himself says proudly: 'I've been thrown out of the Labour Party twice.'

Yet when the Archbishop of Canterbury asked him if he would give up his membership of the Labour Party on his appointment to Southwark, his answer was a good round No.

I once asked him which one of his favourite things he would take with him to his desert island if he could choose – music, painting, architecture, the drama, wine? 'Wine,' he said, 'in a music box – you could pack a great many bottles into one of those old-fashioned cabinet gramophones.'

Wherever two or three of his clergy are gathered together, Mervyn stories fly around. The most often quoted is that of one Good Friday at Southwark Cathedral. Nothing if not an instinctive actor, the Bishop, in procession, staggered down the aisle bent under the weight of that heavy-looking hollow wooden cross which he lowered into a stand at the altar. Then, hands together pointing to Heaven and with an intent face, he knelt. So did his attendant priest, in close proximity. Without abandoning his pious posture, Mervyn said out of the corner of his malleable mouth: 'Six paces *behind* me, boy.'

But wait a minute . . .

What bemused me was that the three clerics who separately recounted the anecdote all claimed to have been there and within hearing distance.

She had, I think, once again, not so much avoided the question as preferred not to grapple with it. She found a comic exit from her consideration of the dilemma. Indeed, her exit might be the last paragraph of a chapter in a comedy-detective novel.

It was Caryl's unswerving intention to punctuate passages of her memoirs with examples of her very favourite form of humour – the Karapat or Armenian joke. In her view, the funniest story ever told was the Armenian joke which she and Skid put through all manner of sketches and stories (see page 51). I have to confess defeat in looking for appropriate places in which to place the others through her narrative, so I have assembled here those she recounted most frequently – and which she had written down before her death. I think she was not aware of the family legend of her Uncle Ned's presence at the Massacre of the Armenians – an event 'so horrible that he could never be persuaded to refer to it'.

There were elements of a frustrated stand-up comedian about Caryl. She cherished an ambition to perform the thankless task of 'warming-up' TV studio audiences . . . an ambition I am afraid I did not allow her to fulfil.

CB I had always supposed that Armenia – the Armenia in which the absurd became a sort of lunatic sense, a land where the impossible became not only possible but extremely probable, where fools were not so much suffered as encouraged – had been totally invented by Skid and me. So it was in a state of mind poised somewhere between pride and pique that I discovered after his death, while I was writing for TW3, that a secretly printed Czechoslovakian satirical newspaper, *Nose Pravda* (Our Justice), plopped through the letterbox of every telephone subscriber in Prague every other week – in itself a somewhat Armenian manner of distribution. A copy arrived in England, and I pounced. In it I found (with the help of a BBC translator) one of my most treasured Karapat stories.

The Director of Radio Armenia was about to visit Moscow. Before leaving he arranged to write to his colleagues in blue ink if he found conditions easier there, and in red ink if he found things were bad. Off he goes and he sends a letter home written in blue ink, which says: 'Everything is fine here in Moscow – only I have not been able to find any red ink!'

The laughter in this publication is secret, grim, and down to earth – laughter applied to the diminishment of terror by ridicule; but before 'applying' you take a good look over your shoulder.

'Dear Editor, My Radio Armenia tells me there is plenty of food in the shops; but my refrigerator is empty. What do I do?'
'Put your radio into your refrigerator.'

The change in Soviet attitude to Stalin's displaced corpse presented a perfect example of Radio Armenia's treatment. They offered his body in a glass coffin to Ben Gurion, who responded: 'We, in Israel, have already suffered unfortunate repercussions from an earlier resurrection.'

A Jew was walking along a street in Armenia and as he walked he sent up a prayer: 'Lord, let me win the Friday sweepstake.'

Friday came round, but the Jew did not win. So he tried again: 'Lord, let me win the Friday sweepstake.'

Friday came round, but still no sweepstake win. So the Jew tried once more: 'Lord, I have asked you twice to let me win the Friday sweepstake. Must I ask you again?'

There was a clashing of clouds and a roll of thunder and the Lord looked down to Armenia: '*Nu*,' said the Almighty, 'but you must play your part, my son. Buy a ticket!'

Caryl looked suddenly older and tireder during the last year of her life, her eighty-first. However, she continued to go regularly to the theatre, to add to and subtract from her memoirs, and to contemplate new projects. The failure of *The Mitford Girls* and *Beecham* to have lengthy and lucrative runs in the West End was a keen disappointment, both financially and because she enjoyed the intimacy of a backstage family. During the couple of weeks before her death she seemed to gather new energy and, perhaps with an unconscious insight into the future, to put her house in order. She took pains, in several cases writing thoughtful letters to people with whom she had had some real or imagined difference, making her peace, as it were, with a considered compliment.

On Friday 4 December she went to a party at the Critics' Circle, seeing a large number of her old colleagues for the last time. On the Saturday afternoon we went to a matinée of *Babes in Arms* at the Arts Educational School near the Barbican. She had always had a particular fondness for the school and had decided that she would give a small annual prize for the best acting performance in a musical. She gave a similar prize at RADA to encourage serious consideration of acting in musicals.

She wanted an early night as the next day, Sunday, we had agreed to start work on yet another stage version of *No Bed For Bacon*. This one, inspired by a recent visit to Mike Alfreds' production of Waugh's *A Handful of Dust*, was to be without music. I left her after a cup of tea and we agreed to meet at my house in Pimlico at 11.30. She called me later, at about ten, to complain that she could not get Channel 4 on which she wished to watch a repeat of *Upstairs Downstairs*. She died suddenly in her bedroom that night.

When I registered her death, the official who took down the particulars raised an eyebrow as he entered her age. 'A very good age,' he said. 'What did she use to do when she was working?'

I did not like to tell him that she had never stopped.

[269]

What follows are virtually the last pages which Caryl wrote and revised. In some measure they illustrate and sum up the central importance of writing to her life, so I place them here as her final statement. They begin with the search for a quotation.

CB *He blew on his pipes and words came tripping round him like pretty little children who are perfectly drilled for the dance.*

I sought it with thimbles, I sought it with care. I chased it down the nights and days – my own and those of my more literate friends. I even toyed with appealing to St Anthony: 'Lost: the source of a quotation.'

The Oxford Dictionary of Quotations failed to come up with it. My friends, having searched each his own Jerusalem with candles, by the waters of Babylon sat down and wept. Then I bethought me of my tablets. They were not of stone, being lined exercise-books in grey board covers. In them I had collected quotations which I used when I was a drama critic to point up a judgement and give my notices a certain scholarly elegance. Who would suppose I had not read the whole of the works from which I quoted? But where were these golden counsellors? I went to the grand dishevelment I call the files. I kept them in the hot-air cupboard. House-proud ladies who spend their afternoons playing bridge and their evenings soporifically boring their husbands with 'I was holding three to the knave of hearts', use hot-air cupboards for airing linen. A quaint conceit. Me, I use mine for keeping my Edwardian picture postcards of English and French actresses, the stationery, oh yes, and my scripts. Well, there they were, my dove-grey books, exactly where they should have been. The shock of this exactitude astounded me. I devoured the Macaulays, the Coleridges, the Lambs, the Hazlitts, the James Agates, the Ken Tynans, the J. C. Trewins, and I came upon the Max Beerbohms. And here, in the wittiest of haystacks, I came upon my needle: Max Beerbohm, writing of Thackeray writing of *The Four Georges*, in which my quotation errant is to be found in the essay on George III.

Does the road of the researcher wind uphill all the way? Yes:

end!

very

the

To

On Writing: 27 September 1982
Because I am not a Sitwell – any one of the glittering three – nor
yet a Grossmith; not a Beatrix Potter and, by the same token, no
Betjeman, no Stoppard, I would wish to be Thackeray; and of those
of his works that I know, the Thackeray who wrote *The Four
Georges*; and, to particularize, that passage which says of the Letters
of Horace Walpole: *'Fiddles sing all through them; wax-lights, fine dresses,
fine jokes, fine plate, fine equipages, glitter and sparkle there. Never was
such a brilliant jigging, smirking Vanity Fair through which he leads
us.'*

What a ballet of words. Gladly I'd settle for being the Poor Man's
Thackeray. He is not troubled by my haunting guilt about not
writing good plain prose; not making the words work for one; even
his use of the colon is a flash of lightning across the inky sky: but
then, I am a humorist, and in the pursuit of laughter there are times
when, as with Dickens, only a torrent of words could do justice to my
writing needs.

Humour is a demanding taskmaster: it places the practitioner in
a poet's strait-jacket. Humour is indeed a strict disciplinarian, finding
its wings and, like a lark ascending, rising on a self-engendered
alcohol, soars until it reaches the hit-or-miss realms of writing
lunacy. At least, this is what happens to this particular humorist.

═══ Postscript ═══

(from *You Were There*)

... At a table in a corner sat a pair of palooka writers ...

The palooka man had a shock of black hair like a Japanese doll without a fringe, a moon-shaped, moon-coloured face that looked like a moon that needed shaving, and ash all over him. His name was S. J. Simon.

The girl palooka looked like a Semitic sparrow. She was Caryl Brahms.

And they didn't know what the future was to hold for them either.

But you could bet your monomark there'd be a lot of laughter in it.

Lament

For Caryl Brahms
(d. 5 Dec 1982)

(i)

Victorian stone children in the trees,
tall under streetlights that increase the dark:
they dream of taxis and of carriages
and of the sun sinking above the park.

High in the flats your window opened out
on a small balcony like a stone shelf
to catch at weather and the distant shout
of the last echoes crying *Know thyself.*

The trees are dying with no noise at all
while the fresh leaf shivers in the fresh light,
leaf by leaf they will turn colour and fall.
The only monument we have is night

(ii)

My dearest, when your childhood had become
a ballet like a transformation scene,
and painful love glowed slowly in the air
never consumed, what you remembered was
dark thousand petalled roses of that time
gathered in thunderstorms of garden scent,
the London thrush heaving his speckled breast,
cigarette smoke like phrases in Chekhov.
The French hill-garden, meagre lemon trees
above the stony dark and sparkling sea.
Poem after poem dissolved away.
Your mother's dresses treasured secretly
because you never could be beautiful,

and a passion for out of date postcards:
heaven opened in them in 1910,
on multicoloured swans that dying sang.
Then the rough wind, the sea's life-giving breath,
and victorious barrenness of the tide.

(iii)

It is the Sabbath now, God has rested,
white snow-showers of stars whirl overhead,
straw-coloured wisps of fire to light the dead
as if time were a clockwork running down,
or the soul ran backward to its own place,
to where a generation hung like breath
among the apple-trees; it was Sabbath.
Will they be happy in two hundred years,
not as we live now, quiet Croydon roads
with bushes, grass and flowers out of hand,
whose hope was visionary in autumn
when the soul cries to her pure origin?
Tall houses, dark nourishment of the soul,
where the piano chimed a thousand hours
expressing hungers blinder than the grave,
and longer than the artifice of life.
Wine pouring into motionless cut glass,
beside bread under velvet and gold thread
with Hebrew lettering white on blood red.
It is the Sabbath now, God has rested.
Cousin, it is time now to light the lamp,
the tide that has carried so many dead
streams away down the bare sand of your life.

(iv)

When it is midday, and when the white fire
of poetry dances above the urns
remember them, my child, they have planted
their conversations in the earth like trees.
How that light foliage unprotected
comes crashing to the ground.
I am tied up with London of those years,

and the whole sky solemn and rose-coloured,
the firemen's bells and sirens and alarms,
when in one moment all houses grew pale
and groaned and blushed and crumbled to ruins.
Canyons of brown brick with their walls on fire,
and the high hoses weakly fountaining
over a wilderness of mad shadow:
your night-times and your wartime in the street,
the dusky fires swarming around your head
and iron clanging tears of molten bells
silted in the dark river of your soul,
when eastern sun, blood-cloud and thunder-cloud
mingled above St Paul's and his high dome,
and the dark angel brooding in the sun
wept at last and in pity turned away.
Cold red fire-weed and cat-infested stones.
Germany is dark. Germany is cold.
Therefore, when I survey the wondrous Cross
I am back in your lightless cobbled streets
that ran once on the south bank of the Thames,
that silence as the great dome rises there,
dreamed in the moons of summer by Shakespeare.
The rain has laid the dust on the plane trees
north of the river, that complaining wood
rustles from tree to tree, till the oldest
extend their heavy branches in the squares
in promises of lightest summer sleep.
Sleep dearest. It is time to sleep now.
Dawn has breasted Thames water like a swan,
she is drifting upstream with the new tide.
The sun is up, soon the milk will arrive,
the street is safe, the city is alive.

(v)

I will stand at the altar of my God
who will be praised in the name of the dead,
and blessed in a wilderness of voices.
All Israel is in the world to come,
as it was said, My people shall be just,

[275]

they shall inherit that land for ever,
branch of my planting, work of my own hand.
How bitter lilies smell in the late year,
where our old tea table has scarred the grass,
white swarms of jasmine climb the wall like bees,
and the tobacco flowers smell at night.
We did not travel through the leafless wood,
we have not seen the edges of mountains
crested with snow, six inches in the sky.
The grape rots on the wall of the greenhouse,
and will it ripen in the world to come?
We have sat warm by the fires of the wise,
but the coals glowed too bright and we were burned:
and their bite is the bite of the fox,
and they sting with the sting of scorpions,
they hiss as a snake hisses, words of fire.
And now the darkening tree drenches the sun,
cool early summer of the world to come;
shall we have visions, cousin, in the grave?
Forget what this world was, what it shall be?
I praise my God in your name and in mine,
Sabbath comes and my tongue is withering
and will wither before the world to come.
Blessed art thou, King of the universe,
creator of the small fruits of the vine.
May we attain the festivals of years
and festivals of seasons in the years,
by God's mercy chanting praises to God.
Our life has been consumed among wonders,
dreamlike before the Sabbath rest of God
done drowsing in the twilight of that day,
and we have passed into the sleep of God.
The red and blue and grey and snow-white glass
that glimmered while your dinner-candles burned
and holy angel gilded on the wall
are gone now and the curtains have fallen,
one complete darkness has extinguished them.
My love is ghostly. I will praise my God.
And where the small car trundled up the lanes
below the pathless ocean of the downs,

while the pale cowslip deepened in the sun,
the spreading thyme and breathless violet
and your green place in every corner sang,
they have sailed out of sight and are silent.
Your hours of time have melted from the clock
and the blue marbling of the moon's white sphere.

(vi)

Now the dry season droning through your head
and the unbodied spirits of the dead
cry out to Venus, where her mild planet
smoulders among the clinkers of sunset.
Now in black shadow while the moon is bright
long silver-throated music chants all night,
the nightingale only nightwalkers see
loud bird of love and painful purity.
He has chanted for you in green branches
in secret muttering river-valleys.
The towers of his leaves are sad and high,
they will paint a fresh colour on the sky:
but we shall not be in the meadow then,
the breath of our words will be forgotten,
these woods and birdsong have buried our day.
What we acted was real. It was no play.

Peter Levi

Index

Index

Benjamin, Arthur, 180
Bennett, Alan, 214
Bennett, Hywel, 257, 266
Benthall, Michael, 32
Bergel, Hugh, xi, 96–7, 110
Bergel, Jack, xi, 52, 58, 60, 71, 73, 76, 79, 84, 89, 92, 97–8, 101–2, 106, 107; death of, 109–10, 111, 112
Beriosova, Svetlana, 164
Berners, Lord, xii, 107
Bernhardt, Sarah, 96–7
Betjeman, John, 266
Billington, Michael, xii, 223
Black, Alfred, 115
Black, George, 115
Bloom, Claire, 250
Blum, impresario, 143, 144
Bradfield, Alyson, 169–70
Bradfield, Bishop of Bath and Wells, 165–70, 265, 266
Bradfield, Mrs, 167–8, 169
Brahms, Caryl (*née* Doris Caroline Abrahams): birth (1901), 1; family and childhood, 1–26; her attitude to religion, 7–10, 165, 263–7; and to money, 14; theatre-going, 15–17; servants and governesses, 17–18; dancing classes, 18–21; boarding schools, 21–4; studies at Royal Academy of Music, 26, 38; early journalism, 28; and poetry, 28, 34–6, 53–4, 175; ballet and theatre criticism, 29–34, 51, 130–1, 140–50, 175, 176; working partnership with S. J. Simon, 38–9, 44–50, 55–115 *passim*, 117–19, 120, 125–38, 150–1, 159; her double portrait of Skid and Ned, 40–4; moves to Ascot Court, 47, 48; Jack Bergel's friendship with, 52, 60, 73, 79, 89, 92, 97–8, 101–2, 109–10, 114; and Second World War, 53–116; ARP work in London, 58, 60, 64–9, 72, 77–8, 81, 89, 122–3; and refugee work in Cambridge, 59, 60–2; job interviews with BBC, 71–3, 74, 110, 113; Richard Sutcliffe's friendship with, 92–3, 114, 119, 208, 209; and death of Jack Bergel, 109–10; flying bombs, 119–21; and shelter patrol, 122; death of her parents, 125; American visits, 143, 217, 220–3; and show jumping, 150, 250–4; dining out, 151–4, 220–2; and Herbert Sidon, 154–9; death of Skid, 159–61, 163, 174; moves to Cambridge Gate, 163–4, 230; her visit to Bishop Bradfield, 165–70; and Dorothy Ward, 171–4; Ned Sherrin's working partnership with, 174–229, 232,

234–7; and Donald Wolfit, 190–5; 'That Was The Week That Was', 199–207; secretaries, 237–40, 241–3; and the law, 243–6; and *faux pas*, 247–50; appointed Governor of National Theatre, 254–5; Bratby's portrait of, 255–7; protégés of, 257–61; and Armenian jokes, 267–9; death of (1982), 269–70
Brahms, Caryl: WORKS:
Away Went Polly, xv, 161–2, 163, 174, 175, 188, 242
Enter a Dragon, Stage Centre, 194, 222
Gilbert and Sullivan, biography of, 216–17, 232
Guy's Grandmother, 262–3
Hear! (short story), 264–5
'It's Peace' (*Punch*), 53–4
Look Back to Lyttletown, 188
Manyana (libretto for TV opera), 180
The Moon On My Left, 34–6; 'Any Boy To Any Ship', 35–6
No Castanets, 216, 237
Palookas in Peril, 59, 69
Reflections in a Lake, 216–17
The Rest of the Evening's My Own, 191–2, 216
Robert Helpmann, Choreographer, 126
A Seat at the Ballet, 33, 34, 140, 171, 175
Stroganoff in Company, 264–5
Tomorrow, Mr Tompion, and About Time Too, 189
Under the Juniper Tree, 180
Variations on Themes by Chekhov, 216–17, 231
IN COLLABORATION WITH NED SHERRIN:
After You, Mr Feydeau, 216
Beecham, 42, 223, 224, 269
Benbow Was His Name, 190, 194
Bigger Beggars, 185; 'Shut Up and Sing' (song), 185
Cindy Ella see *I Gotta Shoe*
Duchess Don't Allow, 189
Hush and Hide, 223
I Gotta Shoe (*Cindy Ella*), 42, 187, 189, 235
Liberty Ranch, 216, 229
The Little Beggars, 184–5
The Mitford Girls, 42, 223–6, 229, 233, 234, 261, 262, 269
Mr Tooley Tried, 189
Nickleby and Me, 217, 218, 258
No Bed For Bacon, stage musical version, 174, 176–8, 180–4, 194–7, 212
Ooh la la!, 216
Parasol, 196, 198
Rappel 1910, xv, 190, 211

[279]

Index

Index

Index